Editing Canadian English

Editing Canadian English

SECOND EDITION

Prepared for the
Editors' Association of Canada
Association canadienne des réviseurs

This edition first published by Macfarlane Walter & Ross 2000
Second printing published by McClelland & Stewart 2003

National Library of Canada Cataloguing in Publication

Main entry under title:

Editing Canadian English

2nd. ed.
Prepared by Catherine Cragg ... [et al.]
Includes bibliographical references and index.
ISBN 1-55199-045-8

1. English language – Canada. 2. English language – Rhetoric.
3. Canadianisms (English).* 4. Editing – Handbooks, manuals, etc.
I. Cragg, Catherine. II. Editors' Association of Canada.

PE3227.E35 2000   427'.971   C00-93063-8

We acknowledge the financial support of the Government of Canada through the
Book Publishing Industry Development Program and that of the Government of
Ontario through the Ontario Media Development Corporation's Ontario Book
Initiative. We further acknowledge the support of the Canada Council for the Arts
and the Ontario Arts Council for our publishing program.

This book is sold with the understanding that neither the author nor the
publisher is hereby rendering legal advice. If such advice is required, the personal
services of a competent professional legal counsel should be sought.

Page design by Robin Brass

Printed and bound in Canada

McClelland & Stewart Ltd.
The Canadian Publishers
481 University Avenue
Toronto, Ontario
M5G 2E9
www.mcclelland.com

2 3 4 5   08 07 06 05 04 03

Prepared for the
Editors' Association of Canada
Association canadienne des réviseurs

Second edition, 2000

Catherine Cragg
Barbara Czarnecki
Iris Hossé Phillips
Katharine Vanderlinden

Coordinator
Sheila Protti

First edition, 1987

Lydia Burton
Catherine Cragg
Barbara Czarnecki
Sonia Kuryliw Paine
Susan Pedwell
Iris Hossé Phillips
Katharine Vanderlinden

Contents

Preface

E*diting Canadian English* began in 1979 as a project of the then fledgling Freelance Editors' Association of Canada (FEAC), when a committee formed to talk about editing "in Canadian." Their hopes were high and their ambitions, they thought, modest: they planned to produce, over the course of a year or so, a booklet of half a dozen chapters that would solve, once and for all, the particular problems of Canadian editors. At that time there were no references that dealt comprehensively with the practical aspects of styling Canadian material for Canadian publications, and the committee set out to fill the gap.

Fortunately for the eventual completion of the project, the committee did not know what they were getting into. Gradually it became clear that they had set themselves a great task of research and debate and that even a few years of work would not produce a once-and-for-all guide. The process from inception through publication of the first edition in fact took eight years.

Moreover, producing a book by committee is neither simple nor swift; when all members of the committee are very experienced editors, the process can be positively Wagnerian. Only other editors can fully appreciate the poignancy of seven editors sitting around a table for an evening debating the series comma or defining the precise distinction between the en dash, the hyphen, and the solidus.

The work of creating this second edition has been immeasurably simpler – largely because the non-prescriptive approach of the first edition has been endorsed by users. Nevertheless, the last decade has witnessed the development of reference works by and for users of Canadian English, the proliferation of electronic resources, and radical changes in many areas that affect editing, including the technology of publishing and attitudes toward the use of non-discriminatory language. Some chapters have required only a modest updating, but others have had to be reconceived. In the first edition, for example, we were all on the brink of "going metric," and yet now we embrace with equanimity a mix of litres and tablespoons, metres and acres.

This second edition of *Editing Canadian English* is once more not the definitive solution to all problems of Canadian editors, nor is it in any way the official style guide of the Editors' Association of Canada. Because of the nature of the association – composed of editors working for many clients and employers and engaged in a wide variety of projects – such a guide is neither possible nor appropriate. What we have produced is a reference work that rarely dictates but instead aims to help its users make sensible editorial choices.

The Editors' Association of Canada welcomes comments and suggestions for revising future editions (<www.editors.ca>). The English language, like all living languages, is constantly changing, as are the conventions that govern its written use. We all take part in this process, and those who deal professionally with the written word are, we hope, always interested in learning and amending their knowledge of it.

About This Book

Editing Canadian English was written for editors, although it will also be useful to writers and all others who work with words. It is intended to help editors who seek to use "Canadian style."

However, to suggest that there is only one Canadian style is a serious oversimplification. In the past, Canadian editors have combined two copy-editing traditions – American and British – to create varying amalgams of the two, with some local colour added. The result was a wide range of styles that were Canadian only by circumstance.

Older editions of Canadian style guides, such as those of Canadian Press and the *Globe and Mail*, presented idiosyncratic choices (such as the **-or** spelling of **color** along with the **-re** spelling of **centre**) that many editors and publishers rejected. Current editions of numerous guides, as well as recent Canadian-based dictionaries, are moving closer to agreement over spelling but still offer divergent choices on other matters.

This book presents a flexible but systematic approach to creating workable Canadian styles. It outlines the contexts in which style alternatives exist, the nature of the alternatives, and the variables to consider in making consistent decisions. The goal is not to impose a uniform Canadian English style but to help editors make informed and appropriate choices for each project.

Many factors determine which choices are appropriate. For instance, editors must consider house traditions, writers' preferences, and target audiences. The prose of a learned journal is treated differently from advertising copy destined for bus shelters; the conference proceedings of a religious denomination are treated differently from the catalogue of an avant-garde art exhibit. We can only advise that an editor's choices be made with the eternal editorial dictum in mind: *Be as consistent as possible.*

The first five chapters of *ECE* – "Spelling," "Compounds," "Capitalization," "Abbreviations," and "Punctuation" – are concerned with general issues of editing, where Canadian practices (or British or American) not only vary but change over time. The last seven chapters – "French in English Context," "Canadianization," "Avoiding Bias," "Measurements," "Documentation," "Editors and the Law," and "Et Alia" – discuss matters specific to Canadian editing; they are more prescriptive because they deal with subjects that have their own conventions.

Chapter 1, "Spelling," presents the categories of words (and the most common individual words) that are spelled in two ways – formerly clearly divided into British and American. Both spellings may appear in Canadian dictionaries. The editor can use this chapter to build word lists so that each manuscript is internally consistent and suitable for its intended readership.

Chapter 2, "Compounds," outlines ways to treat temporary, permanent, and variable compounds. In this area, Canadian practice is highly inconsistent; the goal is consistency within the project at hand. Also treated are end-of-line divisions not only of words but also of numbers, codes, and electronic addresses.

Chapter 3, "Capitalization," examines issues of uppercase vs. lowercase, especially in instances not covered by the major guides. This chapter begins where other guides stop.

Chapter 4, "Abbreviations," reviews traditional and modern ways of treating true abbreviations, suspensions, acronyms, and symbols. In this area of usage, Canadian practice, like the American and the British, is in transition.

Similarly, Chapter 5, "Punctuation," is not an exhaustive treatment but concentrates on style practices that vary (as in the treatment of ellipses) or are contentious (the series comma).

Chapter 6, "French in English Context," sets out guidelines for the treatment of French words and phrases in English-language material to ensure that terms retain their French character and yet fit smoothly into English text.

Chapter 7, "Canadianization," offers advice on working with materials that are being adapted from foreign sources for the Canadian market.

Chapter 8, "Avoiding Bias," discusses ways to avoid denigrating individuals and groups by thoughtless and stereotypical modes of expression. Bias in language has for some time been a target in Canadian educational and government publishing. The chapter provides tools that editors can use to ensure balance and accuracy without resort to euphemism.

Chapter 9, "Measurements," summarizes the principles of SI (Système international d'unités) and surveys current patterns of usage of both "metric" and traditional measurements. The examples given apply to material for general readership; the chapter does not attempt to deal with highly technical copy.

Chapter 10, "Documentation," considers the content and treatment of references, including those that are complex and unusual. The chapter offers a group of matrixes to help editors choose and arrange the essential information consistently and accurately. This edition includes new matrixes for electronic references.

Chapter 11, "Editors and the Law," examines legal issues that editors must be aware of. The topics include libel and current copyright law following the Bill C-32 amendments.

Chapter 12, "Et Alia" (expanded from the first edition's "Glossary"), includes diverse items of special interest to Canadian editors. It also contains entries on miscellaneous topics not covered in other chapters (for example, treatment of quoted material; names of Canadian dailies; McLachlan, McLauchlan, McLachlin, or McLaughlin).

This new edition of *Editing Canadian English* also reflects the change in technology that increasingly determines editors' working practices. The overwhelming majority of EAC's members use the Internet. The means by which resources are consulted, facts checked, sources cited, and advice sought has been transformed. Further changes that will come about before the next edition can only be imagined.

In preparing the manuscript for this book we had, of course, to make our own style choices, which was no easy task. Although we tried to arrive at a consensus, we often had to settle for compromise. Look upon this work, then, as a typical Canadian product: it mixes certain British conventions with American ones, certain traditional treatments with avant-garde ones. Some choices were necessarily arbitrary. But we hope the result is consistent and harmonious and, in a suitably Canadian way, unobtrusive.

Abbreviated forms for standard references

Canadian Oxford	*The Canadian Oxford Dictionary,* 1998
Chicago Manual	*The Chicago Manual of Style,* 1993
Concise Oxford	*The Concise Oxford Dictionary,* 1999
Gage	*Gage Canadian Dictionary,* 1998
Nelson	*ITP Nelson Canadian Dictionary of the English Language,* 1998
Webster's	*Merriam-Webster's Collegiate Dictionary,* 1996

CHAPTER 1

Spelling

Chapter 1 – Spelling

1.1   Canadian English, reflecting our country's historical ties to Britain and its geographical proximity to the United States, has been influenced by both British and American cultures. It is no surprise, then, that Canadians use a hybrid of English that derives from two spelling traditions.

The variant spellings that have plagued Canadian editors and writers (not to mention schoolchildren) are partly the result of the historical development of spelling conventions in the English language. American spelling follows one respectable tradition in English orthography and British spelling follows another. In the early nineteenth century, when lexicographers tried to unify spelling, they had various historical examples to choose from and therefore gave alternative derivations. For example, both **honour** and **honor** had been used in Middle English. Some authorities deemed the word to be derived from the French and others from the original Latin.

Today, of course, neither British nor American usage is uniform. For instance, many words end in **-ize** in the *Concise Oxford* and in **-ise** in other British dictionaries (**recognize/recognise, organize/organise, realize/realise**). Yet the **-ise** endings are extremely rare in Canadian usage except in a few words (see Table 1.12), and those words are treated the same in American usage. To complicate the situation further, spelling preferences – particularly in the British tradition – are changing over time, and some words that once seemed to typify the distinctions are now being treated uniformly. For example, spellings of computer terms such as **disk, icon, analog,** and **program** cross all boundaries, even when the preferred spelling for the non-computer meaning is different. *Concise Oxford* joins American dictionaries in preferring **medieval** without the **-ae-** diphthong, and the **-x-** has been replaced by **-ct-** in **connection, reflection,** and **inflection.**

CANADIAN SPELLING STYLES

1.2   Canadian spelling has been a combination of British and American patterns, often idiosyncratically constructed. Until the end of the twentieth century, there was very little choice in Canadian dictionaries constructed from scratch (that is, other than American publications with the spelling adjusted and some Canadian entries added). As of early 2000, there are three made-in-Canada dictionaries, from Oxford, ITP Nelson, and Gage, as well as the established non-Canadian standbys such as *Concise Oxford* and *Webster's*. The editor may choose among them on the basis of the following considerations.

Market

1.3   Material published in Canada and aimed at distribution in Alberta or the United States may follow an American-influenced style, whereas material for the school market in Ontario or Nova Scotia would follow a British-influenced style. Some Canadian publishers satisfy an American market by using the American variants for **-re** and **-our** words only, as in **center** and **neighbor.**

Client

1.4   An author's insistence or a publisher's house style may determine the dictionary preference.

Subject matter

1.5   In some cases, the subject matter may suggest the choice. Discrepancies in spelling style between the text proper and quoted excerpts cannot always be avoided. However, if the subject is the union movement in the United States, for example, most excerpts and proper nouns will use the spelling **labor;** thus, to use a dictionary reflecting American spelling would avoid a jarring back-and-forth between variants. Similarly, although Canadian dictionaries usually drop the diphthong in **pediatricians,** practitioners may identify themselves as **paediatricians** and would use that form in their publications.

Type of publication

1.6   It used to be the case that established book publishers most often followed British spellings, whereas magazines and newspapers used the mixed spellings of the earlier Canadian Press style. More recently, however, the preferences of Canadian Press's *Caps and Spelling* and other newspapers and magazines have converged with those of book publishers.

1.7   Ideally, an editor chooses an appropriate dictionary and abides by its spelling preferences throughout a given manuscript. The problem is that dictionaries do not necessarily keep categories of spellings "pure"; their first entry for a particular word may be based on the frequency with which that spelling is encountered rather than principles of consistency. (For instance, note the *Canadian Oxford* entries in Table 1.8.) Yet internal consistency is what a particular work requires. Thus editors have to be acquainted with the categories of words that contain variant spellings as shown in the tables. We recommend strongly that spellings not be mixed *within* each of the categories in Tables 1.1, 1.3, 1.6, and 1.11. If **-ll-** is used in **travelled,** it should also be used in **signalling.** Nevertheless, mixing categories – for example, using **labor/neighbor** and **centre/metre** – is truly Canadian.

3

> "Henry Fowler declared that American and British English should not be mixed, an injunction that must leave Canadians speechless."
>
> – Peter Sypnowich, "Our Native Tongue," *Saturday Night*, March 1986

Moreover, we argue against idiosyncratic spelling styles that involve so many exceptions from the main-choice dictionary that the editor has trouble maintaining consistency and the proofreader considers an alternative career. A major purpose of editing is, after all, to make the mechanics of presentation inconspicuous so as not to distract the reader.

CATEGORIES OF VARIANT SPELLINGS

1.8 The tables that follow indicate the first entry for words as they appear in five dictionaries: *Webster's, Gage, Nelson, Canadian Oxford,* and *Concise Oxford.* It is interesting to peruse those categories to see where the Canadian dictionaries lean to the American spelling and where they uphold the British tradition. Where a specific dictionary does not suit the manuscript at hand, the editor can use these categories to build a more suitable style sheet.

Table 1.1   -or / -our

-or	Webster's	Gage	Nelson	Cdn. Oxford	Con. Oxford	-our	Webster's	Gage	Nelson	Cdn. Oxford	Con. Oxford
arbor	●					arbour		●	●	●	●
arboreal						*arboreal*					
ardor	●					ardour		●	●	●	●
armor	●					armour		●	●	●	●
armorial						*armorial*					
behavior	●					behaviour		●	●	●	●
candor	●					candour		●	●	●	●
clamor	●					clamour		●	●	●	●
color	●					colour		●	●	●	●
coloration	●	●	●	●		colouration					●
colorful	●					colourful		●	●	●	●
colorize	●		●			colourize				●	
colorist	●					colourist		●	●	●	●
demeanor	●					demeanour		●	●	●	●

Note: Italics indicate that the same spelling is the preference of all five dictionaries.

Table 1.1   -or / -our – *continued*

	Webster's	Gage	Nelson	Cdn. Oxford	Con. Oxford
endeavor	●				
favor	●				
favorable	●				
favorite	●				
fervor	●				
glamour					
glamorize, glamorous					
harbor	●				
honor	●				
honorable	●				
honorary, honorific					
humor	●				
humorous					
humorist					
labor	●				
laborious					
neighbor	●				
odor	●				
odorous, odoriferous					
parlor	●				
rancor	●				
rancorous					
rigor (strictness)	●				
rigorous					
rumor	●				
savior	●				
savor	●				
savory (taste)	●				
splendor	●				
succor	●				
tumor	●				
valor	●				
valorous					
vapor	●				
vaporize					
vigor	●				
vigorous					

	Webster's	Gage	Nelson	Cdn. Oxford	Con. Oxford
endeavour		●	●	●	●
favour		●	●	●	●
favourable		●	●	●	●
favourite		●	●	●	●
fervour		●	●	●	●
glamour					
glamorize, glamorous					
harbour		●	●	●	●
honour		●	●	●	●
honourable		●	●	●	●
honorary, honorific					
humour		●	●	●	●
humorous					
humorist					
labour		●	●	●	●
laborious					
neighbour		●	●	●	●
odour		●	●	●	●
odorous, odoriferous					
parlour		●	●	●	●
rancour		●	●	●	●
rancorous					
rigour (strictness)		●	●	●	●
rigorous					
rumour		●	●	●	●
saviour		●	●	●	●
savour		●	●	●	●
savoury (taste)		●	●	●	●
splendour		●	●	●	●
succour		●	●	●	●
tumour		●	●	●	●
valour		●	●	●	●
valorous					
vapour		●	●	●	●
vaporize					
vigour		●	●	●	●
vigorous					

Note: Italics indicate that the same spelling is the preference of all five dictionaries.

Table 1.2   Invariant -or (all dictionaries)

rigor (mortis)
languor
liquor
manor
pallor
savory (herb)
squalor
stupor
tenor
tremor

Table 1.3   -er/-re

	Webster's	Gage	Nelson	Cdn. Oxford	Con. Oxford		Webster's	Gage	Nelson	Cdn. Oxford	Con. Oxford
center	●					centre	●	●	●	●	
fiber *fibroid, fibrous*	●					fibre *fibroid, fibrous*	●	●	●	●	
luster *lustrous*	●					lustre *lustrous*	●	●	●	●	
maneuver	●					manoeuvre	●	●	●	●	
meager	●					meagre	●	●	●	●	
meter (device)						*meter (device)*					
meter (SI unit)	●					metre (SI unit)	●	●	●	●	
miter	●					mitre	●	●	●	●	
ocher	●					ochre	●	●	●	●	
philter	●					philtre	●	●	●	●	
saltpeter	●					saltpetre	●	●	●	●	
scepter	●					sceptre	●	●	●	●	
somber	●					sombre	●	●	●	●	
specter *spectral*	●					spectre *spectral*	●	●	●	●	
theater*	●					theatre	●	●	●	●	

*Some theatres in the United States use the **-re** spelling in their names.

Note: Italics indicate that the same spelling is the preference of all five dictionaries.

Table 1.4   Invariant -re (all dictionaries)

genre
lucre
macabre
massacre
mediocre
timbre

Table 1.5   Diphthongs

	Webster's	Gage	Nelson	Cdn. Oxford	Con. Oxford		Webster's	Gage	Nelson	Cdn. Oxford	Con. Oxford
aesthetic						*aesthetic*					
anemia	●	●	●	●		anaemia					●
anesthesia	●	●	●			anaesthesia				●	●
archaeology						*archaeology*					
diarrhea	●	●	●	●		diarrhoea					●
encyclopedia						*encyclopedia*					
enology	●		●			oenology		●		●	●
estrogen	●	●	●	●		oestrogen					●
etiology	●	●	●	●		aetiology					●
fetid						*fetid*					
fetus						*fetus*					
hemorrhage	●	●	●	●		haemorrhage					●
maneuver	●					manoeuvre		●	●	●	●
medieval						*medieval*					
orthopedic	●	●	●			orthopaedic				●	●
pedagogy						*pedagogy*					
pediatric	●	●	●	●		paediatric					●

Note: Italics indicate that the same spelling is the preference of all five dictionaries.

Table 1.6   -yze/-yse

	Webster's	Gage	Nelson	Cdn. Oxford	Con. Oxford		Webster's	Gage	Nelson	Cdn. Oxford	Con. Oxford
analyze	●		●	●		analyse		●			●
Breathalyzer*	●		●	●		Breathalyser*		●			●
catalyze	●		●	●		catalyse		●			●
dialyze	●		●	●		dialyse		●			●
paralyze	●		●	●		paralyse		●			●

* Capitalized as a trade name in *Webster's*, *Gage*, *Nelson*, and *Canadian Oxford*.

Table 1.7   Plurals of foreign words

	Webster's	Gage	Nelson	Cdn. Oxford	Con. Oxford		Webster's	Gage	Nelson	Cdn. Oxford	Con. Oxford
appendixes	●	●	●			appendices				●	●
bureaus	●	●		●		bureaux			●		●
châteaus	●					châteaux*		●	●	●	●
formulas†	●	●	●			formulae (math., chem.)				●	●
						formulas (other)				●	●
indexes† (back of book)						indexes (back of book)				●	●
indexes† (technical)						indices (technical)				●	●
referendums		●	●	●	●	referenda	●				
tableaux						*tableaux*					

* No circumflex accent in *Concise Oxford*.

† *Webster's*, *Gage*, and *Nelson* give both plurals but do not distinguish their use.

Note: Italics indicate that the same spelling is the preference of all five dictionaries.

Table 1.8   Silent -e- plus suffix

	Webster's	Gage	Nelson	Cdn. Oxford	Con. Oxford
abridgment	●	●	●		
acknowledgment	●	●	●		
aging	●		●	●	
judgment	●	●	●	●	
likable	●	●	●		
livable	●	●	●	●	
lovable					
movable					
salable	●		●		
sizable	●	●	●	●	

	Webster's	Gage	Nelson	Cdn. Oxford	Con. Oxford
abridgement				●	●
acknowledgement				●	●
ageing		●			●
judgement					●
likeable				●	●
liveable					●
lovable					
movable					
saleable		●		●	●
sizeable					●

Table 1.9   -c-/-s- plus endings

	Webster's	Gage	Nelson	Cdn. Oxford	Con. Oxford
defense *defensible, defensive*	●				
license (n. & v.)	●				
offense *offensive*	●				
practice (n.&v.)	●				
pretense	●		●		
prophecy (n.) *prophesy (v.)*					

	Webster's	Gage	Nelson	Cdn. Oxford	Con. Oxford
defence *defensible, defensive*		●	●	●	●
licence (n.)		●	●	●	●
license (v.)		●	●	●	●
offence *offensive*		●	●	●	●
practice (n.)		●	●	●	●
practise (v.)		●	●	●	
pretence		●		●	●
prophecy (n.) *prophesy (v.)*					

Note: Italics indicate that the same spelling is the preference of all five dictionaries.

Table 1.10 Certain stems containing -l or -ll (stressed syllable)

	Webster's	Gage	Nelson	Cdn. Oxford	Con. Oxford
annul					
annulment					
appall	●		●	●	
appalling					
compel					
dispel					
distill	●		●	●	
distillation					
enroll	●		●		
enrollment	●		●		
expel					
forestall					
forestallment	●		●		
fulfill	●		●	●	
fulfillment	●		●	●	
fulfilling					
impel					
install					
installment	●		●		
instill	●		●	●	
repel					
repellent					

	Webster's	Gage	Nelson	Cdn. Oxford	Con. Oxford
annul					
annulment					
appal		●			●
appalling					
compel					
dispel					
distil		●			●
distillation					
enrol		●		●	●
enrolment		●		●	●
expel					
forestall					
forestalment				●	●
fulfil		●			●
fulfilment		●			●
fulfilling					
impel					
install					
instalment		●		●	●
instil		●			●
repel					
repellent					

Note: Italics indicate that the same spelling is the preference of all five dictionaries.

Table 1.11 Single or double consonant (unstressed syllable) before other endings

	Webster's	Gage	Nelson	Cdn. Oxford	Con. Oxford		Webster's	Gage	Nelson	Cdn. Oxford	Con. Oxford
benefited						*benefited*					
biased	●		●	●	●	biassed		●			
billeted						*billeted*					
budgeted						*budgeted*					
combating	●		●		●	combatting		●		●	
equaled	●					equalled		●	●	●	●
focused	●		●	●	●	focussed		●			
graveled	●					gravelled		●	●	●	●
imperiled	●					imperilled		●	●	●	●
kidnapped						*kidnapped*					
libelous	●					libellous		●	●	●	●
marshaled	●					marshalled		●	●	●	●
marvelous	●					marvellous		●	●	●	●
outfitted						*outfitted*					
paralleled	●		●	●	●	parallelled		●			
pedaled	●					pedalled		●	●	●	●
signaler	●					signaller		●	●	●	●
targeted						*targeted*					
tranquilize	●			●		tranquillize		●	●		●
traveler	●					traveller		●	●	●	●
woolen	●					woollen		●	●	●	●
woolly						*woolly*					
worshiper	●					worshipper		●	●	●	●

Note: Italics indicate that the same spelling is the preference of all five dictionaries.

Table 1.12 Invariant -ise (all dictionaries except as noted)

circumcise, excise, exercise, exorcise, * *incise*

compromise, surmise

despise

apprise, comprise, surprise *

advertise

advise, devise, improvise, revise, supervise

* For *exorcise,* an **-ize** ending is first choice in *Concise Oxford,* and an alternative in *Canadian Oxford* and *Webster's.* For *surprise,* an **-ize** ending is an alternative in *Webster's* and *Nelson.*

Table 1.13 Miscellaneous

	Webster's	Gage	Nelson	Cdn. Oxford	Con. Oxford
*adviser**					
airplane	●	●	●	●	
analogue†					
artifact	●	●	●	●	
ax	●				
balk	●	●	●	●	
blowzy			●		●
caulk					
catalog	●				
cauldron					
check (verify)					
check (bank draft)	●				
cigarette					
cozy	●		●	●	
dialogue					
disk†	●				
dispatch					

	Webster's	Gage	Nelson	Cdn. Oxford	Con. Oxford
*adviser**					
aeroplane					●
analogue†					
artefact					●
axe		●	●	●	●
baulk					●
blowsy	●	●		●	
caulk					
catalogue		●	●	●	●
cauldron					
check (verify)					
cheque (bank draft)		●	●	●	●
cigarette					
cosy		●			●
dialogue					
disc†		●	●	●	●
dispatch					

Note: Italics indicate that the same spelling is the preference of all five dictionaries.

Table 1.13 Miscellaneous – *continued*

	Webster's	Gage	Nelson	Cdn. Oxford	Con. Oxford
draft (draw up)					
draft (wind, gulp)	●	●	●	●	
drier (comparative)					
dryer (appliance)					
dryer (chem. agent)		●		●	●
dryly	●	●	●	●	
flyer (pilot)		●		●	●
flyer (pamphlet)	●	●		●	●
gauge					
gray	●				
jail					
ikon†	●				
inflection					
inquire	●	●	●	●	
marshal‡					
mold	●				
mustache	●	●	●		
omelette					
peddler	●	●	●	●	
plow	●		●	●	
program†	●	●	●	●	
pajamas	●				
racket (tennis)	●	●	●		●
skepticism	●		●	●	
smolder	●				
story (buildings)	●				
sulfur	●				

	Webster's	Gage	Nelson	Cdn. Oxford	Con. Oxford
draft (draw up)					
draught (wind, gulp)					●
drier (comparative)					
dryer (appliance)					
drier (chem. agent)	●				
drily					●
flier (pilot)	●		●		
flier (pamphlet)			●		
gauge					
grey		●	●	●	●
jail					
icon†		●	●	●	●
inflection					
enquire					●
marshal‡					
mould		●	●	●	●
moustache				●	●
omelette					
pedlar					●
plough		●			●
programme†					●
pyjamas		●	●	●	●
racquet (tennis)				●	
scepticism		●			●
smoulder		●	●	●	●
storey (buildings)		●	●	●	●
sulphur		●	●	●	●

* The **-or** option is widely seen nevertheless, possibly because of its similarity to **advisory.**

† All five dictionaries prefer **analog, disk, icon,** and **program** in computer context.

‡ Occasionally seen as **marshall,** probably in imitation of the spelling of the name.

Note: Italics indicate that the same spelling is the preference of all five dictionaries.

CANADIAN DICTIONARIES AND SPELLING GUIDES

1.9   Canadian editors have welcomed the appearance of all-Canadian dictionaries. An informal survey suggests that they most favour the *Canadian Oxford Dictionary* and the *Nelson Canadian Dictionary*. The extensive encyclopedic entries in these two are valuable for personal and place names and data. Neither offers totally consistent within-category spellings; however, supplemented by the information above, either is a good working tool. *Nelson* has an edge in that it indicates word breaks. The *Canadian Oxford Spelling Dictionary* remedies this weakness in the main dictionary.

1.10   Widely used, especially by editors in journalism, is the Canadian Press's *Caps and Spelling,* an often updated booklet of abbreviations, commonly misspelled words, CP's preferred spelling style, and names of Canadian people, places, and institutions.

1.11   Canadian editors find that the spellcheckers available at time of writing are of limited use. Apart from their inability to pick up typical errors such as *causal* for *casual,* they do not reflect the essentially Canadian practice of selecting from both British and American forms.

SOURCE

Partridge, Eric. *Origins: A Short Etymological Dictionary of Modern English.* New York: Greenwich House, 1983.

CHAPTER 2

Compounds

Chapter 2 – Compounds

2.1   When words, part words (such as prefixes and suffixes), and numbers combine to form a unit of meaning, judicious use of punctuation can clarify the nature of the link. The hyphen and, to a lesser extent, the en dash and the solidus enable writers to eliminate ambiguity and make reading easier. Other choices are to close up two elements or to leave them open (not hyphenated).

     With compound words, especially those involving prefixes, Canadian writers and editors have taken a path somewhere between American and British practices, closing up more compounds than the British and fewer than the Americans. Over time there has been a trend toward treating more compounds as closed rather than hyphenated.

     Some functions of the hyphen are grammatical, clarifying the relationships between words. Although these uses are described here, there is nothing distinctively Canadian in their treatment. Nor is there any particularly Canadian principle for end-of-line breaks. Nevertheless we include a brief discussion at the end of the chapter because novel constructions such as Internet addresses pose a new challenge.

2.2   Unfortunately, dictionaries do not always provide adequate guidance for dealing with compounds: some dictionaries list only (or list first) the form most often encountered by the compilers. Thus, two terms exactly parallel in construction may be treated differently in the dictionary and yet obviously call for a consistent form in the project at hand. For example, the *Canadian Oxford* offers **wood-burning/woodcutting** and **woodworker/metal worker.** It also shows **decision maker** as open and **policy-maker** as hyphenated, and **co-operate** and **coordinate.** In a context in which such compounds have a parallel function, it makes sense to treat them in the same way.

2.3   Tables 2.1 and 2.2 illustrate a few of the hyphenating preferences of some popular dictionaries: *Concise Oxford, Webster's,* and three recent Canadian publications, *Gage, Nelson,* and *Canadian Oxford.* It is clear that their choices are not based on consistent treatment from word to word, although *Nelson* and *Webster's* have a distinct preference for closed constructions.

2.4   In this chapter, as elsewhere, we advise considering the subject matter and the intended audience. The terms encountered in a specialized subject, familiar to those in the field, may more often be either closed or open rather than hyphenated (e.g., **psychopharmacology; small business development loan**). By comparison, less fluent readers, younger readers, and readers encountering unfamiliar vocabulary will appreciate more punctuation clues to clarify meaning. Although a main dictionary may be chosen as appropriate to the particular audience, the style sheet for the project may have to include many exceptions that allow a greater consistency of treatment of compounds.

Table 2.1   Examples of hyphenation: nouns and adjectives

	Webster's	Gage	Nelson	Cdn. Oxford	Con. Oxford		Webster's	Gage	Nelson	Cdn. Oxford	Con. Oxford
Nouns											
backstabber	●		●			back-stabber		●		●	●
catchall	●		●			catch-all		●		●	●
court-martial	●	●	●			court martial				●	●
daycare			●	●		day care	●	●			●
double-talk	●			●	●	double talk		●	●		
facelift		●		●	●	face-lift	●		●		
ladylove	●	●	●			lady love				●	
mind-reader				●	●	mind reader	●	●	●		
Adjectives											
homemade	●	●	●	●		home-made					●
longtime	●		●			long-time				●	
secondhand	●		●			second-hand		●		●	●
yearlong	●	●	●			year-long				●	

Note: Most of these dictionaries agree in hyphenating doubled words such as **putt-putt, bye-bye,** and **pooh-pooh.**

Table 2.2   Examples of hyphenation: prefixes and verb tails

	Webster's	Gage	Nelson	Cdn. Oxford	Con. Oxford		Webster's	Gage	Nelson	Cdn. Oxford	Con. Oxford
antiaircraft	●		●			anti-aircraft		●		●	●
antiinflammatory			●			anti-inflammatory	●	●		●	●
antioxidant	●		●	●	●	anti-oxidant	●				
antisocial	●	●	●		●	anti-social				●	

Table 2.2   Examples of hyphenation: prefixes and verb tails – *continued*

	Webster's	Gage	Nelson	Cdn. Oxford	Con. Oxford		Webster's	Gage	Nelson	Cdn. Oxford	Con. Oxford
multiethnic	●	●	●			multi-ethnic				●	●
coauthor	●		●			co-author		●		●	●
cochair	●					co-chair				●	
cooperate	●		●		●	co-operate		●		●	
coproduce	●					co-produce				●	●
preempt	●		●			pre-empt		●		●	●
preset	●	●	●		●	pre-set				●	
predetermined	●	●	●	●	●	pre-determined					
postgraduate	●	●	●		●	post-graduate				●	
postmortem	●		●			post-mortem		●		●	●
underreport	●	●	●			under-report				●	
pushover	●		●	●	●	push-over	●				
puton	●					put-on		●	●	●	●
putdown			●			put-down	●	●		●	●
faceoff					●	face-off	●	●	●		●

THREE APPROACHES

2.5   After considering the project, its audience, and not least the author and publisher, the editor may choose one of the approaches below and then identify any necessary exceptions. Alternatively, the editor may stay with the preferences of a particular dictionary with minor adaptations.

Temporary vs. permanent compounds

2.6   Use a hyphen when the prefix and root word, or root word and suffix, or any two words form a temporary compound – that is, a handy word put together for the occasion (**teen-proof, widget-maker, fold-away**). Do not use the hyphen in permanent compounds – those so thoroughly fixed in the language that they are distinct words in their own right (**foolproof, shoemaker, tearaway**).

The problem with this approach is that a large number of words are semi-permanent – words "in transition," moving from open to hyphenated to closed status as they become established (**Web site** to **Web-site** to **Website** or **website**). The editor must judge the permanence of each example encountered.

Minimum use of hyphens

2.7   Close the compound after prefixes, between two root words, and before verb tails (**preordained, toolbar, startup**). Some American guides (*Chicago Manual* and *Webster's* dictionary) omit hyphens wherever possible. But this approach includes several cautions and exceptions, particularly with regard to prefixes (see 2.9).

Readability

2.8   Many letter combinations (**ea, ai, oi, ee, oo, ou, th, ph, sh,** for example) can be read as diphthongs. Some editors prefer to separate them. For example, they might put a hyphen in such examples as:

> contra-indicated, photo-offset, meta-analysis
>
> hot-house, glass-house, hop-head

Words that are well established are nevertheless frequently closed up.

PREFIXES, SUFFIXES, AND VERB TAILS

Prefixes

2.9   Canadian writers and editors have traditionally tended to use more hyphens after a prefix (**pre-, re-, anti-, non-, counter-,** etc.) than American writers and fewer than British. Yet recent Canadian dictionaries, as well as the most recent *Concise Oxford*, have been taking these hyphens out by the handful. If the stylistic preference is minimal use of hyphens, the editor can look to these dictionaries for support (see Table 2.2). However, many editors would make the following exceptions:

- when the root word is capitalized (anti-Soviet, pre-Columbian, un-Canadian)
- when there is confusion of meaning (recover/re-cover, reformation/ re-formation, resign/re-sign, coop/co-op, overage/over-age, recreation/re-creation)
- after **cross-, ex-, quasi-,** and **self-** (cross-cultural, ex-president, quasi-judicial, self-deceit)

- when **aa, ii,** or **lll** would result (meta-analysis, anti-intellectual, bell-like)
- when three vowels would result (anti-aircraft, anti-authoritarian, co-author, semi-automatic)
- when two identical consonants would result (dial-like, non-native, counter-revolution, post-traumatic)

The problem with rigidly applying any of these options is that some familiar words (**reorganize, prearrange, crossover**) look strange *with* a hyphen, and yet other words can be difficult to read correctly *without* a hyphen (**demisting, prowar, codriver, cowriter**). Some editors reject all of these rules, reserving the hyphen for specific types of compounds. For example:

- those that would otherwise juxtapose un-English combinations such as **aa** or **ii** (anti-inflammatory)
- those otherwise difficult to read correctly (co-opt)
- those that join a prefix or suffix to a root that is already a compound (anti-free-trade crusader, pro-bilingual-education group, multi-drug-resistant TB, co-op-like). In some cases recasting may be preferable. If the hyphenated version is kept, note that both hyphens in each such example are needed.

(*Webster's* also makes exceptions for many **by-** compounds: bylaw, byline, bypass, byplay; but by-blow, by-election, by-product.)

Suffixes and verb tails

2.10   Verbs with tails – **shut in, put up, let down, throw away, set off, turn over, fall out** – are open; adjectives derived from verbs with tails are hyphenated; derived nouns may or may not be.

- When companies lay off workers, are the laid-off people victims of a layoff or a lay-off?
- Now that you have grown up, are you a grownup or a grown-up?
- When the new sitcom was spun off, was it a spinoff or a spin-off?

Whether a hyphen is used in these compounds depends on a judgment of readability. For example, compounds with **-out, -over,** and **-off** may need no hyphen if the whole word is easily grasped (**burnout, takeover, playoff**).

When **up** is the verb tail, a hyphen may be preferable if the root word is more than one syllable (**follow-up, cover-up**). If the root word ends in an **e,** the hyphen may be unnecessary, particularly in a context where the word is common (**line-up/lineup, make-up/makeup, tune-up/tuneup**).

When **in** is the verb tail, the compound is difficult to read without a hyphen (**sitin/sit-in, cavein/cave-in**).

2.11   Established words ending in **-like** are usually written without the hyphen (**Christlike, birdlike**). Otherwise, if the root word

- ends in **-l,** a hyphen is recommended (dial-like)
- ends in -**ll,** the hyphen is essential (bell-like, mall-like)
- is a proper noun, use the hyphen (McMullen-like, Vancouver-like)
- is long, a hyphen is desirable (alligator-like)
- is a compound, two hyphens are needed (boa-constrictor-like). But many double compounds are awkward if not ludicrous.

Prefixes and suffixes with compound proper nouns

2.12   Proper nouns consisting of more than one word are perceived as a unit because they are capitalized, and do not require a hyphen (**Grey Cup Game party**). Yet a prefix before a compound proper noun looks awkward:

> The ex-Grand Duchess Felicia attended the post-Grey Cup Game party.

Rewording solves the problem:

> The former Grand Duchess Felicia attended a party after the Grey Cup Game.

2.13   The en dash instead of a hyphen between a prefix and a multi-word proper-noun construction is an alternative.

> ex–Grand Duchess
>
> pre–War of 1812 boundaries
>
> anti–Combines Law editorial

The same solution may be used for a suffix or tail following a proper-noun compound:

> James Bond–style shenanigans
>
> Marie Antoinette–like disdain

However, it may be better to reword: the nicety of the en dash may not be sufficient to improve an ungainly construction.

HYPHENS IN COMPOUND MODIFIERS

2.14   The following rules relate to the grammatical function of the words in the sentence, rather than to the spelling of the words themselves.

Adverb ending in "-ly" plus adjective or participle

2.15   A hyphen generally should not be used after an adverb ending in **-ly**, for the **-ly** itself in most cases identifies its modifier function:

> a poorly paid editor
>
> an unjustly accused person

Note that **wholly-owned subsidiary** is often seen in the context of taxation, as the term is so treated in the Income Tax Act.

Many adjectives have the **-ly** form, such as **womanly, lovely, seemly, likely, worldly,** and **comely.** However, their adjectival function is usually obvious.

Qualifying adverb plus adjective or participle

2.16   When the qualifying adverb, such as **well, ill, better, best, little,** or **least,** modifies an adjective, the hyphen is usually omitted:

> the less official version
>
> the least likely candidate

When the qualifying adverb modifies a past or present participle, a hyphen is usually used when the modifying compound precedes the noun:

> a well-regarded principle
>
> the worst-paying jobs
>
> a little-understood phenomenon

The hyphen may be omitted if the meaning is unambiguous. But compare:

> the best funded projects/the best-funded projects

Do not hyphenate when the compound modifier follows the noun:

> The principle is well regarded.
>
> These jobs are the worst paying.

The hyphen is unnecessary when the compound is itself qualified:

> a very well regarded principle
>
> the comparatively less developed economies

Noun plus present or past participle

2.17   If the compound is an adjective, use the hyphen:

> Meat-packing plants are not for the squeamish.
>
> Mama sneers at machine-made noodles.
>
> Hand-knitted sweaters often turn out strangely baggy.

Do not use the hyphen if the compound comes after the noun:

> noodles that are machine made
>
> sweaters may be hand knitted

If the compound is a noun, the hyphen is optional:

> a cat breeding *or* cat-breeding operation

2.18   Many compounds are so well established in everyday language that they may be hyphenated no matter how they are used in the sentence (**arm-twisting, money-grubbing**) or may be one word (**nitpicking, handmade**). These permanent compounds are given in the dictionary. Characteristically they are pronounced with a marked stress on the first element and a minor stress on the second.

Adjective plus noun

2.19   Hyphenate the compound if it comes before the noun:

> Energy at low cost is low-cost energy.
>
> Industry characterized by high technology is high-technology industry.

Similarly, **third-party representation, low-water mark,** etc. If the compound is used after the noun but is still adjectival, the hyphen may be omitted if the meaning is clear:

> All ingredients used are best quality.

In some works, an extraordinary number of these constructions are used. Some editors prefer, for the sake of appearance, to leave open those phrases that are unambiguous in the context. For instance, if the subject is Chinese cuisine, **glutinous rice wine** is readily understood, although the phrase in isolation may give one pause.

> "Keep in mind the advice of the Oxford University Press stylebook: 'If you take hyphens seriously, you will surely go mad.'"
>
> – *The Canadian Press Stylebook*

Noun plus adjective

2.20 Hyphenate a temporary compound if it comes before the noun:

> motion-sensitive light
> child-friendly environment
> frost-resistant strain
> hassle-free travel

Foreign phrases as modifiers

2.21 Phrases of foreign origin used as modifiers are normally not hyphenated, unless they would be hyphenated in the original language:

> per capita income
> ad hoc committee
> 10 per cent (*or* percent) raise
> prix fixe menu
> laissez-faire policy
> tête-à-tête conversation

Some editors treat phrases well established in English usage in the same way as English terms: **per-capita income.**

Series

2.22 When one of the elements of a compound is omitted in a pair or a series, note the appropriate spacing in relation to the hyphen or en dash:

> the 46- and 52-cent stamps
> a 30-, 60-, or 90-day term deposit
> a five- or six-day work week
> pre– and post–Stanley Cup riots
> a network-owned and -operated station
> a well-planned and -executed attack

If the construction looks awkward, either repeat the omitted word or recast.

Ambiguous phrases

2.23 Hyphens should be inserted in any string of words whenever the sense can be missed if no signal links a specific pair or group (as in "50 year old hens for sale"):

> a precooked-tuna and tomato dish; a precooked tuna-and-tomato dish
> high-school dropout rate; high school-dropout rate
> a dog-free play area; a dog free-play area

SOLIDUS AND EN DASH

Equal elements with solidus

2.24 A solidus (forward slash, slant, oblique) may give a clearer signal than a hyphen when elements of equal significance are joined and the relationship is more complex than **and** or **or** would indicate.

> The student/teacher ratio soared as funds shrank. (*ratio*)
>
> Irving was one of the great actor/managers. (*simultaneous roles*)
>
> Labour/management relations were under review. (*between*)
>
> The home-with-mother/quality-child-care debate continued. (*alternatives*)

Some editors avoid such constructions, particularly in formal prose. Solidus constructions can also often introduce a vagueness that would be remedied only by rephrasing.

Compound compounds with solidus

2.25 The solidus is a useful device when the two elements of the balanced compound are themselves compound:

> research in left-brain/right-brain task differentiation
>
> the total Saint John–Halifax/Halifax–Vancouver flying time

Note that the second example calls for the en dash between **Saint John** and **Halifax** and between **Halifax** and **Vancouver** (see 2.27).

Compounds with en dash

2.26 The en dash may join a prefix or a tail to a proper noun of more than one word. It may also join parallel elements where one proper-noun element contains more than one word:

> the member for Toronto Centre–Rosedale
>
> the Tsawwassen–Swartz Bay ferry

2.27 The en dash is preferable to the hyphen for replacing the words **from ... to** or **between ... and** in several types of compounds, particularly those involving numerals:

> pages 30–35 *or* 30–5
>
> member of the provincial assembly 1942–48
>
> a range of 23%–43%

As with numerals, the words **from ... to** may be replaced by the en dash in several contexts:

> the Regina–Saskatoon bus fare
>
> the Mus–Nij volume of the encyclopedia

Note that the en dash replaces *both* words. Either retain both words (**open from 6 to 10 p.m.**) or use the en dash only (**open 6–10 p.m.**).

2.28   Note also how a distinction may be made between an inclusive span of years and a period that overlaps calendar years. The solidus in the first example below is frequently used for the latter purpose:

> the 2002/03 fiscal year (school year, hockey season, winter)
>
> the decade 1982–91

HYPHENS WITH NUMBERS

2.29   The hyphenation of spelled-out numbers gives many writers difficulties.

> two-thirds, one-half (*but* a half, a fifth)
>
> one hundred and twenty-five
>
> thirty-three one-hundredths
>
> four and three-quarters

Note that *all* of the hyphens are required in adjectival forms:

> a four-and-three-quarter-hour flight
>
> a twenty-four-year-old man

With an adjective that combines a numeral and a unit of measure, the hyphen is optional.

> a 4.75-hour flight, a 4.75 hour flight
>
> a 15.5-km drive, a 15.5 km drive

The Globe and Mail Style Book calls for a hyphen in expressions of millions or billions of dollars:

> a $25-million contract; a fortune of $35-billion

END-OF-LINE BREAKS

Word division

2.30　Rules for word division as practised in Canada and the United States are given in the major guides such as the *Chicago Manual*.

The main principle governing word breaks is pronunciation: the portion of the word at the end of the line should be capable of being sounded correctly before the eye sees the rest of the word.

Although the *Chicago Manual* states that British practice is based on derivation rather than pronunciation, in fact the British style is also governed by pronunciation. Yet it forbids many breaks that would be acceptable in North American practice. If the editor and typesetter are asked to use British word divisions, they should invest in a British word-division dictionary, such as the *Oxford Colour Spelling Dictionary*.

The *Canadian Oxford Spelling Dictionary* (1999) also shows word division, basing it on a mixture of etymological and phonological criteria.

Division of numerals

2.31　The end-of-line break of large numbers, when unavoidable, should occur at a comma:

　　3,456, ▌789, ▌654, ▌321

Do not break at the decimal point, and do not break after one digit. Insert a hyphen at the break.

Division of other sequences

2.32　Codes such as ISBNs that contain hyphens may be broken at any of the hyphens. Codes or sequences that include a slash (a forward or a back slash) may be similarly broken after the slash, with no hyphen needed. Note that as with any word, the break would not be placed before only one or two characters.

　　ISBN 0- ▌88894- ▌540-X

　　C87- ▌091062-0

　　Browse to the \VENTURA\ ▌SAMPLES\ ▌TUTORIAL folder

　　IBRS/ ▌CCRI NUMBER: PHQD- ▌4080-mk

2.33　When they first appeared in running prose, Internet addresses and email addresses were never broken no matter what happened to the appearance of the paragraph. They are now seen with breaks occurring at the punctuation marks. The break follows the forward slashes in <http://>, follows a single symbol, and separates two symbols. *A hyphen appears only when it already occurs in the address.*

vicbiz. ▌@pathicom. ▌com

http:// ▌www. ▌editors.ca

www. ▌management. ▌mcgill. ▌ca/ ▌resource/ ▌library/ ▌rosslib. ▌htm

www. ▌ccra- ▌adrc. ▌gc.ca

gopher:// ▌gopher. ▌ipc. ▌apc. ▌org/

SOURCE

Calishain, Tara, and Jill Alane Nystrom. *Official Netscape Guide to Internet Research.* 2nd ed. Scottsdale, Ariz.: Coriolus Group, 1998.

CHAPTER 3

Capitalization

Chapter 3 – Capitalization

3.1 Capitalization is probably second only to spelling as a source of confusion and ambivalence for Canadian editors. Few rules of English-language capitalization enjoy a consensus. In addition, capital letters, more than any other style device, can be value laden and thus likely to provoke debate. In recent years, the trend on both sides of the Atlantic has been toward an increasing use of lowercase. Thus many writers and editors today consider capitals in general old-fashioned and conservative. Others, however, continue to see them as conferring on certain terms a proper authority and importance.

This chapter does not attempt to deal with the numerous conventions of capitalization in normal sentence punctuation, in titles of works, and in headings. These are covered extensively in general style guides such as the *Chicago Manual* and *Words into Type*. Here the focus is rather on the problem terms encountered in text that do not fall under an iron-clad rule. On the editor's style sheet for any manuscript, these are the terms that show two or three changes of mind as the editor tries to discern some principle to follow. This chapter identifies the various factors that govern decisions on capitalization – factors that often overlap and conflict with one another. When such a conflict occurs, the editor's only resort is judgment, with the aim of resolving all analogous conflicts the same way within a given manuscript.

GENERAL FACTORS

3.2 The first decisions an editor must make regarding capitalization concern the manuscript as a whole. Would a more generous or a less generous use of capitals be appropriate for the particular manuscript? Where should the lines be drawn, and are there any peculiarities for which exceptions should be made? Decisions based on context are perhaps the most important, for they set the general style and provide a basis for making later, more specific choices.

Tradition

3.3 Is a traditional or more modern style appropriate to a publication? Although the current trend is toward lowercase, an editor may decide that more capitals are required for more conservative publications and their readers. A business journal or a book put out by the Monarchist League, for example, may well use more capitals than a film-and-video trade paper. The former might note the presence of **a Cabinet Minister** at an opening ceremony, where the latter would refer to the same ribbon-cutting politician as **a cabinet minister.**

Readership

3.4   Readers in a specialized field may be accustomed to more capitals than a general readership would be. Some internal corporate publications, for example, require capitalization of such words as **Company, Board,** and **President.** Legal documents contain more capitals in order to remove every trace of possible ambiguity in the use of special terms. However, manuscripts intended for general readership are edited according to standard modern style guides, which favour a down, or lowercase, style.

Aesthetics

3.5   It is entirely legitimate to make some capitalization decisions purely on the basis of appearance. Editors may decide to uppercase only the most unequivocal proper nouns when it becomes apparent that a more generous use of capitals would result in a daunting thicket.

SPECIFIC FACTORS

3.6   The factors in this section should be considered in making specific capitalization decisions. For additional factors relating to titles, see 3.16–29; on names of organizations, see 3.30–33; for geographical terms, see 3.34–50.

Official vs. less official forms

3.7   Conventional wisdom on capitalization starts from the assumption that place names, names of organizations, and certain titles and positions should be uppercased when in their full, proper, and official forms. These full forms should be given at least at first reference.

> National Film Board
>
> Ministry of Agriculture and Food
>
> Faculty of Law
>
> Selkirk County
>
> Secretary of State (Asia-Pacific)
>
> Minister of Indian Affairs and Northern Development

See also 12.50, "federal government department names," and 12.135, "secretaries of state."

Some editors capitalize only these full blue-ribbon forms, often the easiest practice since it requires the fewest decisions. (It becomes less easy if extensive research is required to determine the official form.) Subsequent references that are partial, inverted, or colloquial versions of the full form may then be lowercased with a clear conscience.

3.8   Other editors also capitalize certain variations of official forms, whether at first reference or later. Commissions and inquiries, in particular, are frequently referred to by the names of the commissioners or by shorter versions of their lengthy official names. Capitalization of these variants is appropriate when they are widely used.

> Commission of Inquiry on the Blood System in Canada/Krever Inquiry *or* Krever Commission
>
> Royal Commission on Bilingualism and Biculturalism/Bi and Bi Commission
>
> Commission of Inquiry into the Deployment of Canadian Forces to Somalia/Somalia Inquiry

3.9   Inverted forms may be capitalized, especially when they are very close to the original forms:

> Agriculture and Food Ministry
>
> Law Faculty
>
> Indian Affairs and Northern Development Minister

3.10   Partial forms, which should be used only rarely at first reference, may be capitalized, especially when they retain the essential *specifying* elements of a name:

> Film Board
>
> Ministry of Agriculture
>
> Agriculture (*where "Ministry of" is understood*)
>
> Minister of Indian Affairs *or* Indian Affairs Minister
>
> Secretary of State (*when the area of responsibility is clear*)

3.11   Use lowercase in partial references that eliminate the specifying element, leaving only the *generic* terms. (For exceptions, see 3.4, 3.24, and 3.25.)

> the board
>
> the faculty
>
> the ministry
>
> the county
>
> the minister

Ours vs. theirs

3.12 A distinction is sometimes made between our dignitaries or organizations and those of other people. This practice may apply to an entire manuscript for a certain readership (see 3.4) or only to certain terms within a manuscript intended for general readership. These terms will vary, of course, depending on who the "we" is in the context.

> the Queen of Canada/the queen of the Netherlands
>
> Governor General of Canada/governor general of Australia
>
> the Alberta Legislature/the Ontario legislature (*in a Calgary newspaper*)
>
> our Mayor/a neighbouring town's mayor

Plurals

3.13 Some editors use lowercase for the generic portion of a phrase in the plural that would be capitalized in the singular:

> Ontario Legislature/Ontario and Alberta legislatures
>
> Lake Huron/lakes Huron and Erie

Other editors, following a traditional practice from the *Chicago Manual,* lowercase plural common nouns that *follow* the proper noun but uppercase common nouns that *precede* their specific components:

> Ontario Legislature/Ontario and Alberta legislatures
>
> Lake Huron/Lakes Huron and Erie

However, these distinctions seem unnecessarily complicated, and many editors ignore them. It is simpler to capitalize the generic term regardless of location. The *Chicago Manual* has in fact adopted this practice in the 14th edition:

> Ontario Legislature/Ontario and Alberta Legislatures
>
> Royal Commission on Corporate Concentration/Royal Commissions on Corporate Concentration and on Periodicals
>
> Burrard and Georgia Streets
>
> Anticosti Island/Anticosti and Pictou Islands
>
> Lake Huron/Lakes Huron and Erie

Ambiguity

3.14 To avoid ambiguity, some words may be capitalized in contexts where their meaning would otherwise be unclear:

> Act (*legislation*)
>
> Conservative (*party member*)

Father (*religious title*)

Fellow (*member of a society*)

Matron (*administrator*)

Speaker (*of the House*)

Witness (*Jehovah's Witness*)

Historical terms

3.15 Some titles and terms are so linked to days gone by that they are all but impossible to lowercase, even in contemporary usage. Often they relate to the monarchy or the judiciary:

Gentleman Usher of the Black Rod (*changed in 1997 to* Usher of the Senate)

the King's Law

Master of the Rolls

Queen's Counsel

Surveyor of the King's Woods

TITLES OF PERSONS

3.16 Inconsistencies both deliberate and accidental are especially frequent in capitalization of titles. It is small comfort to the struggling editor that the average reader rarely notices these inconsistencies.

In addition to the following points, see the general factors discussed at 3.2–5 and the specific factors considered at 3.6–15.

Before the name

3.17 A common starting point is to capitalize titles when they directly precede the name of the titleholder (but see 3.18–22). Most authorities capitalize titles in this construction only:

Prime Minister Chrétien/Chrétien, the prime minister

Attorney General Ujjal Dosanjh/Ujjal Dosanjh, who is attorney general of British Columbia

Lieutenant O'Keeffe/O'Keeffe, the lieutenant in charge at the front

Archbishop Maurice Couture/Couture, archbishop of Quebec City

President Letitia Bloggs/Bloggs, president of BigCorp

Appositives and modifiers

3.18   If a title has a modifier – an article or an adjective – immediately preceding it, it may be an appositive rather than a true title. (For the use of commas with appositives, see 5.9–11.)

3.19   If the appositive is non-restrictive, use lowercase:

> A prince, Louis of Flanders, was born here.
>
> the New Brunswick premier, Bernard Lord
>
> BigCorp's president, Letitia Bloggs

3.20   When the modifier applies to a titleholder's *role or position,* treat the title
as a restrictive appositive and lowercase it:

> British prime minister Blair
>
> BigCorp president Letitia Bloggs

3.21   With other uses of articles and adjectives, the meaning of the modifier can
be significant. When the modifier applies to a titleholder as a *person,*
uppercase the title:

> Ebullient Mayor Tanaka stole the show.
>
> The late Premier Greenbaum was greatly respected.

3.22   In some cases an adjective may be construed as modifying either the person or the role. The context will determine the editor's choice:

> dynamic premier René Lévesque (*a person whose premiership, his* role,
> *was dynamic*)
>
> dynamic Premier René Lévesque (*a dynamic* person *who happened to be
> premier*)

Former, acting, designate, etc.

3.23   Many editors capitalize only the current titleholder, even when the title
precedes the full or partial name. Terms such as **former** act as modifiers
that allow the use of lowercase (see 3.20):

> former solicitor general Herb Gray
>
> acting mayor Giovanni Schwarz
>
> retired chairman of the board O'Hara

The time frame of the manuscript governs what is "current." For example,
in a discussion of parliamentary business in 1885, capitalize as follows:

> During the debate, Prime Minister Macdonald blamed the trouble on the
> policies of former prime minister Alexander Mackenzie.

In a discussion of British Columbia politics in 1999:

> As the catastrophes mounted, Premier Clark continued to insist that everything was fine, right up to the day he announced his resignation.

High rank

3.24 Some conservative editors and style guides suggest that titles of high rank should always be capitalized, regardless of context, in order to signal the elevated status of these positions:

> our Prime Minister, the Premiers
>
> Chief Justice
>
> a General, two Admirals
>
> Pope, Cardinal
>
> the new Chief (*of a band*)
>
> President (*of a country*)
>
> King, Queen, Prince, Princess

Tradition and context must be considered in determining how high is "high" rank. For example, editors who usually lowercase the title **duke** might capitalize **Duke of Edinburgh** because tradition accords a queen's consort a higher status than that enjoyed by other dukes:

> The duke of Norfolk won his polo match.
>
> The duke won the match.

> The Queen and the Duke of Edinburgh raced for the bus.
>
> The Queen and the Duke raced for the bus.

Title standing alone

3.25 Some editors capitalize a title without a person's name when context indicates that a specific person is referred to:

> The Archbishop returns today from Rome.
>
> Noisy reporters demanded answers from the Premier.
>
> We regret that the Councillor is not available to comment.

Many style guides apply this rule to titles of high rank only, using lowercase for titles of lesser dignitaries standing alone:

> A rally to oppose the demolition has been called by the alderman.
>
> The director of human resources is firmly against unionization.
>
> Could you help the deacon at Friday's bake sale?

3.26 Most corporate titles are lowercased when standing alone in material intended for a general readership (see also 3.4).

A title standing alone without reference to a specific person is not properly a title (see 3.27–28).

Titles as generic terms

3.27 Capitals are unnecessary in the following constructions, where the titles serve as generic terms:

> Bloggs became captain of the polo team.
>
> The polo team named Bloggs captain.
>
> As the captain, Bloggs led the team to victory.

3.28 A title standing alone that describes a role rather than the person fulfilling it is not a true title, and is lowercase:

> The director of human resources approves promotions.
>
> The governor general represents the monarch.
>
> Day-to-day crises are dealt with by the managing editor.

Exceptions may be made for readership (see 3.4) and rank (see 3.24).

Title vs. job description

3.29 Job descriptions are not generally capitalized. It is easy enough to recognize that **Premier Bloggs** should be capitalized and **architect Bloggs** should not. The difficulty lies in that grey area where true titles designating rank and simple job descriptions meet – for example, **principal, headmaster.**

True titles are largely political, military, religious, or academic. Corporate designations tend to be treated as titles only in corporate or legal contexts or in material intended for a corporate readership.

ORGANIZATIONS AND DEPARTMENTS

3.30 Many common problems of capitalizing names of organizations and departments are treated among the general factors discussed at 3.2–5 and the specific factors examined at 3.6–15. Frequently the deciding factor in capitalizing the name of a department, committee, association, or similar body is whether the name is considered official (see 3.7–11).

The prevailing trend is toward a down style in names of organizations, but tradition weighs heavily in this regard, and many editors choose a mixed style.

Status

3.31 As is the case with titleholders (see 3.24), some organizations seem to hold higher status than others. Some editors capitalize both federal and provincial bodies but draw the line at regional, county, and municipal ones:

> (*national*) Council on Drug Abuse/Guysborough county council/ Vancouver city council/Assiniboia town council
>
> Manitoba Department of Environment/York Region planning department/Charlottetown planning department

A few style guides locate the boundary dividing greater and lesser status between those departments or bodies that make policy and those that implement it:

> Department of Justice/police department
>
> Ministry of Health/sanitation department
>
> Board of Regents/department of administration

3.32 Similar hierarchies of status can be delineated for most academic, religious, military, and corporate organizations.

Following "status" as a guide, however, often requires substantial background (or even backroom) information. Although it may be necessary to observe fine distinctions in academic and highly specialized manuscripts, simpler rules will suffice in most material.

Political and judicial entities

3.33 The following terms of the Canadian judiciary and political system are usually capitalized as either nouns or adjectives:

> Crown (*the monarchy*)
>
> Grit, Tory
>
> Hansard
>
> House of Commons, the House, the Commons
>
> Opposition (*official*)
>
> Parliament (*but* parliamentary)
>
> Red Chamber
>
> Senate
>
> Supreme Court of Canada, Federal Court of Canada, all provincial and territorial superior courts (*names vary: see 12.111–23, "provinces and territories"*)

The following terms are seen both ways:

cabinet/Cabinet (*noun or adjective*)

city hall/City Hall

federal/Federal

government/Government

leader/Leader

official opposition/Official Opposition/official Opposition

party/Party (*in a party name; but always* New Democratic Party, Parti Québécois, Saskatchewan Party)

provincial legislatures (*names vary: see 12.111–23, "provinces and territories"*)

question period/Question Period

speech from the throne/Speech from the Throne

The following terms are usually lowercased:

the bar

the bench

opposition (*noun or adjective; all parties in opposition, or any opposition party other than the official one*)

provincial

upper/lower house

GEOGRAPHICAL TERMS

3.34   Certain common geographical terms receive muddled treatment in capitalization because Canadians cannot agree on whether our regions have "official" names. In the United States, regional designations such as **the South** and **the Northeast** are capitalized without a second thought, but in Canada the parallel terms are a matter of vigorous debate. Our preferences are given below.

    See also the discussion of general factors at 3.2–5 and specific factors at 3.6–15.

West, East, North, South

3.35   When simple direction is intended, use lowercase.

Drive 10 km south on Highway 27.

The sun sets in the west.

3.36   In Canada, **the West** and **the East** designate certain groups of provinces, but the groups are defined differently in different parts of the country:

> the West: British Columbia, Alberta, Saskatchewan, Manitoba
>
> the East: Nova Scotia, New Brunswick, Prince Edward Island, Newfoundland and Labrador *or* (*as seen from the West*) these four plus Ontario and Quebec

Uppercase is especially appropriate in political contexts but may be used in others as well. Sometimes lowercase is used to avoid confusion with the global **West** (the capitalist system) and **East** (the former communist system).

3.37   **The North** may designate Yukon, the Northwest Territories, and Nunavut only, or it may include the northern parts of the West and of Ontario and Quebec as well. **The Far North** designates the territories or, when contrasted to **the North,** the lands beyond the Arctic Circle.

3.38   **The South** is considered a region only when contrasted to or viewed from **the North.** (It is often said that Canada "has no south.")

3.39   Capitalization is unnecessary when **Canada** or **Canadian** is part of the phrase, although **the Canadian North** is often seen.

> the Canadian north
>
> the west of Canada

Eastern, Easterner, et al.

3.40   Use lowercase for simple direction.

> It's in the eastern part of town.

3.41   Uppercase is rarely necessary when **Canada** or **Canadian** is part of the regional designation.

> eastern Canada, western Canadian farmers
>
> central Canada: Ontario and Quebec

These terms may be uppercased when **Canada** or **Canadian** is omitted but implied.

> Eastern fisheries, Western lumber, Northern settlements
>
> Easterner, Westerner, Northerner

See also 3.50.

Coasts

3.42   **The East Coast** usually means the Atlantic provinces. **The West Coast** usually means only British Columbia, or even just part of the province. **The Northwest Coast** usually includes Washington State and Alaska with British Columbia. All three terms are lowercase to designate shorelines.

> The minister is touring the East Coast.
>
> Sushi started as a West Coast phenomenon.
>
> A tanker spilled oil off the east coast.

3.43   The names of interior coasts or parts of coastlines in several provinces have become official enough to be capped. Examples are the **North Shore** and **South Shore** in Quebec, the **North Shore** in New Brunswick, and the **South Shore, North Shore,** and **Eastern Shore** in Nova Scotia.

Fog warning on the coasts

3.44   Editors should approach coastal designations (and perhaps regions in general) with caution, as they are often a matter of some debate, not to say confusion. Newfoundland's south coast, for instance, is known as both the **South Coast** and the **Southern Coast** and variously defined as the entire length, running from Cape Ray to Cape Race, or just the section from Hermitage Bay to Rose Blanche. Neither of these is to be confused with the **Southern Shore,** which is the east coast of the Avalon Peninsula from Bay Bulls to Trepassey, and thus the easternmost coast of the province – unless you believe the theory claiming it to be a stretch of road running south from St. John's.

Prairie, Maritime, Atlantic, Arctic

3.45   It is not necessary to capitalize **province** when used with these terms.

3.46   **The Prairie provinces** or **the Prairies** are Alberta, Saskatchewan, and Manitoba. Do not capitalize **prairie** as a noun or adjective describing landscape.

> The wind blew across the prairie.
>
> The band played to ecstatic audiences in towns throughout the Prairies.

3.47   **The Maritime provinces** or **the Maritimes** are Nova Scotia, New Brunswick, and Prince Edward Island. These three plus Newfoundland form **the Atlantic provinces.**

3.48   Capitalize **Maritime** and **Prairie** as adjectives only when they refer to political designations. (**Atlantic** is always uppercased.)

> The tax deal annoyed Prairie homeowners.
>
> What can be done about Maritime unemployment?
>
> Fogs/grasshoppers are a fact of maritime/prairie life.

3.49   **The Arctic** is the region north of the Arctic Circle. As an adjective it is uppercased when referring to the region and lowercased when referring to frigid temperature. In established names of Arctic flora and fauna, **arctic** is usually lowercased.

> Arctic communities
>
> arctic char
>
> arctic gale

Regions

3.50   Areas within some provinces, or including parts of more than one province, have become official enough to be uppercased, especially in local contexts. These include:

> Western Arctic, Eastern Arctic (*distinct regions in the North*)
>
> Interior, Lower Mainland, Sunshine Coast (*British Columbia*)
>
> Badlands, the Foothills (*Alberta*)
>
> Palliser Triangle (*Alberta and Saskatchewan*)
>
> Prairie Pothole Region (*southern Alberta, Saskatchewan, and Manitoba*)
>
> Barren Lands, Barren Grounds, the Barrens (*Northwest Territories*)
>
> Fruit Belt, Golden Horseshoe (*Ontario*)
>
> Northern Ontario (*but* Southern *or* southern Ontario)
>
> Eastern Townships, the Townships (*Quebec*)
>
> the Island (*Prince Edward Island, Vancouver Island*)
>
> French Shore (*Newfoundland*)
>
> Rainbow Country (*British Columbia, Ontario*)

"THE" IN TITLES AND NAMES

3.51   A familiar editorial question is whether to capitalize **the** in the titles of newspapers and other publications and in the names of companies, associations, and other organizations. A reasonable starting point is to choose between two principles: strict adherence to accuracy, and editorial expediency.

An editor who chooses the accuracy principle must determine through research whether, for instance, **the** is part of the masthead of each newspaper referred to in a manuscript. In editing a historical work, it might be necessary to follow records back through masthead changes that oblige the editor to capitalize (and italicize) **the** in a reference with a 1920s context but to lowercase (and not italicize) it in a current reference. Considerable effort may be required to locate exact names of distant, obscure, or defunct publications.

Editorial expediency, in contrast, is much less demanding: with a few simple exceptions, an editor may choose always or never to capitalize **the.** Some exceptions are scholarly studies, in which expediency must unquestionably yield to accuracy, and technical or legal materials, in which names must be given in full and proper forms. Journalistic traditions present idiosyncrasies too: in some magazine circles, for example, **the** in *The New Yorker* and *The Times* (London) is always capitalized.

3.52   The same principles may be applied in styling names of organizations. In practice, however, even when uppercase **the** appears on a body's letterhead, the editor generally lowercases it. Except in technical, legal, or internal material, an uppercase **the** in a corporate or organizational name is puffery.

MISCELLANEOUS CANADIANA

3.53   The following are usually capitalized:

Auto Pact

Bluenose (*Nova Scotian*)

Canadian Shield (*topographical feature*)

Centennial Year (*1967*)

Charter of Rights and Freedoms, the Charter

Confederation

Constitution

Dominion

Family Compact (*influential circle in Upper Canada, 1800s*)

Great Lakes

Group of Seven

Iceberg Alley (*off Newfoundland and Labrador*)

Lotusland/Lotus Land (*British Columbia*)

Loyalist (*pro-British immigrants of 1700s and their descendants*)

Maple Leaf (*flag*)

Musical Ride (*RCMP*)

National Capital Region

Quiet Revolution (*Quebec, 1960s*)

Riel Rebellion

The following are usually lowercased:

allophone

chinook (*wind or salmon*)

medicare (*in Canada;* Medicare *in the United States is different*)

The following are seen both ways:

anglophone, francophone/Anglophone, Francophone

anglo-, franco-/Anglo-, Franco-

For capitalization of terms denoting ethnicity, including **native/Native,** see 8.15–21.

CHAPTER 4

Abbreviations

Chapter 4 – Abbreviations

4.1   Abbreviations serve a highly useful purpose in specific contexts. However, an overabundant or overinventive use of them is unwieldy and confusing. In general, a term should be spelled out in full at first use if there is any likelihood that the readers are not familiar with it.

　　　A trend toward simplified punctuation and less fussy typography is gaining support. There is an overwhelming tendency toward all caps and no periods in acronyms and initialisms (see 4.8–10). For example, **C.B.C.** is not wrong, but it has become old-fashioned. In contrast, geographical initialisms, such as **P.E.I.,** often retain the periods (see 4.18).

　　　Abbreviations are particularly useful in tables, notes, lists, or catalogues and in other contexts where space is tight. Tabular matter may require extremely short forms of abbreviations, which should be consistent and make as much sense as possible.

TYPES OF ABBREVIATIONS

True abbreviations and suspensions

4.2   A true abbreviation is a shortened form in which the end of the word is dropped. For example:

p.	page
Sask.	Saskatchewan
Co.	Company
Can.	Canada

The period that has traditionally been used to end true abbreviations represents the dropped letters.

4.3   A suspension is a shortened form in which the middle of the word is dropped or "suspended." For example:

Alta.	Alberta
Dept.	Department
Ltd.	Limited
Mrs.	Mistress

Some editors omit the period in suspensions because the last letter of the form is the last letter of the complete word. They do not consider this form a true abbreviation.

4.4   In the many manuscripts that contain both true abbreviations and suspensions, a mixture of period and no-period styles can be distracting. In such cases, editors may choose either to omit the period or to use it after both suspensions and abbreviations. The former style is a trend favoured by the *Chicago Manual* and may suit texts with few types of abbreviations. (In this book, given the large variety of abbreviations, using the period after both abbreviations and suspensions was considered more appropriate. However, note that no period is used after SI symbols: see 9.23.)

4.5 **Ms.,** now widely used as the female parallel to **Mr.,** is an artificial creation, neither abbreviation nor suspension but inviting similar treatment. **Mr., Mrs.,** and **Dr.** are rarely spelled out, except in dialogue or direct address, when they are substitutes for a name: "Doctor, could you help me?" When phonetic representation is called for, **Ms.** may be shown as "Miz," and **Mrs.** as "Missus."

4.6 The Department of National Defence uses its own style for abbreviations of military titles. Useful lists of military titles and abbreviations are in *The Canadian Style* and *The Canadian Press Stylebook.*

4.7 French practice requires a strict differentiation between true abbreviations and suspensions:

Mlle *or* Mlle	Mademoiselle
Mme *or* Mme	Madame
MM. *or* Messrs	Messieurs
M.	Monsieur
St, Ste *or* S^t, S^{te}	Saint/Sainte

Acronyms

4.8 An acronym is a shortened form in which the initial letters or parts of a compound term stand for the compound and are usually pronounced as a word. Acronyms often appear as small caps.

CUPE	Canadian Union of Public Employees
GATT	General Agreement on Tariffs and Trade
laser	light amplification by stimulated emission of radiation
NAFTA	North American Free Trade Agreement
PEN	International Association of Poets, Playwrights, Editors, Essayists, and Novelists
RAM	random access memory
scuba	self-contained underwater breathing apparatus

Care must be taken to avoid redundancy (e.g., *not* RAM memory).

The following acronyms are created from parts of a compound term rather than from the initial letters of words making up the term:

CANDU/Candu	Canadian deuterium uranium
Oxfam	Oxford Committee for Famine Relief
quango	quasi-autonomous non-governmental organization
radar	radio detecting and ranging
SaskPool	*successor to* Saskatchewan Wheat Pool
StatsCan	Statistics Canada

Note that **laser, quango, radar,** and **scuba** have become bona fide words spelled in lowercase.

A few acronyms are sometimes treated as proper nouns (upper- and lowercase): **Unesco, Unicef,** and (less often) **Cuso, Nato, Opec.**

Initialisms

4.9   An initialism is a shortened form with the same construction as an acronym, but usually spoken letter by letter. For example:

CBC/SRC	Canadian Broadcasting Corporation/Société Radio-Canada
CEO	chief executive officer
CLC	Canadian Labour Congress
CMHC	Canada Mortgage and Housing Corporation (*formerly* Central Mortgage and Housing Corporation)
CNIB	Canadian National Institute for the Blind
CNR	Canadian National Railways
CPR	Canadian Pacific Railway, cardiopulmonary resuscitation
CRTC	Canadian Radio-television and Telecommunications Commission
CSA	Canadian Standards Association
EI, UI	employment insurance, *formerly* unemployment insurance
EU, EC	European Union, *formerly* European Community
HTML	Hypertext Markup Language
NFB	National Film Board
NGO	non-governmental organization
NMR	nuclear magnetic resonance
RCMP	Royal Canadian Mounted Police

As with acronyms, care must be taken to avoid redundancy in use of some initialisms:

HIV	human immunodeficiency virus (*not* HIV virus)

ATM	automated teller machine (*not* ATM machine)
SIN	social insurance number (*not* SIN number)

4.10 Abbreviations made up of letters within a single word do not take periods and are conventionally set in caps:

IV	intravenous
TB	tuberculosis
TV	television

Note **CD-ROM** (compact disc read-only memory), a curiosity that is part initialism and part acronym.

SPECIFIC USES OF ABBREVIATIONS

Titles preceding names

4.11 Ordinarily, a civil, military, or religious title that precedes a surname alone should be spelled out:

Rear-Admiral Dixon

Senator Schmidt

Professor Gonzales

Governor General Dégas

Monsignor Chiu

With full names, most of these titles are abbreviated:

Rear-Adm. Josiah Dixon

Sen. Renata Schmidt

Prof. Rafael Gonzales

Gov. Gen. Ryan Dégas

Msgr. Szi Sun Chiu

Some editors prefer always to spell out **Admiral** and **Senator.**

Honours and titles after names

4.12 It is not customary to use **Mr., Mrs., Ms.,** or **Dr.** before a name if another title follows the name:

Wilma Atherton, Ph.D. (*Doctor of Philosophy*)

Edwin Samuels, FRSC (*Fellow of the Royal Society of Canada*)

(The exception would appear to be doctors who produce self-help books.)

The now rarely seen abbreviation **Esq.** is used after the name alone and never with a title before or after the name.

4.13 Persons of eminence may collect a variety of degrees and honours to follow their names. The order in which these appear is generally thus:

1. honours, orders, decorations, and medals
2. academic degrees, diplomas, and licentiates
3. academic and professional associations and affiliations

For example:

John Pinofsky, OC [Officer of the Order of Canada], MC [decoration], Ph.D., LL.B. [academic degrees], FRSC [affiliation]

Francis Delaney, M.A., D. ès L., LL.D. [academic degrees], FRSA, FRHistS [affiliations]

Academic degrees

4.14 Academic degrees may appear with or without periods.

B.A.	BA
B.Sc.	BSc
Ph.D.	PhD
LL.B.	LLB

Other honours and affiliations

4.15 Other strings of letters after names may or may not include periods depending upon how strange or familiar they are to the intended audience:

Siegfried Bloggs, FRSC
André Fortier, SJ

Company names

4.16 The formal titles of companies, here and abroad, may include such abbreviations as:

AG	Allgemeine Gesellschaft, Aktiengesellschaft
Co.	Company
Corp.	Corporation
GmbH	Gesellschaft mit beschränkter Haftung
Inc.	Incorporated
Ltd.	Limited
Ltée	Limitée
PLC, plc	Public Limited Company

Pty	Proprietary
SA	Société anonyme, Sociedad anónima
Spa, SpA	Società per Azione
Srl	Società a responsabilità limitata

"Saint/Sainte" and "St./Ste."

4.17 When **Saint** is part of a name, it should be spelled and punctuated according to the bearer's preference:

St. Clair Balfour
HMCS *Ste. Thérèse*
Saint Albert Collegiate
Saint Demetrios Greek Orthodox Church
St. Vincent de Paul Society

When the saint as a person is referred to, **Saint** is spelled out unless space is a concern.

Saint Francis of Assisi is the special protector of the poor.

Saint is almost always abbreviated in place names in English Canada to **St.:**

St. Lawrence River/Gulf of St. Lawrence
St. Boniface (Manitoba)
St. John's (Newfoundland) *but* Saint John (New Brunswick)
St. Marys (Ontario) *but* Sault Ste. Marie

For the conventions governing names with **Saint** in French Canada, see 6.43.

Geographical designations

4.18 Table 4.1 lists the two-letter symbols for provinces and territories used by Canada Post, together with the more traditional abbreviations. As noted in 4.1, some editors treat geographical initialisms as a separate category from other initialisms and retain the periods (**B.C., N.B., P.E.I.**).

4.19 Abbreviations for names of countries can be used in special circumstances (tables, charts, lists). In text copy, names are usually spelled out; common exceptions are:

U.K. *or* UK	United Kingdom
U.S. *or* US	United States
U.S.S.R. *or* USSR	Union of Soviet Socialist Republics

Since the breakup of the last, a new abbreviation has developed:

F.S.U. *or* FSU   Former Soviet Union

Table 4.1   Abbreviations for provinces and territories

	Canada Post	Traditional
Alberta	AB	Alta.
British Columbia	BC	B.C./BC
Manitoba	MB	Man.
New Brunswick	NB	N.B./NB
Newfoundland and Labrador	NF/NL from 2002	Nfld. and Lab.
Nova Scotia	NS	N.S./NS
Northwest Territories	NT	N.W.T./NWT
Nunavut	NT/NU from 2000	
Ontario	ON	Ont.
Prince Edward Island	PE	P.E.I./PEI
Quebec	QC	Que. or P.Q./PQ
Saskatchewan	SK	Sask.
Yukon Territory	YT	Y.T./YT

4.20   Two-letter codes often identify countries in Internet addresses:

at   Austria
ca   Canada
uk   United Kingdom

A Web search for "ISO country codes" will yield sources that offer a complete list.

4.21   Compass directions conventionally are not interrupted by periods:

N, E, S, W/NE, SE, NW, SW
N by NE
60°N

Latin abbreviations

4.22   Latin abbreviations are generally set in roman type, although Latin words are sometimes italicized in English text.

a.m./p.m., am/pm, A.M./P.M., AM/PM, *or* A.M./P.M. (*ante meridiem/post meridiem, before/after noon*)

c. *or* ca   *circa* (*about*)

cf.   *confer* (*compare*)

e.g.   *exempli gratia* (*for example*)

et al.   *et alia* (*and others things*), *et alii* (*and other people*)

etc.   *et cetera* or *etcetera* (*and so forth*)

ibid.   *ibidem* (*in the same place*)

i.e.   *id est* (*that is*)

Dates and times

Numeric abbreviations for dates

4.23   The all-numeric style of abbreviating dates is used in government documents in Canada and in documents of international organizations. It follows the sequence *year/month/day*. In other contexts, however (e.g., software, VCRs), the sequence used may be *day/month/year* or *month/day/year*. In dates before the turn of 2000, the sequence was often easily understood: 11/24/99 would necessarily be November 24, 1999. However, dates from 2001 through 2031 may be ambiguous in all-numeric forms. Either the chosen sequence must be clarified at the first occurrence, or the month must be spelled out, and all four digits should be used for the year:

99/12/02 = December 2, 1999

2004/12/09 = December 9, 2004

00/06/14 = June 14, 2000

The 24-hour clock and the Universal Time System

4.24   The 24-hour clock is a convenient and universal measurement. The hours and minutes are separated by a colon in both French and English:

00:00   12 A.M. (*midnight*) (see 4.22 for A.M. and P.M.)

00:30   12:30 A.M.

12:00   12 P.M. (*noon*)

15:45   3:45 P.M.

18:00   6:00 P.M.

Note that 18:00 is "18 hours," not "eighteen hundred hours" except in military parlance.

The 24-hour clock is not likely to replace current usage completely, especially in non-technical material. Convention allows the following forms:

We meet at 1:00/1:00 p.m./1 p.m./one o'clock/one in the afternoon/one.

The word **o'clock** should not be used with **a.m.** or **p.m.,** or with numerals. No matter how bad things may be, it is *never* "3 a.m. in the morning."

4.25   In the context of worldwide instantaneous electronic transmission, there is a need to express date and time in terms that do not depend on specification of time zone. Hence the use of **UT** (**Universal Time**), **UTC** (**Universal Time Coordinate**), or sometimes just **U** designations: time is quoted, for example, as **UT 23.35,** which is the time (in the 24-hour system) at the prime meridian (Greenwich, U.K.).

    This system also expands to specify date: for example, **UT 001 083 18.25.30,** which translates as year 2001, 83rd day (March 24), 18:25 and 30 seconds Greenwich Mean Time. Further detail is available at <www.universal-time.org>.

Designation of eras

4.26   The abbreviations for the traditional Christian year designations are often set in small caps:

> AD 1000   Anno Domini (*in the year of our Lord*)
> 1000 BC   before Christ

More commonly seen now are abbreviations that de-emphasize the Christian origin of these terms (also often set in small caps):

> BP   before the present
> BCE   before the common era
> CE   of the common era

MULTIPLE REPRESENTATION

4.27   Some abbreviations represent dozens of designations. It is therefore necessary to spell out the full title at first use should any doubt exist. For example:

> CBC   Canadian Broadcasting Corporation
>   Caribbean Broadcasting Corporation
>   Ceylon Broadcasting Corporation
>   Children's Book Council
>   Contraband Control
>   Corset and Brassiere Council
>   Cyprus Broadcasting Corporation

PLURALS OF ABBREVIATIONS

4.28   Plurals of abbreviations (or of letters) are formed by adding an **s**. Modern usage no longer places an apostrophe before the **s** unless it is needed to prevent misreading.

> four VIPs
>
> several MPs
>
> uncollected IOUs
>
> Oakland A's

SYMBOLS

Currency

4.29   Monetary symbols are among the most familiar. Globalization and the advent of the European Monetary Union bring a variety of national currencies into the news. The core unit of the EMU is the euro:

€   euro

Other commonly encountered symbols for currency include:

£   British pound, Irish punt, or any of many pound currencies
(Before decimalization in 1971, pounds/shillings/pence was written variously as £1.8*s*.6*d*., £1.8.6, or £1/8s/6p.)
    Where pound currencies need to be differentiated one from another, the symbol is preceded or followed by an identifying letter or letters. For example:

IR£   Irish punt

£C   Cyprus pound

£S   Syrian pound

$ dollar, peso, peseta, and others:
Can$, CDN$ Canadian dollar

A$ Australian dollar

Col$ Colombian peso

C$ Nicaraguan cordoba

HK$ Hong Kong dollar

¥   Japanese yen

Most other currency values are preceded by a letter identifier, such as zl (Polish zloty).

See <pacific.commerce.ubc.ca/xr/currency_table.html> for an example of other currencies treated in this manner. Note, however, that different sources may give different identifiers: the Swiss franc, for example, turns up variously as SwF, SFr, and HF.

4.30   The system of the International Organization for Standardization (ISO) uses no symbols but rather a three-letter code preceding the figure: two letters identify the country and the third the currency type. For example:

CAD   Canadian dollar

GBP   British pound

CHF   Swiss franc

A Web search for "ISO 4217 currency codes" will yield complete lists.

Scientific/mathematical symbols

4.31   Chemical, scientific, and mathematical symbols require particularly careful and accurate use. Such symbols can be checked by consulting dictionaries, major style guides, and technical references.

The SI symbols (metric abbreviations) do not take periods. See chapter 9 for abbreviations, symbols, and punctuation in SI usage.

SOURCES

Antweiler, W. *Pacific Exchange Rate Service* [online]. Pacific Policy Analysis Computing and Information Facility in Commerce, University of British Columbia. [Three-letter currency codes.] UBC, 1999. [Cited February 17, 2000.] <pacific.commerce.ubc.ca/xr/currency_table.html>.

Canadian Tax Foundation. *Style Guide.* Toronto: the Foundation, 1995.

Universal Time Organization. *Promoting a Metric Based System* [online]. [Cited November 7, 1999.] <www.universal-time.org>.

Wearing of Orders, Decorations and Medals. Ottawa: Chancellery, Office of the Secretary to the Governor General, 1998.

Punctuation

Chapter 5 – Punctuation

5.1 Punctuation marks clarify the author's meaning by expressing the relationship among the parts of the sentence. Their role is both structural and stylistic.

5.2 There are two styles of punctuation: *closed* (sometimes called "close") *punctuation,* which uses all the punctuation marks suggested by the grammatical relationship between the parts of the sentence, and *open punctuation,* which uses only those punctuation marks necessary to prevent misinterpretation. Modern style favours open punctuation and is especially evident in newspapers and magazines.

5.3 Usage in Canada is often a combination of conventional British and American punctuation styles, which may fall in the spectrum of open and closed styles. This chapter clarifies the distinctions, urges consistency in a preferred choice, recommends certain usages, and explores those areas of punctuation that cause the most confusion and error. It is not intended to be a complete guide to punctuation.

For treatment of the solidus, en dash, and hyphen see chapter 2 and 9.37–39.

COMMA

5.4 Grammarians agree that the comma has more uses than any other punctuation mark. Although it is obligatory in a small number of grammatical constructions, more often its use is a matter of judgment. Some editors omit optional commas when the meaning and context of the sentence are clear. Consult a standard grammar text for detailed guidelines (see Sources).

In series

5.5 The series comma (or serial comma) separates items in a list or in a series consisting of three or more elements. The series can be composed of single words, phrases, or clauses. There are two approaches to the treatment of the final element in the series. Many authorities recommend the use of the comma before **and** or **or** in the final element because it avoids ambiguity and possible misinterpretation. Other authorities prefer to omit the final comma on the grounds that **and** with a comma is redundant. Editors who favour the series comma should use it consistently. Editors who do not favour it must nevertheless sometimes use it to avoid ambiguity:

The police arrested two thugs, a pimp, and a drug dealer.

The police arrested two thugs, a pimp and a drug dealer.

Did the police arrest two or four people? The absence of the series comma before **and** leaves the reader in doubt. The series comma signals the reader that the police arrested four people.

Confusion also arises when the items in the series are complex grammatical units such as prepositional phrases and dependent or independent clauses. With complex structures it is often difficult to recognize where one series ends and the other begins. The final series comma prevents confusion among the elements.

> With the rise of science, technology, and industry and the accompanying development of large nation-states, the productive capacities of industrial societies have increased immensely, the standard of living has increased proportionately, and the necessity of continued expansion becomes paramount.

Many major Canadian publishing houses use the series comma. However, it is rarely used in magazines and newspapers (see *Maclean's,* the *Globe and Mail*); an exception is *Saturday Night.*

5.6   In a long series, the semicolon is useful when the elements are complex and include other punctuation:

> He expected the imminent arrival of his sister, with or without her egregious "companion," Lester; possibly her former husband – a contingency promising a very long and rancorous evening; probably her anorectic Russian wolfhound; and undoubtedly her four totally superfluous children.

At the end of a series with semicolons, **and** or **or** may sometimes be omitted; however, the final series semicolon cannot be omitted, regardless of style preference on the series comma.

With independent clauses

5.7   The comma should be used between independent clauses introduced by conjunctions – such as **and, but, or, nor, for, yet** – except in very short sentences. Most style guides concur on this use of the comma.

> The analysis was carefully conducted by both the company and independent reviewers, but the final results were dismissed as shoddy by the minister, and the originators of the scheme suggested another course of action.

In Canadian magazines and newspapers this comma is often omitted if there is no ambiguity of meaning.

Note that **for,** in particular, needs the comma in front of it to avoid its being read as a preposition:

> They raced up the slope, for the river was rising at great speed.

Sentences with independent clauses are often confused with sentences in which one subject governs two verbs.

> He went to the party with high hopes[,] but stayed only 10 minutes.

No comma is required in such constructions, although some editors use the comma as a pause in a long sentence.

> Mary Smith edited five manuscripts and wrote a best-seller last year[,] but had trouble with her income tax.

With appositives

5.8   Appositives can be restrictive (defining, limiting terms that are essential to the meaning of the sentence) or non-restrictive (descriptive, non-limiting terms that merely add information).

5.9   Non-restrictive appositives are enclosed by commas. Both commas are necessary unless the appositive is at the end of the sentence:

> "My wife, Belinda, will be unable to attend the awards dinner," Jeremy said bitterly.

Unless Jeremy is a bigamist, he has only one wife. He has identified the person he is talking about with the words **my wife**. Her name is an extra piece of information that doesn't alter the meaning of the sentence; therefore, it is non-restrictive.

> The governors heatedly discussed the implications of the committee's final report, *Salary Adjustments.*

Although the title adds information, the words **final report** are sufficient to identify which report caused the heat. The title is non-restrictive and requires a comma.

5.10   Restrictive appositives are not set off by commas:

> My friend Sam and I are taking a tour of Italy.

Presumably the speaker has more than one friend; the name **Sam** identifies which friend is going on the tour. It is essential to the meaning and therefore is a restrictive appositive.

> The novelist Margaret Laurence wrote *The Stone Angel.*

Her name defines which novelist we are talking about; it is a restrictive appositive and does not take commas.

5.11   Appositives are the source of much confusion, and error in the use of commas is common. Some periodicals seem to have chosen a one-solution-fits-all approach and enclose all appositives by commas. This practice leads to such familiar absurdities as:

    ✗ Hockey star, Wayne Gretzky, announced his retirement today.

Gretzky's name is not parenthetical but essential to the meaning of the sentence; the commas should not be there.

    ✗ David Cronenberg's movie, *Crash*, explored familiar terrain but in an especially provocative manner.

If we believed the commas, we would think Mr. Cronenberg had made only one movie. The title is necessary to distinguish this movie from the many other films the director has made; it is restrictive and should not have commas.

Note that there are classes of full and partial apposition. Consult Randolph Quirk et al. for a detailed description. (See also 12.142, "that/which.")

In dates

5.12   There are several styles of setting out dates in general text. For numeric styles of dates see 4.23 and 4.25.

5.13   The style used in most trade books, magazines, journals, and newspapers gives the date in the order *month/day/year* with the month spelled out or abbreviated. When the day is given, the year must be enclosed in commas.

December 16, 1983, was the coldest day in recorded history.

Dec. 17, 1983, was slightly warmer.

A frequent error is the omission of the comma after the year.

When no day is given, the commas are unnecessary and should be omitted:

December 1983 was the coldest month in recorded history.

5.14   The second style uses the sequence *day/month/year*. No commas are used to separate the sequence:

On 16 December 1983 the members of the climbing expedition filed their last report.

This form, which is becoming increasingly common, is the traditional European date style. It is used in some Canadian government documents and in some Canadian textbooks at school and college levels, as well as in scientific and technical works.

In place names

5.15   Commas set off the second, identifying element in geographical entities (names of towns, counties, provinces, and countries), whether abbreviated or not.

> The representative from Nairobi, Kenya, spoke first.
>
> The delegates from Saskatchewan, Canada, and Montana, United States, led the contingent.
>
> The miners from Sudbury, Ont., refused to strike.

Omission of the second comma is a frequent error.

APOSTROPHE

5.16   Apostrophes perform three basic functions: they indicate the possessive, they substitute for letters and numerals that are omitted, and they sometimes form the plural of letters, numbers, and abbreviations without periods. Some common problems are discussed here.

"It's" and "its"

5.17   Confusion in usage between **it's** and **its** is commonplace. **It's** is the contraction of **it is** (or infrequently **it has**) and **its** is a possessive pronoun.

> It's a wise dog that knows its own fleas.

With names ending in "s" or "z"

5.18   There is little agreement in the treatment of the possessive of proper nouns ending in a sounded **s** or **z**. Some authorities advocate adding **'s** to form the possessive; others prefer to add the apostrophe only.

> Keats's poetry/Keats' poetry
>
> Berlioz's opera/Berlioz' opera

Many editors prefer the spellings on the left. Where the double sibilant is thought to sound awkward, the sentence can be recast.

In nouns of foreign origin, in particular French proper nouns, in which the final **z, x,** or **s** is silent, the **'s** is needed for sounding:

> Duplessis's cabinet
>
> Malraux's art
>
> Agassiz's population
>
> corps's marching band

See also 6.15.

Exceptions

5.19 The traditional exceptions to the **'s** rule are many Greek and hellenized names and the names Jesus and Moses. They form the possessive by adding the apostrophe alone:

> Jesus' name
>
> Moses' leadership
>
> Ulysses' travels
>
> Socrates' wisdom

Phrases in which **sake** is preceded by a word ending in a sibilant traditionally use the apostrophe alone:

> for goodness' sake
>
> for conscience' sake
>
> for righteousness' sake

False possessives

5.20 Certain descriptive expressions seem to call for the possessive apostrophe because the final **s** makes them *sound* like possessive forms. In fact, these forms are only plural nouns used as adjectives, and no apostrophe should be added.

> the first Beatles album (*but* the Beatles' first album)
>
> A Canucks defenceman knocked out an Avalanche forward.
>
> An autoworkers representative met with a management flunky.
>
> a complaints office

Adjectival possessives

5.21 The practice of deleting the apostrophe in phrases where the possessive noun becomes an adjective is gaining in popularity:

> two weeks holiday/two weeks' holiday
>
> thirty days sentence/thirty days' sentence

However, those who prefer this method use the apostrophe for the singular: **a day's work.**

Ways to skirt the inconsistency include using a hyphen and recasting the phrase:

> a two-week holiday/two weeks of holiday
>
> a 30-day sentence/a sentence of 30 days

Official names

5.22 Company, institutional, and geographical names often omit the apostrophe. Follow the official and recognized form:

> A group of junior aides took time off from the conference in Smiths Falls to attend a Lions Club function, to lunch at McDonald's, to shop at Zellers, and to treat themselves to a bag of M&M's.

Many Canadian companies with a presence in Quebec dropped the possessive **'s** from their corporate names in that province to comply with Bill 101, the Charter of the French Language.

Plurals

5.23 There are two styles for forming the plural of letters, numbers, and abbreviations without periods. The current trend forms the plural by adding **s** alone on dates and uppercase letters:

> three Rs
>
> 1950s
>
> YWCAs

The older style, which is seen occasionally, forms the plural by adding **'s:** "three B's," "the 1800's," "YMCA's."

However, with single characters and some phrases many editors use the apostrophe to avoid possible ambiguity and to facilitate reading:

> There are four s's in Mississippi.
>
> The Oakland A's are improving their baseball game.
>
> The teacher put three 1's on the board.

ELLIPSIS POINTS

5.24 The vexed question of the editorial and typographical treatment of omissions within quotations is examined in detail in standard reference books. Some of the questions that try editors' patience are:

- Should the three points of ellipsis be set with word spacing or set tight (three to the em)?
- Should a fourth point be added to an ellipsis to indicate a period preceding or following the omission?
- In "three-point" style, should word spaces precede and follow the ellipsis? Should spaces be added only according to the rules normally applied to "four-point" style?

- Can the editor be sure, without seeing the author's sources, that the author who has used "four-point" style has correctly distinguished between omissions at the beginning, end, and middle of sentences?

In the face of such hairsplitting, we recommend a sanity-saving approach, which we have used in this book: three points only, with the points set tight and word spacing fore and aft, regardless of location. A slight variation that would cause no appreciable increase in anxiety would use word spacing between the points as well.

SINGLE AND DOUBLE QUOTATION MARKS

5.25 American practice uses double quotation marks to enclose quoted sentences, phrases, and words. Single quotation marks enclose quotations within quotations. In the case of further quotations within quotations, the double and single quotes alternate.

> "He said, 'Why can't we shout "Fascist pig!" without getting busted?'"

5.26 British practice is usually the reverse: single quotation marks are first, and then double quotation marks enclose the quote within the quote. This style is no longer popular in Canada.

> American style: The poet stated emphatically: "The whole purpose of the phrase 'ironic iconic iron-crusted coruscation' is to scratch the rhinoceros epidermis of the era."
>
> British style: The poet stated emphatically: 'The whole purpose of the phrase "ironic iconic iron-crusted coruscation" is to scratch the rhinoceros epidermis of the era.'

Sometimes a visual problem arises with the use of single quotes as primary, for example when the single close-quote and the possessive apostrophe occur together:

> The formation of 'workers' governments' and use of the factory council in support of the issue created havoc.

Most Canadian newspapers, magazines, and journals and a large number of book publishers follow the American double-quote usage, which we recommend. However, a few publishers, including the University of Toronto Press and Oxford University Press Canada, use British style for some publications.

5.27 Double or single quotation marks (depending on which is the preferred style of a text) are used to set off significant words or phrases, words used ironically, and slang. Double or single quotes are sometimes used to enclose individual words that express the author's ironic distance.

American style: He knows that in the final analysis there are no "minor" surgical procedures.

British style: ... 'minor' surgical procedures.

5.28 Single quotes are also used for special terms in the fields of theology, philosophy, and linguistics in some American and British styles:

The 'divine' was discussed in the "Anglican Mysticism" seminar.

PUNCTUATION WITH QUOTATION MARKS

5.29 In Canada, most magazines, newspapers, journals, and book publishers usually follow American style, which always places the period or comma inside the closing quotation marks. However, a few follow British usage, which places the period or comma outside the quotation marks (unless it rightly belongs to what is within the quotation marks, such as a full sentence).

American style: The director told us that the group "could prevent insipid posturing," as well as avoid conflict, if it was willing to implement the suggestions "at once."

British style: The director told us that the group 'could prevent insipid posturing', as well as avoid conflict, if it was willing to implement the suggestions 'at once'.

Some texts combine the two punctuation traditions, using American style of double quotes and British order of punctuation, or British style of single quotes and American order of punctuation.

5.30 Colons and semicolons are always placed outside the quotation marks. A question mark or an exclamation point should be placed inside the quotation marks when it is part of the quoted material; otherwise, it is outside.

COLON AND CAPITALIZATION

5.31 Although some grammarians recommend that the first word after the colon be capitalized if it begins a complete sentence, many editors lowercase the first letter because the capital breaks the continuity and balance of the sentence:

He was not a misogynist: four wives later he still claimed a fondness for women.

Canadian usage is divided, although there is a definite trend toward lowercase in such constructions. Some styles capitalize the first letter after the colon if emphasis is necessary:

> Verdict: Not guilty.

When a direct quote contains a complete sentence or sentences, the first letter of the quote is capitalized:

> The question is this: "Is she aware of her rights?"

The capital is used after the colon when the elements following consist of more than one sentence:

> She considered the joys of the day to come: At ten o'clock would come a group of irate citizens opposing the project. At eleven would come an equally irate delegation supporting it. At noon, if she was lucky, she could make it to the periodontist.

INTERNET ADDRESSES

5.32   In running text, angle brackets around the address enable a distinction between the punctuation of the address and that of the sentence: for example, <jmcleod@interpret.org>.

SOURCES

Guide to Canadian English Usage. By Margery Fee and Janice McAlpine. Strathy Language Unit, Queen's University. Toronto: Oxford University Press, 1997.

The New Fowler's Modern English Usage. Edited by R.W. Burchfield. 3rd ed. Oxford: Clarendon Press, 1996.

Quirk, Randolph, et al. *A Comprehensive Grammar of the English Language.* London: Longman Group, 1985. 1779 pages.

————. *A Grammar of Contemporary English.* London: Longman Group, 1972.

Stilman, Anne. *Grammatically Correct: The Writer's Essential Guide to Punctuation, Spelling, Style, Usage and Grammar.* Cincinnati: Writer's Digest Books, 1997.

French in English Context

Chapter 6 – French in English Context

6.1 When French appears in an English-language manuscript – a word or phrase, a line of dialogue, a block quotation, a name or title – it must often be treated differently from either English alone or French alone.

6.2 One consideration for the editor is how the work's intended audience might react to the presence of French. In some cases the political attitudes or educational level of readers will suggest that editors should translate or edit out French words or phrases. But in general, editors can assume that Canadian readers know some French and are not totally unwilling to look up what they do not know. That is, we enjoy a greater knowledge of and receptiveness toward French than would be found in countries not officially bilingual. It should not be necessary to translate every word of French that creeps into a Canadian English text, although we might translate every word of Finnish or Swahili.

6.3 In dealing with the untranslated French that remains, editors can't always simply apply the rules of good French usage, even if they know them. Doing so can result in awkwardness and inconsistency that irritate English and French readers alike. This chapter offers some guidance in cases where the two languages must bend a little to accommodate each other and in cases where French material may safely be left as editors find it without risk of confusing readers.

6.4 Two cautions: Editors whose knowledge of French is shaky should seek the advice of more fluent colleagues. And editors working with material that must be approved by governments, especially the Quebec government, will probably be asked to follow style guidelines that are less flexible than those stated in this chapter.

ACCENTS, DIERESES, CEDILLAS

On capital letters

6.5 In Canadian usage, letters retain diacritics (accents, diereses, and cedillas) when capitalized.

À Â Ç É Ê Ë È Î Ï Ô Û Ü Ù

6.6 Initialisms (*sigles*) and acronyms using only capital letters are normally written without any periods, hyphens, or accents that appear in the spelled-out forms:

> OCDE (Organisation de coopération et de développement économiques)
> ALENA (Accord de libre-échange nord-américain)

6.7   However, most abbreviations that contain periods, hyphens, or lowercase letters retain the accent:

>   N.D.É. (note de l'éditeur)
>
>   É.-U. (États-Unis)
>
>   S. Ém. (Son Éminence)
>
>   *but*
>
>   B.Ed. (Baccalauréat en éducation)

To be sure of correct usage, check the many useful lists in *Le guide du rédacteur.*

6.8   Editors may encounter seemingly anomalous abbreviations such as **cégep** (Collège d'enseignement général et professionnel) and **cédérom** (CD-ROM). These are examples of the French phenomenon *sigles lexicalisés,* in which initialisms have been made into pronounceable common nouns by adding accents or new letters. These coined words are usually seen all lowercase, although spellings may vary: **cégep,** clearly still a word in transition, may also occur as **Cégep, CEGEP,** or (breaking all rules) **CÉGEP.**

In personal names

6.9   Every effort should be made to determine, then follow, the preference of the person named in regard to diacritics, since these are as much a component of correct spelling as the letters they appear with. Note that some francophones with names that have historically taken accents and other diacritics do not use them (e.g., Celine Dion omits the accent in English; Jean-Luc Pepin, a Trudeau-era cabinet minister, omitted the accent in both languages). Their preferences should be respected. Newspapers are not a good source for checking these marks, since many use them irregularly if at all; standard library references such as *The Canadian Encyclopedia* and its French edition, *L'Encyclopédie du Canada,* are more reliable.

In French words and phrases

6.10   Use accents, diereses, and cedillas correctly when treating a word or phrase as French, whether this entails the use of quotes, italics, or neither. Dictionaries vary in their judgment of the extent to which particular French words and phrases have been assimilated into the English language. *Webster's* and the *Concise Oxford* deem **protégé** a French word or at least an English word with accents. *Canadian Oxford,* on the other hand, considers **protege** an English word and spells it without accents. Similarly, *Canadian Oxford* and *Webster's* retain the accent on **café,** whereas the *Concise Oxford* omits it. *Webster's* keeps both accents on **résumé;** *Canadian*

Oxford retains only the second one; *Concise Oxford* drops both. Editors can only look up all contentious words in the dictionary they're using and follow its recommendations.

For the special case of **Montreal** and **Quebec** (the city), see 6.34.

ITALICS AND QUOTATION MARKS

6.11   Italics or quotation marks may be used at first reference when treating a word or phrase as French – that is, when the dictionary or style book being followed deems it a foreign term. Italics are preferable, for aesthetic reasons, but quotation marks are acceptable if used consistently. Further references may be in roman type, without quotation marks, especially if they are numerous. Avoid overusing italics or quotation marks with words and phrases that are familiar to a given readership.

6.12   In certain subject areas where there are many French terms – such as cooking, ballet, and fencing – roman type may be used throughout. Similarly, individual works in general disciplines that contain a large number of French terms – such as a popular history of Quebec – may be easier to read without the constant visual interruption of italics.

6.13   Do not use italics or quotation marks with names of persons, places, or organizations simply because they are in French. For titles of published works, see 6.48–54.

PLURALS AND POSSESSIVES

6.14   Avoid imposing English constructions on French words and phrases. For instance, in a noun-adjective phrase such as **caisse populaire,** form the plural in the French way: by adding **s** to both the noun and the adjective.

>   one caisse populaire
>
>   two caisses populaires

6.15   Reword to avoid constructions where the possessive ending -'**s** or -**s'** might be added to a French word:

>   the members of the Parti (*not* the Parti's members)
>
>   the protagonist of two *causes célèbres* (*not* the two *causes célèbres'* protagonist)

6.16   Possessives of personal names in French are treated the same way as English personal names (e.g., **Louis's keyboard**). See 5.18.

NAMES OF ORGANIZATIONS

6.17   The names of organizations, institutions, corporations, and other such bodies, in French as in English, can be highly idiosyncratic. Although "rules" exist in both languages – quite complex ones in the case of French – many organizations ignore them.

The names of organizations such as businesses are especially likely to follow the trends of the times. In English, the modern gimmick is lowercasing, particularly to suggest associations with the Internet. In French, by contrast, capitalization seems to be on the rise. The Alliance Française, standard-bearer of the French language around the world, now uppercases its **F** in contradiction of generations of instruction.

English editors can be forgiven for wondering whether it is their responsibility to impose a traditional consistency on quirky organization names in any language. Following an organization's own style at least achieves accuracy. But English editors with a good understanding of the parts of speech in French can consult a standard reference such as *Le guide du rédacteur* if they prefer to implement more conventional patterns.

We recommend that English editors use an organization's own preferred name style, including hyphenation, accents, and capitalization, as a starting point; check with the organizations themselves. The section below deals with questions and difficulties that can arise from the placement of these names within English context.

French or English

6.18   When there is an official English name, use it together with the French name or in place of it:

> Association des collèges communautaires du Canada/Association of Canadian Community Colleges
>
> Musée des beaux-arts de Montréal/Montreal Museum of Fine Arts

6.19   If there is no official English name, use the French name, generally without translation:

> Sûreté du Québec
>
> Office de la langue française

Where context demands translation, give it in parentheses:

> Sûreté du Québec (Quebec provincial police)

Do not treat an unofficial translation as an official English name; in the example above, therefore, do not capitalize **provincial police.**

Definite articles

6.20 The zone where French and English styles in organization names are most likely to collide is the treatment of the definite article (**the** in English, **le, la, l', les** in French).

In an organization's internal documents or in any legal setting, use the article as shown in the official style. For other contexts, we recommend the following.

English definite article

6.21 Use **the** to replace the French definite article (even if the French definite article forms part of the official name) in the following circumstances:

- when it modifies a generic noun (**association, comité, compagnie, musée, organisation,** etc.):

   Meet me at the Grand café des amis.

   What happened to the Union nationale?

- when the article modifies a noun that is not generic but is well understood in the English context:

   I'll take the Métro.

   No one can see all the Louvre in one day.

- when the organization name is used adjectivally:

   We went to the Nostalchics concert last night.

   The premier addressed the Parti Québécois convention.

French definite article

6.22 Many French organization or institution names that are not based on generic nouns begin with a definite article in their official forms:

   Les Gens de l'air

   La Francophonie

   Les Nostalchics

   La Relève

In most English contexts these articles can be retained without risk of misunderstanding (but see adjectival uses, 6.21).

   Negotiations are continuing with Les Gens de l'Air.

   The breakaway state seeks to join La Francophonie.

6.23 Do not lowercase the French article or combine it with an English one:

✗ She's an accompanist for les Nostalchics.

✗ Ottawa has devoted massive resources to the La Relève.

Clowning around

6.24 Cirque du Soleil, styled "le Cirque du Soleil" in French, omits the article entirely in English text (and uppercases *soleil* in both languages):

No animals appear in the productions of Cirque du Soleil.

Capitalization

6.25 On the Canadian linguistic landscape, the French organization names that are exceptions to the traditional rules of capitalization are so numerous and so prominent as to cast doubt on the continuing relevance of those rules. These are all official styles of the organizations:

Banque Royale

Centre national des Arts

Conseil des Arts du Canada

Grands Ballets Canadiens

Bloc Québécois

Parti Québécois

Cirque du Soleil

Alliance Française

Option A

6.26 Following official organization style in capitalization is the simplest option. Other choices require that the editor have sufficient knowledge of French to be able to distinguish between parts of speech.

Option B

6.27 Capitalize the first word after the article and all proper nouns. If the article is in French (see 6.22–23), capitalize it as well.

Option C

6.28 Editors who wish to impose the conventional French style can follow *Le guide du rédacteur*. In brief, the *Guide* capitalizes the first noun, any preceding adjectives, and all proper nouns.

Option D

6.29　English style for organization names may at times be suitable, especially in texts where only a few French names appear. Consider the readership carefully, and proceed with caution.

Table 6.1　Options for capitalizing names of organizations

Option A	Option B
Les Petits Violons de Noël	Les Petits violons de Noël
the Grands Ballets Canadiens	the Grands ballets canadiens
the Union nationale	the Union nationale
the Direction des services linguistiques	the Direction des services linguistiques

Option C	Option D
Les Petits Violons de Noël	Les Petits Violons de Noël
the Grands Ballets canadiens	the Grands Ballets Canadiens
the Union nationale	the Union Nationale
the Direction des services linguistiques	the Direction des Services Linguistiques

---

An official exception

6.30　In the names of Quebec ministries, French style lowercases **ministère,** in contrast to other generic nouns. For English text, *The Canadian Style* endorses a treatment that is a sensible exception to its basic rule of following the official French form. Follow the official capitalization for the rest of the name, but uppercase **Ministère:**

　　the Ministère des Relations avec les citoyens et de l'Immigration

　　the Ministère des Ressources naturelles

　　the Ministère de la Santé et des Services sociaux

Italic vs. roman

6.31　Do not italicize the French names of organizations, institutions, and corporations simply because they are in French.

PLACE NAMES

6.32　Rules governing the official style of place names in French, especially in capitalization and hyphenation, are intricate; only a few points are touched on below. Fortunately, it is rarely necessary to deviate from the official form in an English context, and many references are available for checking French place names in Canada (see Sources).

6.33 English translations of Quebec place names are no longer officially accepted (for exceptions see 6.34). For example, **Trois-Rivières** (formerly Three Rivers) and **Sept-Îles** (formerly Seven Islands) are now the accepted forms in both languages. The Treasury Board of Canada (Circular 1983-58) approved a list of 81 names of pan-Canadian significance that have official forms in both languages; for example, **Baffin Island/Île de Baffin, St. Lawrence River/Fleuve Saint-Laurent, Quebec/Québec** (province). This list appears in *The Canadian Style* and on the *GeoNames/Toponymes* Web site, which is maintained by the Canadian Permanent Committee on Geographical Names.

Accents

6.34 French place names in Canada retain their accents in English text. Legitimate exceptions are **Montreal** and **Quebec** (the city), although they are not listed as names of pan-Canadian significance (see 6.33). **Quebec** province, however, is on the list and is shown without an accent in English.

   Montreal and **Quebec** (the city), although very similar to their French counterparts, are well established in both spelling and pronunciation as English words, just as **Londres** is established as the French word for London, England. Most francophones would not write "Elle est allée à London," and there is no reason for anglophones to write "She has gone to Montréal." **Montréal** and **Québec** often appear affected in English text. The form **Québec City** makes no sense in either language.

   However, the accented forms are increasingly evident in some publications. *The Canadian Style* states that **Montréal** and **Québec** (the city) must retain their accents in English federal documents.

Geographical features

6.35 In French text, names of geographical features are written with the generic – **baie, mont, rivière** – in lowercase and the specific capitalized: "la baie des Anglais," "le mont Tremblant," "la rivière Noire." In English text, the editor may either retain the French generic or translate it. (The specific element of a name is never translated.)

6.36 With the first option, which we recommend, the generic must be capitalized and the article omitted:

   Baie Laval
   Rivière Noire

6.37   The second option – **Laval Bay, Noire River** – is discussed in *Le guide du rédacteur* and *The Canadian Style*. Acceptable English generic terms are listed in *The Glossary of Generic Terms in Canada's Geographical Names* (see Sources). However, editors who decide to translate the generic should be aware of the exceptions to that option. The exceptions are outlined and discussed in *Canada's Geographical Names Approved in English and French* (see Sources). For example, the generic is not translated if it is separated from the specific by one or more particles (short linking words): **lac aux Sables/Lac aux Sables, baie de la Mouette/Baie de la Mouette.**

6.38   Names that are well known to anglophones in their French forms, such as the **Mont Tremblant** resort, should not be translated.

6.39   Short-form references should be in English (the **bay,** the **river**).

Streets, structures, and public places

6.40   In French text, the generic in names of roadways, bridges, parks, and squares is lowercase, whether part of an address or used alone: "la rue Cartier," "le pont Jacques-Cartier," "le parc Lafontaine," "la place Royale." In English text, the editor may either retain the generic with a capital and omit the article (an option we recommend), or translate the generic.

Rue Cartier	Cartier Street
Chemin de la Côte-des-Neiges	Côte-des-Neiges Road
Pont Jacques-Cartier	Jacques-Cartier (or Jacques Cartier) Bridge
Parc Lafontaine	Lafontaine Park

6.41   Well-known French street names and names of squares and other features are generally not translated:

Grande-Allée

Place Royale

Bois Joli

6.42   Street names in Quebec should be left in their French forms except when usage, audience, political slant of text, or historical context demands translation. For example, a novel set in Montreal in the 1920s would refer to **Mountain Street** and **St. James Street,** and not to the current French versions, **Rue de la Montagne** and **Rue Saint-Jacques.**

"Saint(s)" and "Sainte(s)"

6.43   In Quebec, **Saint** and **Sainte** in place names are usually spelled out and joined to the following word by a hyphen. When they must be abbreviated, as in maps or graphs, use **St, Sts, Ste, Stes**, without periods and with hyphens:

> Ste-Agathe-des-Monts
>
> Cap-St-Jacques
>
> Sts-Anges

Populated places

6.44   Multiple-word names of inhabited places in Quebec are hyphenated:

> Trois-Rivières
>
> Stanstead-Est
>
> Notre-Dame-du-Bon-Conseil
>
> Saint-Louis-du-Ha! Ha!

6.45   Place names derived from geographical features are generally formed by capitalizing the generic and adding a hyphen: the town of **Mont-Tremblant,** the town of **Baie-Comeau,** the village of **Île-d'Entrée.**

French place names outside Quebec

6.46   French names in provinces other than Quebec follow their own rules for hyphenation, abbreviation, and capitalization.

> Sault Ste. Marie, Ontario
>
> St. Boniface, Manitoba
>
> St-Laurent-Grandin, Saskatchewan
>
> Petit-De-Grat, Nova Scotia
>
> Saint-Martin-de-Restigouche, New Brunswick

Italic vs. roman

6.47   Do not italicize the French names of streets, buildings, structures, or geographical features simply because they are in French.

TITLES OF WORKS

Capitalization

6.48   Editors have two choices in styling the titles of published works, films, plays, TV productions, etc.

Option A

6.49 The first option is to capitalize only the first word and all proper nouns, a system that has the virtue of being very easy to apply. The *Chicago Manual* and the most recent editions of *Le Ramat de la typographie* and *Le guide du rédacteur* adhere to this system (with exceptions as noted in 6.50):

> *Un zoo la nuit*
>
> *Du côté de chez Swann*
>
> *Le matou*

Old-fashioned types

6.50 Even among followers of Option A, periodical titles are capitalized according to the traditional system, shown here as Option B.

> *Le Devoir*
>
> *La Presse*

A generally recognized exception in Canada is *L'actualité*.

Option B

6.51 The second option is the more traditional system, although it is gradually falling out of use. Briefly, the principal rules are:

- Uppercase the first word and all proper nouns.
- If the first word is a definite article, uppercase also the first noun and any intervening adjectives:

> *Le Rêve inachevé*
>
> *Les Cordes de bois*
>
> *Les Bons Débarras*
>
> *L'Entre-deux-guerres*
>
> *La Nausée*
>
> *Le Devoir*

- If the first word is anything other than a definite article, only the first word and any proper nouns are capitalized:

> *Au bord du lac*
>
> *Un chapeau de paille d'Italie*
>
> *Ces enfants de ma vie*
>
> *Mort à crédit*
>
> *Cité libre*

- If the title is composed of two or more *equivalent* nouns joined by **et** or **ou,** capitalize both, plus any preceding adjectives (but not articles):

  Un Homme et une Femme

  Le Rouge et le Noir

  Le Petit Homme et la Grande Femme

  Note that these conjunctions do not necessarily denote an equivalence:

  L'Homme et son milieu

- If the title is a complete sentence, uppercase only the first word:

  Les fées ont soif

  Le gendarme est sans pitié

Table 6.2   Options for capitalizing titles of works

Option A	Option B
Le rêve inachevé	*Le Rêve inachevé*
Les bons débarras	*Les Bons Débarras*
Le Devoir	*Le Devoir*
Au bord du lac	*Au bord du lac*
Un homme et une femme	*Un Homme et une Femme*
Les fées ont soif	*Les fées ont soif*

Italics and quotation marks

6.52   Do not italicize a French title merely because it is French. Use the same rules for italicizing titles that apply in English. For example, set song titles in roman and enclose in quotation marks:

"La vie en rose"

"Mon pays"

Translation of titles

6.53   Translations of titles should be set within parentheses, in roman type without quotes, and using sentence capitalization rather than title style. (In documentation, some editors would substitute square brackets for parentheses if the translation does not appear in the book.)

Dictionnaire des noms propres (Dictionary of proper names)

When the work has been published in translation, the English title should be in italics or quotes, as appropriate to the genre:

> *Bonheur d'occasion* (Second-hand happiness; published in English as *The Tin Flute*)

> "Les feuilles mortes" (Dead leaves; published in English as "Autumn Leaves")

6.54 Many Canadian publications have bilingual titles, such as the journal *Canadian Public Policy/Analyse de politiques*. Both titles should be given at first text reference. At second reference use the title in the language of the article cited, or, if the reference is to the entire publication, use the English title.

QUOTED MATERIAL

6.55 Readers who understand the content of French quoted material are not likely to be confused by French typographical conventions, different as they are from English ones.

Editors may be tempted to anglicize French punctuation within quoted material in order to impose stylistic consistency. The extent to which an editor may alter quoted material, in any language, is never a clear-cut question (see 12.127, "quoted material"). In the case of French quotation style, French differs from English in so many small ways that anglicizing large amounts of French copy may be more trouble than it is worth.

Presented below are the most common conventions of French typography in Canada (according to *Le Ramat de la typographie, Le guide du rédacteur,* and *The Canadian Style*) to assist typesetters and proofreaders in reproducing French punctuation accurately. If the punctuation of a French passage presents too much difficulty for a given English-language readership, it may be wise to add or substitute a translation rather than anglicizing its typography.

Spacing

Dashes

6.56 A dash is always set off by spaces in French:

> L'énigme torturante – ce qu'est la vie, ce qu'est la mort – m'y ramenait de force.

> – Gabrielle Roy

Ellipses

6.57 Ellipsis points – always three, never four – are set tight (three to the em) in French, with no space before and one space after:

> Parce que… parce que… Je ne sais pas.

Colon, dollar sign, per cent

6.58 A thin space or full space is left before the colon, the dollar sign, and the per cent symbol.

> Il y a des mots comme cela : une fois dits, on les entendra toujours.
>
> – Gabrielle Roy

> Le budget est de 26 000 $, soit une hausse de 14 % par rapport à l'année dernière.

Note that the dollar sign follows the figure.

Semicolon, exclamation mark, question mark

6.59 The semicolon, the exclamation mark, and the question mark generally have the same spacing as in English.

For the spacing of French quotation marks, see 6.65.

Superior letters

6.60 Many abbreviations in French traditionally use superior (superscript) letters. These letters are set smaller than the body copy.

> n^o
>
> Mme, Mlle
>
> 1er (1re), 2^e
>
> S^t, S^{te}

Note that in **n^o**, the **o** is a letter, not the numeral zero.

Superior letters can be set in ordinary type instead unless the resulting form could be confused with another word.

> n^{os} (numéros), *not* nos
>
> M^e (Maître), *not* Me

For more on French abbreviations, see 4.7 and 6.6–8.

Punctuation of numbers

6.61 It is in the punctuation of numbers that variations among traditional French style, traditional English style, and SI style pose the highest risk of misleading the reader. The three styles use different markers to separate groups of three digits:

population of 25,000 (*English*)

25.000 (*older French*)

25 000 (*SI*)

And the decimal marker varies between English and French:

2.125% (*English*)

2,125 % (*French*)

Both styles for the decimal marker are valid in SI: the period in English text and the comma in French text.

6.62 In many instances, context will provide sufficient clues to the meaning of the numbers in a passage of French, and the French can therefore be reproduced with its original punctuation intact. But if editorial intervention is necessary, consider the following three options.

- Adopt SI style throughout the document, including the "English SI" decimal marker. An explanatory note in the front matter may be required.
- Translate or paraphrase the French passages that present difficulty.
- Replace French numbers with English numbers inside square brackets (and add an explanatory note):

population de [25,000]

taux d'interêt de [2.125] %

Quotation marks

6.63 French conventions in punctuating quotations and dialogue differ markedly from English rules. Fortunately, the possibility of using French quotation marks (« ») – called guillemets or chevrons – arises in English texts in limited circumstances only: in block quotations and in internal quotations within French quoted material. (Many an English manuscript, of course, will contain neither.)

6.64   A passage of French run into English text carries the same quotation style as the surrounding text: that is, English quotation marks. Other French punctuation inside the passage should be left intact:

> As Gabrielle Roy wrote, "Il y a des mots comme cela : une fois dits, on les entendra toujours."

Spacing

6.65   A space is set after an opening guillemet and before a closing one.

> « Elle est en pleine évolution. »

Interlocutory phrases

6.66   In French, phrases such as **he said** are not always set off with quotation marks:

> « Il pleut, dit Jean, et je n'ai pas mon parapluie. »

See also 6.69.

Multiple punctuation

6.67   For the order of quotation marks and other punctuation, French style is based on grammatical logic rather than typographical efficiency, which largely informs Canadian and American English style practices (see 5.29–30). Therefore, French punctuation is often found outside the guillemets.

> « Je me demande qui c'est », dit Chloë.

French style also allows certain combinations of punctuation that are less acceptable in English:

> « C'est monstrueux! », s'écria-t-elle.

Internal quotations

6.68   French style for delineating internal quotations varies. English-style quotation marks (called in French guillemets anglais) or italics are common in modern Canadian French.

> Louise m'a dit, « J'ai entendu dire que ton cabaret est un "succès fou" ».

In an older style, guillemets fulfill the functions of both single and double English quotation marks. In this style, when an internal quotation closes at the same point as the direct quotation, only one guillemet is used:

> Louise m'a dit, « J'ai entendu dire que ton cabaret est un « succès fou ».

Dashes

6.69　Dashes are sometimes used in French instead of or in combination with guillemets to introduce dialogue.

> – Je te vois, Jean Le Maigre, dit Grand-Mère, tu te crois à l'abri mais je te vois.
> – Tu ne peux pas me voir puisque personne ne me voit pas quand je lis, dit Jean Le Maigre.
>
> – Marie-Claire Blais

> « Comme vous avez l'air sérieux aujourd'hui, avec ce manuscrit impressionnant.
> – Si j'en avais le loisir, chère madame, c'est avec plaisir que je prendrais congé de ce monument poussiéreux!
> – Courage, lui dit-elle en riant, avant de se diriger vers le centre de la salle. »
>
> – Jacques Desautels

Note that in the second example, the entire conversation is enclosed within one set of guillemets, with dashes indicating a change in speaker. In the last sentence, only "courage" is actually spoken; the rest of the sentence is description, which, like short interlocutory phrases (see 6.66), is included inside the guillemets as part of the exchange.

WORD DIVISION

6.70　French rules of word division should be followed whenever a French word must break at the end of a line, whether in excerpted material or in running text. The 1978 Statistics Canada publication *Word Division in French* (sadly, long out of print) has roughly 50,000 entries, and many standard references, including the *Chicago Manual* and *The Canadian Style,* give basic rules for French word division.

SOURCES

Baudot, Alain, and Thérèse Lior. *Basic Rules for Typesetting in French: Where They Differ from Rules for English.* Toronto: Groupe de recherche en études francophones, 1984. 10 pp. Out of print.

Canadian Permanent Committee on Geographical Names. *Canada's Geographical Names Approved in English and French.* [Ottawa]: CPCGN Secretariat, 1998. May be ordered free through CPCGN Web site: <geonames.nrcan.gc.ca>.

Commission de toponymie du Québec (for official forms of Quebec place names)
Édifice Marie-Guyart
1060, rue Louis-Alexandre Taschereau, 4e étage
Quebec, QC G1R 5V8
Tel. (418) 643-2817; fax (418) 644-9466
<www.toponymie.gouv.qc.ca>
(With older browser software, enter site at
<www.toponymie.gouv.qc.ca/index.htm>.)

The Glossary of Generic Terms in Canada's Geographical Names/Glossaire des génériques en usage dans les noms géographiques du Canada. Ottawa: Department of the Secretary of State, Department of Energy, Mines and Resources, and Translation Bureau, 1987. Terminology Bulletin 176.

Le guide du rédacteur. 2nd ed. [Ottawa]: Bureau de la traduction, 1996. First edition was titled *Guide du rédacteur de l'administration fédérale.*

Ramat, Aurel. *Le Ramat de la typographie.* 3rd ed. Saint-Lambert, Que.: Ramat, 1997.

Villers, Marie-Éva de. *Multidictionnaire des difficultés de la langue française.* Montreal: Québec-Amérique, 1997.

Word Division in French/La division des mots en français. Compiled by Gérard D. Fontaine. Ottawa: Statistics Canada, 1978. Out of print.

Works quoted

Blais, Marie-Claire. *Une saison dans la vie d'Emmanuel.* Montreal: Alain Stanké, 1980.

Desautels, Jacques. *Le quatrième roi mage.* Montreal: Les Quinze, 1993.

Roy, Gabrielle. *La détresse et l'enchantement.* Montreal: Boréal Express, 1984.

Canadianization

Chapter 7 – Canadianization

7.1   A Canadian edition is a work originally published in another country (usually but not always the United States) in which changes are made to reflect the Canadian context. The process of creating this edition is often referred to as Canadianization or adaptation.

7.2   Canadian publishers – or more often Canadian subsidiaries of foreign publishers – are likely to undertake the preparation of a Canadian edition when the substance will serve a Canadian audience but details (examples, references to regulations, or prices, for instance) must be adapted. Consider a post-secondary textbook in financial accounting as an example: the theory is the same on both sides of the border, but as each country has its own nationally regulated procedures, the latter must be altered to show Canadian practice. A guide rating current models of automobiles would have to take into account factors involved in the Canadian selling price that may not apply in the United States, as well as Canadian laws regarding safety features, emission standards, and the like.

Nevertheless, for Canadian publishers, Canadianizing an existing work can save labour and reduce financial risk. The basic structure has been provided by the foreign book. Elements such as end-of-chapter exercises are generally much easier to modify than to create from scratch. The original text, including artwork that would be expensive to recreate, is nowadays usually available electronically. When the book is a proven success in its own country, the Canadian adapting author or editor and publisher have the advantage of working with a product that has already been market tested. Also, before the final decision to Canadianize is made, the publisher can have a number of potential users of the adapted text review the existing edition to get a fairly accurate sense of what their level of enthusiasm for the final product will be, as well as to determine what features should be retained or enhanced.

7.3   Budget remains a major consideration in Canadianization. The original work has usually been created for many times the potential market available in this country, and it may be economically impossible to match the original production job. The publisher must make decisions early about possible ways to reduce costs: Could the Canadian book be shorter? Could four-colour artwork be reproduced as two-colour? Could photos be eliminated without sacrificing clarity of presentation? These decisions will affect not only the price of the book but also the way the editor handles its preparation.

WHEN IS CANADIANIZATION APPROPRIATE?

7.4   Both content and reading level must be considered when adapting a foreign work for a Canadian edition. In primary reading series, the early how-to-read books tend to focus on technique rather than content, and so materials developed elsewhere may be appropriate for Canadianization. As children progress from simple "decoding" and begin to read, the cultural content becomes increasingly important, and the pervasive changes that would be required in an adaptation make Canadianization less feasible. Mathematics and science texts, however, are less culture-dependent; thus a Canadian series can be based on an existing work that has already undergone extensive (and expensive) development and classroom testing.

7.5   For other elementary and high school texts, original Canadian works are much more common than adapted ones, partly because the market is large enough to support the cost of producing Canadian books, and partly because provincial course guidelines are so specific that books must be written to fit them.

7.6   In college and university textbooks the emphasis changes. Students at this level can be expected to use mathematics and physical science textbooks published elsewhere. It is in social science and business texts that Canadian legislation, history, and context are significant if not central concerns; texts in these fields are therefore prime candidates for Canadianization.

7.7   In trade publishing, it is possible (though uncommon) to Canadianize how-to books and other non-fiction. Usually the same considerations that affect the Canadianization of college texts apply.

CANADIANIZING CONTENT

7.8   A minimal adaptation would change only those facts or passages in the original that have little or no meaning for Canadian readers. Since there are seldom exact parallels in moving from one culture to another, the Canadianizing or adapting author and editor must check every change against its context to ensure that the revised version still rings true. The original may quote a survey stating that 42 per cent of the American population favours private schools over public ones. It is inexcusable, but not uncommon, to change "American" to "Canadian" in the adapted work. There may be no survey to support such a claim about the Canadian population. Even the concept of public schools is somewhat different in the minds of Canadians. In such areas, the adapting author and editor must take care to ensure that statements are based on Canadian research and reflect the specific Canadian situation. Alternatively, statements in the original that cannot be Canadianized may be specifically identified as non-Canadian, or they may be deleted if the point is not central.

The Canadianizing author

7.9 Increasingly, market considerations influence publishers to request more than minimal changes and the insertion of a multitude of Canadian examples. Such is the case in the post-secondary textbook market where a Canadian author, generally a faculty member experienced in teaching the course in which the text would be used, is hired to adapt the material for the Canadian market. Because of the experience these adapting authors bring with them to the writing of the text, they are not limited to just changing examples in order to make the content Canadian but are encouraged to make the book their own.

The market

7.10 Before the adapting author is hired, a survey of the potential market for the text is undertaken to determine what needs to be changed. It is understood that spelling, examples, and references to laws, regulations, and standards need to be changed throughout the book. However, a survey of the market will also determine whether the order and emphasis of topics is in line with average Canadian curriculum. This type of research can lead to a decision to eliminate or add a chapter, or to completely change the emphasis of one that will be retained.

THE EDITOR'S ROLE

7.11 The technical accuracy of a major adaptation will need to be confirmed by reviewers from the field. However, there are a number of areas that the publisher and editor should check to ensure that the Canadianization does not come across as a "patch job":

- If the adapting author is not sensitive to the nuances of the original work, some of the new examples may not accomplish the same results as the ones they replace. Every example must be tested against its context to ensure that it in fact reinforces the point being made. An informed editor can often help by suggesting alternative examples to replace inappropriate or ineffective ones.

- In an illustrated work, the adapter must be alert to foreign landmarks, customs, and situations in the original illustrations: the American flag on the desk; American currency; the American black or Hispanic slum to illustrate urban poverty. New photographs should be substituted to reflect Canadian ethnic representation and Canadian social settings. If a precisely parallel illustration is impossible to find, the inappropriate original must be deleted – no illustration is often better than a blatantly American one.

- In books containing a large number of fictitious names, special care must be taken that they, too, reflect Canadian ethnic representation including francophone groups. The predominance of Anglo-Saxon names in many American texts is increasingly unacceptable in the Canadian market. Departments of education are particularly insistent that text and illustrations reflect the diverse ethnic mix of their student population, as well as a gender and age balance.

Substantive and structural editing

7.12   It is often assumed that substantive, structural, and stylistic editing of an adaptation will be a minor task, for "we already have a book." Certainly the process should be faster – if the work was well edited in the first place. If it was not, editor and publisher must come to an agreement as to how much the editor should tinker with the form and wording of the original. Financial constraints are often the major reason for compromise, but contractual and ethical concerns may also come into play.

    Canadianization is often regarded as a specialized form of editing, but it requires only an extra level of awareness in addition to the usual editorial functions. The editor's main concerns should be the following.

7.13   *Has the Canadianizing author followed changes through to their logical conclusion?* It is very easy to recognize a problem area and make changes but then miss one or more of the less obvious corollaries, especially if they are buried "insignificantly" elsewhere in the book. American introductory business texts, for example, usually describe three forms of private business ownership – sole proprietorship, partnership, and corporation. In Canada, especially in the Prairie provinces, a fourth form – the cooperative – is important. Canadianizing authors usually recognize this element and modify the initial descriptions of forms of ownership appropriately, but may miss allusions elsewhere in the text to the "three forms of private ownership."

7.14   *Have features peculiar to the Canadian situation been added?* The author may concentrate so hard on Canadianizing the existing material that uniquely Canadian topics that should be covered are forgotten. For example, because a much larger proportion of Canadian workers are unionized, it may be necessary to expand related material rather than just Canadianize what exists.

7.15   *Is the original structure still appropriate to the Canadian context?* Different
conditions may dictate different emphases, which in turn dictate a different ordering of the material and the downplaying or highlighting of
different aspects. For example, an American economics text may have a
substantial chapter about foreign exchange, in effect introducing the
entire subject to readers who know nothing about it. For Canadian readers, however, foreign exchange is an unavoidable feature of business and
personal life, and awareness of the basics can be assumed.

7.16   *Are the Canadian examples truly parallel?* Are the examples as strong as the
original ones? Has too little effort – or too much – gone into substituting
Canadian examples? It is foolish to substitute a Canadian incident that no
one has heard of for George Washington and the cherry tree. In some
cases, examples with an international aspect may be an improvement on
both the original and the proposed Canadian substitutes.

7.17   *Should elements be dropped?* What if no parallel Canadian example can be
found? If the original example must be cut, it may not be necessary to
substitute a Canadian one; perhaps the chapter can survive without. Material that should probably be cut is not limited to examples. Discussion
that may be unnecessary in Canada (e.g., detailed definitions of the metric system or parliamentary democracy) should be dropped as well.

7.18   *Should new elements be added?* Just because the original work did not offer
an example of a certain subject does not mean that the Canadianization
cannot. Canada may offer a marvellous example where the original text
had none.

7.19   *Are underlying attitudes appropriate for Canadian readers?* For example, is
there an unconscious extolling of the American way of life at the expense
of the rest of the world? Be aware, though, that Canadians have their fair
share of North American insularity; do not replace one extreme with
another.

Copy-editing

7.20   Copy-editing of a Canadianization does not differ greatly from copy-
editing of an original work. For example, the editor would still flag a sus-
pect statement of fact. However, Canadianizing text can lead to certain
inconsistencies that may require special attention.

Writing style

7.21   In the adaptation of the text, the adapting author probably replaced whole
sections of prose with entirely new material yet retained other sections
with only the spelling changed. The editor must note and address any

inconsistencies in writing style across this material. Is the phrasing conspicuously more complex in some paragraphs? Does the vocabulary level vary?

Spelling and punctuation

7.22   The editor must verify the spelling convention that is to be used in the adaptation. Guidelines of provincial departments of education may restrict the choice for some books. For other books, it is up to the Canadian publisher. Generally, the adapting author will have followed the decided-upon convention when reworking passages or writing new ones. However, if no change was made to a paragraph, it may still follow the American spelling in the original work. Alternatively, there may be no remnants of the American spelling because the author made global changes – including inappropriate ones, such as changing the spelling of official names (U.S. Department of "Labour").

Punctuation may be more inconsistent in an adaptation than in most single-author works. The editor must ensure that the style of punctuation and the format for lists, captions, and so on are consistent throughout.

Terminology

7.23   Use of some terms is determined by regulation, of others by convention. For instance, in the United States, the owners of companies are known as "stockholders," whereas in Canada they are called "shareholders." Canadians vote in "ridings" and nibble on "chocolate bars" while Americans vote in "electoral districts" and snack on "candy bars." Canadians "write" exams and Americans "take" them (but Britons "sit" them). Normally the author can be expected to be familiar with the relevant usages, but the editor must be careful to ensure that *all* appearances of such terms are altered.

7.24   The most common forms of nationally regulated terms are currency and standards of measurement. Works originally published in the United States are likely to use the U.S. system of measurement (loosely related to, but not entirely the same as, the British imperial system). Books intended for Canadian schools must be converted to SI/metric units of measurement, as must most college and university texts (see chapter 9). For trade books, the decision on which system of measurement to use will be made on a book-by-book basis.

RIGHTS – AND WRONGS

The authors in an adaptation

7.25 Canadianization is usually undertaken by a Canadian subsidiary of the publishing company that first published the work. The author of the original work may not be consulted and may not even be aware that an adapted version is being prepared. Legally, the original publisher is usually covered by a clause in the author agreement that gives the publisher the right to produce foreign editions or to sell that right. Ethically, the publisher may be on questionable ground. If the author's examples are an organic part of the work, changing them may destroy the essence of the work. Original authors may find that a book issued in Canada with their names on the cover contains ideas that they consider distasteful or untenable. The integrity of the original author should always be considered when the work is adapted for Canadian readers.

Ethical standards dictate that a Canadianization be clearly identified as an adaptation of a non-Canadian work. An editor may be in a position to suggest a way of wording the author credit on the cover and the title page so that the specific contributions of the original author and the Canadianizing author are clear.

Some books provide the preface from the original work as well as the preface to the Canadian edition. This practice is more ethical than that of simply rewriting the original preface to fit the Canadian edition. If the original preface is rewritten, only the name of the Canadian author should appear after it, unless the author of the original work has read and approved the revision.

Copyright information

7.26 Copyright information should show the history of both the original book and the adaptation:

© 1994, 1997 John Wiley & Sons, Inc.
© 1999 John Wiley & Sons Canada, Ltd.

Permissions

7.27 The original work may contain material quoted or reproduced from other sources. The editor should not assume that the permissions granted for the original edition will cover the Canadian adaptation; the contracts for the original work and for the adaptation will specify permissions liability, which can vary greatly from work to work. In addition, each permission letter must be checked to verify that it covers editions other than the original work.

Avoiding Bias

Chapter 8 – Avoiding Bias

8.1 Bias in writing stems from a failure to acknowledge in other groups the same human qualities that one takes for granted in one's own group. This failure is frequently expressed as a stereotype – a fixed image or phrase that is a substitute for the effort of serious thought. When people are treated as stereotypes, they are denied their complexity and individuality.

We live in a country and in a time of diversity among people – diversity of heritage, of capacities, of goals and life choices. Canadians are becoming more sensitive to bias and to the ways in which language can respond to or perpetuate bias in our pluralistic society, and many Canadian editorial reference works now reflect that society's changes in attitude. The editor's task is still to revise copy so that it avoids offensive terms while skirting the traps of euphemism, stiltedness, tokenism, and condescension. Bias is, after all, a distortion of fact; the goal of revision is the usual one of enhancing accuracy and clarity. Much of the backlash against "political correctness" is a revolt against replacing not only negative clichés but also clear descriptive terms with saccharine absurdities that are no improvement.

However, what is considered acceptable vocabulary changes over time. Particularly when a group is subject to prejudice, a term that may have come into use as a corrective to offensive terms (such as "retarded" to replace "imbecile" and "moron") may itself take on a negative connotation and prompt efforts to find a replacement.

The suggestions in this chapter point to ways to avoid expressions that are insensitive or offensive. We have focused on four specific areas: ethnicity and race, gender, sexual orientation, and disability. In addition to these, editors should be aware of other areas of bias, such as age (the suggestion that everyone over 65 is in mental decline); height and weight (tall/slender people are more competent than short/plump ones); geography (there is nothing worthy of notice outside Ontario); religion (we are pious; they are superstitious).

As with so many other aspects of editing, context (the author's point of view, the purpose, and the audience) will influence the editor's decisions. The editor should use judgment and discretion – in consultation with the author and publisher – to find the appropriate vocabulary for that context. A note of caution, however: In specialized fields and in the area of human rights, terminology may be highly specific and unlike that in general use. The editor is advised to consult the agencies concerned with such fields.

COMMON PITFALLS

Stereotyped portrayals

8.2 Avoid hackneyed attributions of characteristics to members of a particular group – thoughtless teenagers; ignorant peasants; flamboyant homosexuals.

Well-meaning stereotypes are no less damaging: when people are categorized as helpless, oppressed victims (fragile seniors; sweet, passive, sexless people in wheelchairs), they risk being deemed unable to determine their own best interests.

8.3 In photographs, drawings, and captions, the repeated portrayal of individuals or groups in a particular way equally constitutes stereotyping.

Overgeneralizations

8.4 Watch for sweeping statements attributing characteristics to all members of a particular group.

> ✗ Hungarians are a proud people, jealous of their honour.
> *(All Hungarians? Day in and day out?)*

Another facet of overgeneralization is *underspecification* – sweeping statements about what is purported to be a group but is in fact many different groups:

> ✗ Canada's black community still reflects the influence of British colonialism.
> *(There isn't a dominant black "community" in Canada comparable to that in the United States. Black Canadians born in Barbados, for example, might be referred to here, but those of Somali, Haitian, or American descent do not fit the generalization, nor do those whose forebears arrived in the eighteenth century.)*

> ✗ Feminists oppose the hierarchical structures of the capitalist system.
> *(Feminism comprises a wide range of political views and economic interests. One subgroup does not speak for all.)*

Irrelevant reference

8.5 Consider whether reference to a person's race, sex, sexual orientation, marital status, number of children, age, ethnic affiliation, disability, personal appearance, and the like is relevant or a distraction.

> ✗ Mother of three is the new head of Western Utilities.
> *(When professional achievement is the point, personal information may trivialize the accomplishment.)*

✘ Mr. Robbins, who immigrated to Montreal from Jamaica when he was five, was charged with assault.
(Unnecessary and selective reference to country of origin, race, culture, or religion in a context such as crime or social problems creates or reinforces a spurious association of a problem with a particular group.)

Condescension

8.6 Watch for backhanded praise that carries the unjustified assumption of lesser ability or achievement in another person or group.

✘ Women are much better than men at repetitive, monotonous tasks.
(The implication is that they are thereby less suited to complex, challenging tasks.)

✘ The Polynesian peoples have a natural gift for musical harmony.
(A skill that in one's own culture could be gained only through considerable application and practice – musical, athletic, rhetorical, or oral memory, for example – is no more "natural" in other people.)

Omission

8.7 A version of history may ostensibly tell the complete story and yet systematically omit all mention of many of the events or participants. For example, until recently, Canadian history books took minimal notice of inhabitants other than French and British males – and mostly explorers and politicians at that.

> "This is a milestone for us. People of colour in this country are trying to say, 'This isn't our history in addition to Canadian history, it *is* Canadian history.'"
>
> – Rev. Darryl Gray at 1999 ceremony honouring the black Canadians who worked as porters on the CPR

Unbalanced juxtaposition

8.8 Two or more persons of equal significance to the story should not be identified differently in a manner that denies their equality.

✘ Dr. Luis Estevez and his associate, Martin Pereira, accepted their Nobel Prize.
(If one individual is identified by an honorific, such as "Dr.," check that others equally entitled to it are similarly identified.)

✘ The plane last seen carrying Duluth Volvo dealer Fred Simpkins and an Indian guide was spotted north of Kenora.
(If two people have identical roles – for example, as missing persons – they should be identified in parallel fashion.)

Hypersensitivity

8.9   Misguided zeal in correcting the errors listed above may lead to bowdlerization, distorting tokenism, and new stereotypes.

For example, illustrations in a children's book may include every possible type of family structure except the "traditional nuclear." Excessive delicacy in describing alcohol-related problems among aboriginal populations avoids stigmatizing all aboriginal people but denies the very serious reality of the effects of alcoholism.

ETHNICITY AND RACE

8.10   Colour, race, and culture are especially likely to invite overgeneralizations.

General terms

8.11   The term **race** should be used with great caution. The word commonly refers to a category of people that *the user* identifies on the basis of similar visible physical characteristics and geographical origin. **Race** is wrongly used to account for the behaviour, attitudes, and aptitudes of groups or individuals – characteristics that are shaped by culture, ethnicity, education, income, and other features of environment. In anthropology, the term has been abandoned. However, in the field of race relations, **race** has a specific meaning more akin to that of **ethnicity** in general use.

8.12   An **ethnic group** is the group with which individuals are identified, or identify themselves, on the basis of cultural characteristics associated with a common origin. Every Canadian has at least one ethnic origin, although not all Canadians identify themselves strongly with a particular ethnic group. Thus **ethnic** should be used carefully. It does not mean "not of the mainstream"; the "mainstream" itself may be an assumption rather than a reality. Ethnic groups are also referred to as **minority groups;** however, not all minority groups in Canada are ethnic groups (e.g., Mormons), and ethnic groups are not always minorities (e.g., the French in Quebec). Note that **ethnic** is an adjective, not a noun.

In the Balkan upheavals of the 1990s, **ethnic Albanians** and **ethnic Serbs** were phrases used to distinguish cultural/linguistic groups from citizens of Albania and Serbia.

8.13   The term **visible minority** usually refers to people who are not of European origin in a context where those of European origin are assumed to be in the majority. Yet "visibility" depends on the perspective of the viewer: Roma (Gipsy) people are highly "visible" to Eastern Europeans, for example, but not to those Canadians who have no history with them. Jews may be "visible" in rural Saskatchewan but invisible in downtown Montreal. Be alert to the implications of perspective.

   Visible minority is sometimes also used to refer to people with perceptible disabilities.

8.14   **Citizenship** relates to one's legal status in a particular state. Especially in contexts of righteous protest, **citizens** has the ring of higher status, although residents, voters, or taxpayers are actually meant. **Nationality** is now out of use, being vague; it has been used to mean citizenship and ethnic origin.

Specific terms

8.15   Oxford's *Guide to Canadian English Usage* is but one source advising that terms of the type discussed below should be adjectives rather than nouns: for example, instead of "blacks" or "natives," use a phrase such as **black people** (or citizens, residents, students, etc.) or **native people** (or representatives, youth, councillors, etc.).

8.16   On the tricky question of capitalization, the same guide recommends that **aboriginal, native, indigenous, black,** and the like be capitalized "to parallel other broad ethnic, linguistic, and geographic designations such as Asian, *Hispanic*, and *Nordic*." Yet other guides, such as those of the *Globe and Mail* and Canadian Press, keep them lowercase. The editor's choice will (as always) be influenced by context. For example, **white** is rarely capitalized; where **white** and **black** are juxtaposed, the editor will probably decide to either capitalize or lowercase both. (In this chapter, the decision to lowercase is arbitrary: the discussion of terms as terms, apart from a context, removes the basis for one choice rather than another.)

8.17   **Anglophone** and **francophone** designate language use (English speakers and French speakers), not ethnic origins. **Allophone** is a well-established word in Canada for speakers of other languages, particularly in relation to Quebec.

8.18   **Race,** however slippery the meaning may be, is much associated with references to skin colour. The context of the work may govern which terms are appropriate. **Negro** (uppercase and applying to both sexes) is acceptable in certain historical contexts, and **coloured** in others (e.g., as a term with official definition in apartheid-era South Africa). **Coloured** is also used by some older people in self-reference. In contemporary use, **black** is common. It is possible in certain contexts for a black person to use the word **nigger** in self-reference, but seriously offensive for others to use it.

Negro and **black** usually apply only to people with some perceptible degree of black African ancestry. **African-Canadian** has similarly limited application, and thus excludes non-black Africans. **People of colour** is a phrase frequently used in a political context of anti-racism and race relations. It refers to all non-whites (another deplored term, for it suggests white as the norm).

No general terms appear to be in use for other dark-skinned peoples, such as Melanesians or Tamils. They are usually identified by ethnicity or citizenship.

8.19   **Oriental** is a highly ambiguous term that was used historically to refer to those whose origins could be anywhere between the Bosporus and the Pacific. For a general modern reference, the following terms are helpful, although there is no official consensus about which countries bound each division:

Southeast Asia	Burma (Myanmar), Thailand, Laos, Cambodia, Vietnam, Malaysia, Indonesia, the Philippines
Central Asia	the area of the Asiatic former republics of the U.S.S.R., some autonomous regions of China, Mongolia
East Asia	China, Japan, North and South Korea, Taiwan
South Asia	India, Pakistan, Bangladesh, Sri Lanka, Nepal, Bhutan
West Asia	Turkey, Syria, Iraq, Israel, Jordan, the Gulf states, Iran, Afghanistan, possibly Armenia, Georgia, Azerbaijan

Given the diversity of peoples within any of these divisions, generalizations of a racial or cultural nature may be misleading. Consider, for example, that West Asia includes Kurds, Iraqis, Armenians, Kuwaitis, Israelis, Turks, and Bedouins, among many others.

8.20   **New Canadian** used to be a common term for recent immigrants generally. **Permanent resident** has replaced **landed immigrant** as the official term for a legally resident person who has not taken Canadian citizenship.

Immigrants *to* Canada are **emigrants** *from* another country. Although the use of **migrants** to replace either term is increasing, some consider it derogatory.

Some people object to "hyphenated" terms such as **Italian-Canadian** on the grounds that they identify a person as less Canadian than the unhyphenated variety. Others value the dual affiliation. Personal preference should be considered. Many style guides call for the hyphen only when the term is an adjective: **Armenian-Canadian organization.**

8.21   In Canada, **Indians** is a term used in two main ways: to mean those abo-
        riginal Canadians defined as Status or Non-Status Indians by the federal
        Indian Act; or to mean people of or from India. In the past, **East Indian**
        was used to distinguish the latter, yet it too is ambiguous, for it may refer
        to the former Dutch East Indies (Indonesia).

        Other terms (capitalized or not) for aboriginal Canadians include **na-
        tive people, First Nations peoples, First Peoples, natives,** and **indig-
        enous people** (see 12.15–16, "aboriginal peoples"). Some individuals
        nonetheless prefer to identify themselves as **Indian.**

GENDER

8.22   Few aspects of language cause as much rancorous debate as the attempt
        to promote gender-fair writing. On the one hand are those who are mor-
        ally outraged when asked to change "chairman" to "chair," and on the
        other are those who take umbrage at a casual conversational reference to
        "the girls." Almost a half-century after feminist writers first brought pub-
        lic attention to the issue, there is still a gap between theory and practice.

        Sex and **gender** are often used synonymously. However, many academ-
        ics use **gender** to refer to socially defined roles and characteristics and **sex**
        to refer to anatomical, genetic, or biological attributes.

        Editors are wise to keep in mind these sensitivities, while focusing on
        the goal: accurate, clear language that respects the world in which we live
        and conveys the writer's intended message and tone. Editors will differ, as
        will their clients, on whether grammatical correctness – or even clarity –
        should be sacrificed to a political agenda, and no two people will apply the
        same weight to each factor, even from one sentence to the next.

        Following are suggestions for amending language to be gender-inclusive;
        these may be useful in discussion with writers, readers, and other editors.
        However, use common sense in applying the examples: in historical or fic-
        tional contexts, for instance, contemporary non-sexist terms may be out
        of place.

Replacing generic "man"

8.23   Research has confirmed what was long suspected: when they hear or read
        the generic **man,** people form mental pictures of males. Experience has
        shown too that when they write, they may often create the same picture:
        "Prehistoric man was a hunter. He ..."

        Words including the generic **man** as prefix or suffix are clearly inaccu-
        rate when applied to all of humanity and to roles and occupations that
        today are also filled by women. However, replacing **man** with **woman,**
        where this is possible, still constitutes an unnecessary gender specifica-

> "Words that speak too strongly of past male domination of the work force (manpower, man-hour) can be avoided. But words that do not have an exclusively male connotation (craftsmanship, sportsmanlike, brotherhood) need not be changed."
>
> — *Canadian Tax Foundation Style Guide*

tion. Changing **-man** to **-person** is one solution, although it often seems awkward or artificial. (Some well-intentioned writers will call a man a "chairman" and a woman a "chairperson.")

Consider the following alternatives:

mankind	humankind, humanity, people, human beings, the human species
man-made	manufactured, machine-made, synthetic, artificial, fabricated
chairman, chairwoman	chair, chairperson, presiding officer, moderator, convenor
businessmen, businesswomen	business people, people in business
salesman, saleswoman	salesperson, sales clerk, clerk, sales representative
repairman, repairwoman	car mechanic, electrician, plumber (as applicable)
to man	to staff, to operate, to manage
workman	worker, employee
manpower	workforce, labour, labour force, staff, personnel
the common man, the man in the street, the average man	ordinary person, average person, typical citizen (resident, etc.)

There is not always an easy solution. For example, in 1998 attempts to replace the word "fisherman" with "fisher" in federal government documents were met with strenuous objections from women in the East Coast industry; they insisted on being called "fishermen." Other terms that lack exact gender-neutral equivalents include **handyman, bondsman,** and **gunman,** although time may produce them.

In several instances, the suffix **-man** may simply be dropped:

chair, news anchor, ombud

Replacing generic "he"

8.24   Personal pronouns referring to an unspecified person have traditionally been masculine. Editors have had much practice in recent years experimenting with various ways of making them gender-fair.

    The use of **she or he, he/she, her/him, his/her, hers/his, himself/herself** constructions is one solution, but best applied frugally. Text littered with these shotgun pairings is offensive to the eye and ear. "S/he" constructions are aberrations to be avoided at all costs.

    In many instances, a slight rewording can remove the pronoun entirely. Consider these alternatives:

> A good teacher learns from his students.
>
> A good teacher learns from the students.

> Ask him to explain the problem.
>
> Ask the writer to explain the problem.

> When a service rep deals with a complaint, he must be tactful.
>
> When we deal with complaints, we must be tactful.
>
> When one deals with complaints, one must be tactful.

> A small child can often climb a high fence by himself.
>
> A small child can often climb a high fence without help.

> Everyone who travels feels guilty as he approaches customs.
>
> All travellers feel guilty as they approach customs.

In instances where a non-specific personal pronoun is called for, the feminine and masculine pronouns can alternate from example to example or from section to section. This strategy is common in magazines and in school materials.

8.25   Plural pronouns (**they, them, their, theirs, themselves**) have always been used as common-gender singular pronouns in informal speech. They sometimes appear in informal written works as a way to circumvent using **he or she** etc. to refer back to indefinite pronouns (**everyone, everybody, anyone, anybody, someone, somebody, no one, nobody**). *The New Fowler's Modern English Usage* (1996), which uses the construction in some examples, concludes: "The process now seems irreversible." Yet many writers and editors prefer to avoid this solution.

    Consider whether numerous sentences will have to be recast entirely to avoid **he or she.** In the following examples, the editor would have to decide whether the meaning is enhanced if the plural pronouns are eliminated.

If your child thinks the teacher doesn't like them and the other kids are picking on them, they will not thrive.

Can you imagine how anyone could allow their name to be attached to such a dubious project?

The person who sent that message obviously did not want to be identified. They deliberately excluded all hints as to their location, their personal characteristics, and even their motivation. Yet the intensity of their emotion was unmistakable.

Avoiding unnecessary feminine forms

8.26   Words such as **poetess, manageress, authoress,** and **sculptress** have long been objected to as suggesting a less serious, paler version of the masculine function. They are now used far less often, for the root word has become understood as gender-neutral. **Stewardess** has given way to **flight attendant,** and **waitress** is often replaced by **server** or **waiter. Hostess** remains in both private and working life. Although many females in the theatre call themselves **actors,** the word **actress** remains in use, possibly because many roles are specifically female.

Aviatrix has been replaced by **pilot** or **flyer** (as has **aviator** by and large). Inasmuch as **executrix** and **dominatrix** carry no implication of genteel amateurism, they need not be abandoned.

Avoiding gender stereotyping

8.27   Gender stereotyping assumes that certain functions, behaviours, or roles belong to one sex but not the other. One practice that stands firmly in the way of clear, accurate, bias-free writing is the inclusion of information (usually about women) that is superfluous, is irrelevant in the context, or confuses private roles with public ones. Reporting off-topic personal details, such as appearance and marital status, distracts attention from the significant information. The acid test is whether the parallel information would be used in the description of a man.

> Spunky manager Louise Tellier convinced the vice-president to fund the proposal.
>
> Bank charged widow $2 to break a $20.
>
> Grandmother elected mayor for second term.

Such adjectives as "spunky" are extraneous when the sentence speaks for itself. Examples unfortunately abound of women being described as widows, mothers, grandmothers, petite, redheaded, smartly dressed, and so on when the detail is irrelevant to the substance of the information.

Also to be avoided is the specification of sex (woman doctor, female police officer, male nurse) except, as in the following, where sex is relevant to the meaning.

Are female pediatricians more sympathetic to new mothers' concerns?

Parallel treatment

8.28 In general, use **men and women** or **girls and boys** depending on the age groups referred to. (Exceptions are when women and men escape from adult responsibility in **a night out with the boys/girls;** or when they are an audience for an after-dinner speech and become **ladies and gentlemen.**) There are, however, still a few job terms, such as **best boy** and **showgirl,** that have no mature equivalents.

8.29 Terms of address should be used symmetrically. If a man's name is given in full, so should a woman's.

Gerard Tanaka and Maria Cosentini

Ms. Cosentini and Mr. Tanaka

8.30 In some contexts an editor may wish to accommodate women who prefer **Mrs.** and **Miss.** Many forms to be filled in now offer only two choices, **Mr.** and **Ms.,** and many publications use only those two.

8.31 Spousal designations are appropriate when the reference is to a purely spousal role:

Madam Justice Hélène Palardeau and Mr. Palardeau welcomed guests at the door.

The ambassador and Mrs. Rasmussen returned to the Paris embassy last Thursday.

The spousal designation is not appropriate when the reference is to individual pursuits:

While Guthrie McDuff devotes his energies to workplace health, Maria McDuff promotes health goals through the Board of Education.

One may no longer assume that wives and husbands use the same surname.

Treating traditional roles

8.32 Avoid expressions that tend to deny the skill and effort involved in traditional feminine roles. The assumption still rears its head that household management and child rearing, not to mention fields such as nursing, teaching, and social work, come naturally to women and demand only low levels of skill. Balanced and thoughtful presentation may be more important here than use of one term rather than another (e.g., **homemaker** for "housewife").

Members of both sexes can be shown performing the full range of human roles and situations in both text and illustrations.

Be especially careful that a working or professional role or status is not omitted or obscured. For example, "pioneers and their wives" and "farmers' wives" have never been particularly accurate terms, as the wives are generally also themselves pioneers and farmers.

SEXUAL ORIENTATION

8.33   There is continual debate, even among homosexuals, over what terms constitute acceptable, non-pejorative designations. This debate often involves self-identity politics, demands for inclusion, and the requirements of political correctness. As well, most minorities have double standards about terms they use for themselves: idioms that some groups use and accept among themselves may not be welcomed from outsiders. Always consider context when choosing appropriate terminology.

There is a vast vocabulary of slang and code words in written materials about homosexuality. Editors unfamiliar with the jargon are advised to seek expertise.

8.34   People who are attracted to both men and women are called **bisexual.**

8.35   **Dyke** and **fag** are terms best left for use by lesbians and gay men to refer to members of their own community. In all contexts, these words are slang; in many contexts, they are pejorative.

8.36   Both **gay** and **gays** can be used for homosexual men and women, as long as it is clear that both sexes are included; but consider using **gays and lesbians** or **gay men and lesbians** instead. Avoid the term "gay lifestyle"; there is as much variety in lifestyle among homosexuals as among heterosexuals.

In a historical context, to designate some homosexuals, **gay** can be accurate as far back as the early twentieth century. In the 1970s, the word became associated with politically active lesbians and gay men.

Although some older people prefer **homosexual** as a self-identifier, many gays find it too clinical. Avoid the term "practising homosexual," unless celibacy is part of the context.

Many homosexual women prefer **lesbian** as a self-identifier; others use **gay woman;** a few use **dyke.**

8.37   **Heterosexism** is the often subtle assumption that everyone is hetero-sexual or that heterosexuality is the only acceptable sexual orientation.

8.38   **Homophobia** and **homophobic** mean a hatred or fear of homosexuality, but they are often applied to any form of discrimination against homosexuals.

8.39   **Partner** and **spouse** are used with nearly equal frequency in same-sex relationships. **Spouse** is often preferred in legal matters. Since **partner** can be used in other contexts (e.g., professional partnership), the ambiguity may or may not be intended. **Companion** is sometimes used by older homosexuals.

8.40   Although **queer** is used by some homosexuals as a self-identifier, this re-claimed derogatory word has become associated with political activity about and commitment to gay issues. **Queer** is similarly used by people of various orientations who reject traditional sexual labels. In some contexts, it can be pejorative.

8.41   The adjective **same-sex** is used to describe gay attraction, sexual activity, or relationships. It is also often used in connection with government, cor-porate, and legal policies and programs that apply to partners of gay men and lesbians.

8.42   The term **sexual orientation** refers to a person's sexuality, widely believed to be innate. It is also used by those involved in securing human-rights protection for gay people. **Sexual preference** is not synonymous; it refers rather to the particulars of what a person finds attractive (e.g., red hair, leather clothing).

8.43   Although **transgendered** usually refers to people who live, occasionally or permanently, as members of the opposite sex, without surgery, it is be-coming an umbrella term for both transsexuals and the transgendered. **Transsexual** usually applies to people who are in the process of having, or who have had, sex-change surgery or hormone therapy. **Intersex,** the con-dition of being between sexes, is used particularly with infants or children whose anatomy or physiology differs from their culture's definitions of male and female.

A homosexual, especially a male, who dresses in the clothing of the opposite sex for emotional or sexual gratification is called a **transvestite.** Anyone who wears the clothes, makeup, etc., of the opposite sex, regard-less of motivation, can be called a **cross-dresser.** When any person wears the clothes of the opposite sex to entertain other people, that person can be said to be **in drag** or **doing drag.**

DISABILITY

8.44 Statements supporting non-discriminatory hiring practices and the like often refer to "the disabled." Like **visible minorities,** the term implies that most people constitute some sort of "normal" mainstream, in contrast to which there are those who are in some way defective. In reality, many people with no obvious "disability" are limited by some physical or mental characteristic – myopia, hay fever, fear of math, colour blindness, shyness, or tennis elbow. Yet someone with a conspicuous handicap in one aspect of functioning may be outstanding in another.

> "Disabled. I hate the term. It sounds as though we have been put out of commission."
>
> – Beryl Potter, activist

The more visible the disability, the more vulnerable a person is to being described only in terms of the disability. Using the name of the disability to describe the person – for example, "the epileptic" – reduces the person to the condition. If writing about a disability is to be clear and accurate, the disability should be seen as only one aspect of the person.

A good beginning is to substitute **people who are disabled** or **people with a disability** for "the disabled" and proceed from there to more specific language as the context dictates. At the time of writing, a scan of the entries in *Sources* of organizations dealing with disability illustrates a variety of wordings on this pattern:

    athletes with disabilities

    those coping with Huntington's disease

    those living with schizophrenia

    individuals with Tourette's syndrome

The specific situation may suggest more exact description:

    customers and employees unable to climb stairs

    passengers requiring assistance boarding

    telephone clients employing TDD

8.45 Avoid "disabled" as an adjective; concrete language conveys more information. "Disabled workers," for example, is too general to be useful; **workers using wheelchairs** specifies a context.

"Handicapped" as noun and adjective presents the same issues as "disabled." Focus on the person rather than the handicap and be as specific as possible.

8.46 Beware, however, of unnecessary euphemistic substitutes. Editors and writers may be inclined to edit out vivid descriptive expressions even in contexts where they are appropriate – in fiction, for example. Although **crippled,** for instance, is a questionable term to use in a non-fiction work about disability, it may have a place in fiction, poetry, metaphor, or polemic. Note also that some older persons with disabilities may refer to themselves in terms now considered offensive. Use judgment and common sense before making sweeping changes.

8.47 Similarly, in a non-fiction context, depressing clichés can unnecessarily emphasize the pathetic-victim picture of disability. **Affected by, with,** and similarly neutral terms are usually preferable to "afflicted with," "stricken by," or "suffering from." "Needs crutches" or "is confined to a wheelchair" can be replaced by **walks with crutches, hops about the park on crutches,** or **makes her rounds in a wheelchair** as neutral or positive alternatives.

General terms

8.48 Avoid using "normal" to describe those without the disability in question. A preferable term would specify what characteristic they would have:

> Crescent Nursery School integrates children who use wheelchairs with their walking peers.
>
> Those with hearing impairment may be more aware of nuances of facial expression than those with full hearing.

8.49 Distinguish clearly between **disability** or **impairment** and, on the other hand, **disease.** For example, a person unable to walk as a result of spinal injury has a disability but not an illness.

Mental illness/intellectual impairment

8.50 Choosing appropriate vocabulary to describe mental illness or intellectual impairment is particularly delicate, for both are stigmatized and widely misunderstood.

Mental illness

8.51 Certain terms, such as **insanity** and **incompetence,** have a specific meaning in legal contexts and should be used with care in other contexts. Clinical terms such as **schizophrenia, bipolar disorder, psychosis,** and **psychopathology** must be used accurately; they may often be inappropriate in general text without elaboration.

As with any disability, avoid labelling the person as "a schizophrenic," "a manic-depressive," or "a paranoid." Use more specific possibilities:

> those coping with schizophrenia
>
> a person showing paranoid symptoms

8.52   A very small proportion of people with mental illness present a danger to others. Nevertheless media reports focus attention on such incidents of violence as do occur, and the unfortunate effect is to create an identification between mental illness and dangerousness.

The after-effects of an episode of a mental illness vary so greatly that generalizations are totally inappropriate. Some people may recover completely and never have another episode. Others may function fully with or without continued medication or other treatment.

Most conspicuous in the public eye are those who are "odd" – withdrawn, perhaps talking to themselves, moving jerkily, often unable to function without some community support. Such people may be displaying habits developed over a period of active mental illness, or they may have some quite different condition such as cerebral palsy or Tourette's syndrome. Editors should be alert to unthinking association of "oddness" with illness, and particularly of "oddness" with dangerousness.

Intellectual impairment

8.53   In the 1980s the euphemism "challenged" had a vogue as a way to describe intellectual disability – "intellectually challenged" or "developmentally challenged." However, its pretentious artificiality prompted a whole raft of jokes ("metabolically challenged" for dead; "follically challenged" for bald). The terms **person with intellectual (developmental) disabilities** and **person who is intellectually (developmentally) impaired** have returned to favour among those in the field.

Deafness

8.54   Language referring to deafness is undergoing significant change in response to the Deaf Culture movement.

The general term **deaf** refers to people with a range of hearing loss. Like **hearing impaired, deaf** does not specify whether they communicate by speech or sign. Those who are **hard of hearing** have some hearing loss but still communicate primarily through speech.

"Deaf mute" and "deaf and dumb" are widely considered offensive by people who are deaf. In most instances, it is unnecessary to refer to a deaf person's inability to speak; where it must be specified, **who cannot speak** is more appropriate.

The term **Deaf** is claimed as a cultural identification by deaf people who communicate primarily through one of the world's sign languages, such as ASL (American Sign Language) or BSL (British Sign Language). Because signing makes use of many conventions that spoken languages lack, the exchange of information is rich and deep and the speed of conversation is comparable to that of speech. Those who belong to the Deaf community value deafness not as a disability but rather as a characteristic of this community's cohesive cultural identity; their position challenges some assumptions about the best way to treat and educate deaf children.

Blindness

8.55 **Blind** implies having no sight whatever. **Visually impaired** or **having low vision** is more appropriate to describe the partially sighted. **Legally blind** refers to those who have roughly 10 per cent or less of normal vision; it is a benchmark degree of impairment that guides programs and services of organizations such as the Canadian National Institute for the Blind.

SOURCES

Maggio, Rosalie. *The Bias-Free Word Finder: A Dictionary of Nondiscriminatory Language.* Boston: Beacon Press, 1991.

————. *The Dictionary of Bias-Free Usage: A Guide to Nondiscriminatory Language.* Phoenix, Ariz.: Oryx Press, 1991.

Ethnicity and race

Guide to Canadian English Usage. By Margery Fee and Janice McAlpine. Strathy Language Unit, Queen's University. Toronto: Oxford University Press, 1997.

Magocsi, Paul Robert, ed. *Encyclopedia of Canada's Peoples.* Toronto: University of Toronto Press, 1999. Published for the Multicultural History Society of Ontario.

Gender

King, Ruth. *Talking Gender: A Guide to Nonsexist Communication.* Mississauga, Ont.: Copp Clark Pitman, 1991.

Miller, Casey, and Kate Swift. *The Handbook of Nonsexist Writing: For Writers, Editors and Speakers.* 2nd ed. New York: Harper & Row, 1988.

————. *Words and Women: New Language in New Times.* Updated. New York: HarperCollins, 1991.

Ontario Women's Directorate. *Words That Count Women Out/In.* 2nd ed. Toronto: OWD, 1993.

Sexual orientation

Canadian Lesbian and Gay Archives. P.O. Box 639, Station A, Toronto, ON M5W 1G2; <www.clga.ca/archives/>; email <queeries@clga.ca>.

Chauncey, George. *Gay New York: Gender, Urban Culture, and the Making of the Gay Male World, 1890–1940.* New York: HarperCollins/BasicBooks, 1994.

———. *The Making of a Modern Gay World: 1935–1975.* Toronto: HarperCollins Canada, 1998.

GayCanada [online]. Canadian Gay, Lesbian and Bisexual Resource Directory, 1999. [Cited January 6, 2000.] <www.cglbrd.com/>.

Gender and Sexuality [online]. Carnegie-Mellon. [Cited January 6, 2000.] U.S. source. <eserver.org/gender/>.

GLAAD Online [online]. Gay and Lesbian Alliance Against Defamation. [Cited January 6, 2000.] U.S. source. <www.glaad.org/>; email <glaad@glaad.org>.

Nelson, E.D., and Barrie W. Robinson. *Gender in Canada.* Toronto: Prentice Hall, 1999.

Queer Resources Directory [online]. [Cited February 17, 2000.] Contains 24,489 files. <www.qrd.org/>.

Disability

Arthritis Society
393 University Ave., Suite 1700
Toronto, ON M5G 1E6
Tel. 1-800-321-1433
<www.arthritis.ca>; email <info@on.arthritis.ca>

Canadian Association for Community Living
Kinsmen Building, York University
4700 Keele St., North York, ON M3J 1P3
Tel. (416) 661-9611; fax (416) 661-5701
<www.cacl.ca>; email <info@cacl.ca>

Canadian Hearing Society
271 Spadina Rd., Toronto, ON M5R 2V1
Tel. (416) 964-9595
<www.chs.ca>; email <info@chs.ca>

Canadian National Institute for the Blind
1929 Bayview Ave., Toronto, ON M4G 3E8
Tel. (416) 480-2131 or (416) 486-2500
<www.cnib.ca>

Canadian Paraplegic Association
1101 Prince of Wales Dr., Suite 230
Ottawa, ON K2C 3W7
Tel. (613) 723-1033; fax (613) 723-1060
<www.canparaplegic.org>

Council of Canadians with Disabilities
294 Portage Ave., Suite 926
Winnipeg, MB R3C 0B9
Tel. (204) 947-0303; fax (204) 942-4625
<www.pcs.mb.ca/~ccd>; email <ccd@pcs.mb.ca>

Epilepsy Canada, National Office
1470 Peel St., Suite 745
Montreal, QC H3A 1T1
Tel. (514) 845-7855 or 1-800-860-5499; fax (514) 845-7866
<www.epilepsy.ca>; email <epilepsy@epilepsy.ca>

Schizophrenia Society of Canada
75 The Donway West, Suite 814
Don Mills, ON M3C 2E9
Tel. (416) 445-8204 or 1-888-772-4673; fax (416) 445-2270
<www.schizophrenia.ca>; email <info@schizophrenia.ca>

Measurements

Chapter 9 – Measurements

9.1   The Canadian duality is evident in the use of measurements, where both traditional and metric units are common. Both systems are considered in this chapter.

    The hesitant introduction of "metric" in Canada in the 1970s made it necessary for editors to familiarize themselves with this new (to many) way of expressing measurements. Although its proponents' hopes for wholesale acceptance were not fulfilled, an understanding of metric measurement remains an essential item in any editor's toolkit.

9.2   The metric system was developed in France in the late eighteenth century, during the French Revolution, in order to reform the chaotic system of weights and measures then in use. The metric system is the basis for SI, the Système international d'unités, which is the most recent (1960), or modern, version of the metric system. Canada adopted SI as its measuring system in 1971 but never fully implemented it. One reason why the metric bandwagon stalled was that it hit a roadblock at our southern border: the United States has made little progress in implementing SI, although it remains, in the *Chicago Manual*'s phrase, "an officially recognized goal." Since the mid-1980s the Canadian government's policy has been to let the marketplace decide where SI, traditional, or dual measurements are appropriate; no intervention to impose (or remove) SI is likely.

9.3   This chapter provides only an overview of traditional measurements and Canadian SI usage for editors working with general-interest materials. Detailed information about measurements may be found in standard references, the Sources at the end of this chapter, and technical or scientific style guides.

TWO SYSTEMS OF MEASUREMENT

9.4   Canadian practice remains a hodgepodge: SI in the sciences, in many industries, in educational publishing, and in government; traditional or mixed measurements in the lumber, construction, and food industries and in many fields of everyday life. As in so many editorial matters, editors must be conversant with all the possibilities and make choices according to context, content, and convention.

    Since Canadian schoolchildren are being taught SI, the newer generations of editors, writers, and teachers are more comfortable with it than their predecessors. Textbooks for elementary and high schools and for colleges and universities contain some of the most consistent examples of

SI usage. Other works containing SI usage include technical and scientific manuals and government publications.

At a more informal, everyday level, established SI usage in Canada is found in the following measurements:

- distance (**km,** except marine and aerial distance)
- temperature (degrees **Celsius**)
- packaged food, drug, household, and agricultural products (**kg, g, L, mL**)
- gasoline and all liquid products (**L**)
- height (**cm**) and weight (**kg**) measurements for medical records and in official documents

9.5   Some imperial units – the link, the scruple – have already been relegated to historical or specialized usage, but most are part of our language and will remain in common idiom. Expressions like "Give them an inch and they'll take a mile" and "An ounce of prevention is worth a pound of cure" may still be appropriate even in contexts where distance and weight are otherwise expressed in SI.

9.6   Some general-interest publications use parenthetical conversions of traditional or SI measurements with every numerical designation. Often these conversions are approximate and rounded off. This dual mode is, understandably, not encouraged by the guardians of SI but will no doubt continue. See 9.40–44 and Table 9.4.

9.7   Where SI is the sole standard, it must be used with care. Its punctuation, capitalization, and usage are very strict: for example, see 9.27 for restrictions on the use of italics with SI. The Canadian authority on SI usage is the *Canadian Metric Practice Guide* (*CMPG*), a National Standard of Canada. In less technical material, the rules of SI may be applied less rigidly.

SI MEASUREMENTS

Units used in SI

9.8   The foundation of SI is its seven *base units* (shown in bold in Table 9.1). Most other units in the SI lexicon are *derived units,* which are either base units with powers or combinations of base units. For example:

Base units	Derived units
metre	square metre
metre, second	metre per second
metre, kilogram, second	metre kilogram per second squared

9.9   Some derived units have been given special names, often the names of scientists:

Derived units	Special names
metre kilogram per second squared	newton
newton per square metre	pascal

SI or not?

9.10   Despite its generally rational structure and the appearance of rigid standardization, SI is by no means monolithic. SI permits the use of many important units that are acknowledged to be "outside the SI," according to the *CMPG*. These include measurements of time – **minute, hour, day,** and **year** – and some widely accepted units such as **hectare, litre,** and **tonne.** Even the **nautical mile** may be used with SI, but only "for a limited time" (the *CMPG* gives no deadline).

Table 9.1   SI units and units permitted for use with SI

The seven base units are shown in bold. See the *CMPG* for additional terms from specialized disciplines.

Name	Symbol	Quantity measured
ampere	**A**	electric current
bel	B	sound intensity
candela	**cd**	luminous intensity
coulomb	C	electric charge
day	d	time
degree (angle)	°	plane angle
degree Celsius	°C	temperature
farad	F	electric capacitance
hectare	ha	area
hertz	Hz	frequency
hour	h	time
joule	J	energy, work
kelvin	**K**	temperature
kilogram	**kg**	weight (mass)
knot	kn	marine and aerial speed
litre	L	volume
lumen	lm	luminous flux

Table 9.1   SI units and units permitted for use with SI – *continued*

Name	Symbol	Quantity measured
lux	lx	illuminance
metre	**m**	length
minute (angle)	'	plane angle
minute (time)	min	time
mole	**mol**	amount of substance
nautical mile	M	marine and aerial distance
newton	N	force
ohm	Ω	electric resistance
pascal	Pa	pressure
revolution	r	plane angle
second (angle)	"	plane angle
second (time)	**s**	time
siemens	S	conductance
tonne	t	weight (mass)
volt	V	electric potential difference
watt	W	power
year	a	time

Sources: *CMPG;* NIST Web site.

9.11   Note the following peculiarities.

- The **litre** (L) is accepted as the name for the cubic decimetre (dm^3). Some non-Canadian references give the symbol for litre as **l** (lowercase), but **L** is "preferred" in Canada, according to the *CMPG*.

- **Nautical mile** and **knot** are imperial units but are accepted for use with SI in navigation. The nautical mile equals 1852 metres, and the knot is a rate of one nautical mile per hour. Symbols and abbreviations for the two terms are not universal. When used in a context with other traditional units, the nautical mile is usually abbreviated **n.m.**

- The **tonne** is also called the **metric ton** (1000 kilograms, or 1 megagram). In French, *tonne* may mean either the metric ton or one of the imperial tons; be careful with references translated from French. (Tonnage in relation to shipping is another story altogether; consult specialized references.)

Weighty issues

9.12 **Weight** in everyday usage is called **mass** in SI standards and other scientific and technical sources. Scientists reserve **weight** to describe the force of gravity (measured in newtons).

What is the mass of this apple?

However, the verb **to weigh** may be used in scientific contexts.

I weighed the apple; its mass is 200 g.

In non-scientific contexts **The apple weighs 200 g** is correct and likely to remain so.

Prefixes

9.13 SI adds standard prefixes to unit names and symbols to indicate multiples and submultiples, in steps of 10 up to 1000, and in steps of 1000 thereafter. The prefixes are joined directly to the names or symbols, without spacing or hyphenation – for example, **centimetre (cm)**, **kilometre (km)**, **milligram (mg)**.

Table 9.2   SI prefixes

Name	Symbol	Meaning	Multiplier	Power
tera	T	one trillion*	1 000 000 000 000	10^{12}
giga	G	one billion*	1 000 000 000	10^9
mega	M	one million	1 000 000	10^6
kilo	k	one thousand	1 000	10^3
hecto	h	one hundred	100	10^2
deca	da	ten	10	10^1
deci	d	one-tenth	0.1	10^{-1}
centi	c	one-hundredth	0.01	10^{-2}
milli	m	one-thousandth	0.001	10^{-3}
micro	μ	one-millionth	0.000 001	10^{-6}
nano	n	one-billionth*	0.000 000 001	10^{-9}
pico	p	one-trillionth*	0.000 000 000 001	10^{-12}

* Be careful with the terms **billion** and **trillion.** This table shows Canadian definitions. In Britain, among other countries, a billion is 10^{12} and a trillion is sometimes read as 10^{18}.

For prefixes ranging up to 10^{24} and down to 10^{-24}, see *The Canadian Style*, section 1.23.

9.14   Use only one prefix with each name or symbol.

millimetre (*not* decicentimetre)

Gg (*not* Mkg)

9.15   **Kilogram** is the only base unit that already has a prefix. When forming multiples or submultiples, start from **gram** instead of kilogram:

gigagram (*not* megakilogram)

milligram (*not* microkilogram)

9.16   **Hectare** (10 000 square metres) combines **hecto-** with **are** (100 square metres), which is no longer used in SI. Instead of combining prefixes with **hectare,** use the appropriate numerical expression plus **square metres** or **square kilometres.**

0.01 hectares = 100 square metres (*not* 1 centihectare)

1000 hectares = 10 square kilometres (*not* 1 kilohectare)

9.17   The **millilitre** is the same as the **cubic centimetre** (**cm³**). The abbreviations **cc, c.c.,** and **cu. cm.** are not correct SI usage.

Energy in flux

9.18   The **kilojoule** and the **megajoule** are increasingly familiar sights on nutritional information charts and electricity bills. The joule and its multiples are the correct SI units for measuring energy.

The term **calorie,** or **Calorie** in nutritional contexts, has a wide variety of meanings, in both dietetics and other sciences, creating confusion. Food packages now often use dual measurements to indicate that a serving of cereal, for instance, yields **105 Cal/440 kJ** of energy. Some utility companies have begun billing their customers in kilojoules or megajoules instead of kilowatt hours, a term no longer in favour in SI.

Style of SI names and symbols

9.19   Each SI unit has a symbol (see Table 9.1). In SI, the symbol is not called an abbreviation.

Capitalization

9.20   All SI unit *names* are lowercase, including those derived from persons'
names. However, in expressions using **Celsius** (for example, **degrees Celsius**), this name is uppercase.

> metre
>
> newton

9.21   The first letter of *symbols* for units named after persons is uppercase;
other symbols are lowercase, except **L** for **litre** (see 9.11).

> m (metre)
>
> N (newton)
>
> Pa (pascal)

9.22   Prefix symbols are lowercase up to **k** (kilo) and capitalized for **M** (mega)
and greater values.

Punctuation

9.23   The SI symbols are never followed by periods (unless, of course, the symbol occurs at the end of a sentence).

> Willa's gerbil is 10 cm long.
>
> From head to tail, Graeme's iguana measures 45 cm.

Plurals

9.24   Most unit *names* may be pluralized by adding **s**: metre, metres; pascal,
pascals, etc. **Hertz, lux,** and **siemens** remain unchanged in the plural. The
adjective **Celsius** is not pluralized; instead, **degree** is given in the plural:

> The temperature rose about three degrees Celsius.
>
> The temperature was 3°C.

9.25   The *symbols* for SI units are never pluralized:

> We jogged 2 km [*not* kms].
>
> The rock's mass is 30 kg [*not* kgs].

Multiplication and division

9.26   Derived units are formed by multiplication or division.
In strict SI style, the product of two units expressed as unit *names* is
indicated by a space. The product of two or more units expressed as *symbols* is indicated by a raised dot.

> newton metre, N·m
>
> pascal second, Pa·s

Division is indicated by **per** between unit *names* and by a solidus between unit *symbols:*

kilometres per hour, km/h

grams per millilitre, g/mL

Italics

9.27 In technical and scientific usage, where SI is the standard measurement system, all SI symbols must be printed in roman type. Quantity symbols, which use many of the same letters, must be italicized to distinguish them from SI symbols.

SI symbol	Quantity symbol
F (farad)	F (force)
m (metre)	m (mass)
a (year)	a (acceleration)
t (tonne)	t (time)

The *CMPG* gives an extensive list of quantity symbols and specifies whether they are uppercase or lowercase. In highly technical work, consult specialized style guides for other conventions for the use of italics and, in a few instances, boldface. In more mainstream publications, it is rare for italics to cause confusion in expressions of measurement.

TRADITIONAL MEASUREMENTS

9.28 Units of the imperial system of weights and measures remain in use in common parlance and in specialized areas of trade and industry.

Unlike the highly standardized SI measurements, imperial and other traditional measurements sometimes vary from country to country; the gallon, for example, is smaller in the United States than in Canada. Within Canada some measurements used in real estate have different values in Quebec than elsewhere.

9.29 Abbreviations may also vary in their spelling and style. Most Canadian style authorities use periods in traditional abbreviations, whether true abbreviations or suspensions; some omit the periods in compound abbreviations such as **mpg** (miles per gallon). Some government agencies have removed all periods, especially in contexts where traditional measurements and SI measurements appear together.

> "Only in Canada can a river be half a mile wide and thirty metres deep. At building supply yards, you buy 100 square metres of shingles and a box of three-quarter-inch nails to hold them down. Only in Canada can you be given the following directions to an auction sale: 'Drive ten kilometres down the road, and you'll see a barn about 200 feet from the highway.' That's simperial."
>
> – Wayne Grady, "The Metric System (Sort of)," *Saturday Night*, March 1999

9.30 Traditional measurements are usually lowercased, in both full form and abbreviation. The plurals of the full names add **s,** but plurals of abbreviations do not.

Table 9.3   Traditional units of measure

Name	Abbreviation/symbol	Quantity measured
acre	acre	area
bushel	bu.	volume
carat	ct.	weight (mass)
chain	ch.	length
cubic yard	cu. yd.	volume
day	d.	time
degree (angle)	°	plane angle
degree Fahrenheit	°F	temperature
dram	dr.	weight (mass)
fluid ounce	fl. oz.	volume
foot	ft.	length
gallon	gal.	volume
gill	gi.	volume
grain	gr.	weight (mass)
hour	hr.	time
hundredweight	cwt.	weight (mass)
inch	in.	length
knot*	kn.	marine or aerial speed
link	li.	length
mile	mi.	length
minute (angle)	′	plane angle

Table 9.3   Traditional units of measure – *continued*

Name	Abbreviation/symbol	Quantity measured
minute (time)	min.	time
nautical mile*	n.m.	marine or aerial distance
ounce	oz.	weight (mass)
peck	pk.	volume
pint	pt.	volume
pound	lb.	weight (mass)
quart	qt.	volume
second (angle)	"	plane angle
second (time)	sec.	time
square foot	sq. ft.	area
stone	st.	weight (mass)
ton	ton	weight (mass)
troy ounce	t. oz.	weight (mass)
yard	yd.	length
year	yr.	time

* See also 9.11.

Sources: *Canadian Oxford Dictionary; Concise Oxford Dictionary; Oxford Dictionary for Writers and Editors; Oxford Dictionary of Abbreviations.*

NUMBERS WITH UNITS OF MEASURE

9.31   This section highlights similarities and differences between SI style and the conventions used with traditional measurements. For more details on treatment of numbers generally, consult standard references.

Spacing

9.32   Use a space between the numeral and the unit symbol or abbreviation, except between numerals and symbols that are not letters.

> 3 kg (*not* 3kg)
>
> 200 mi. (*not* 200mi.)
>
> *but*
>
> 15°C (*not* 15° C *or* 15 °C)
>
> −3°F (*not* −3° F *or* −3 °F)
>
> 45°30' angle (*not* 45 ° 30 ' angle)

Spelling out

9.33   In technical writing, the preferred combination is numerals with SI unit symbols.

> The typical dose is 5 mg as needed.

In non-technical writing, more variety is permissible:

> She ran about 12 km. (*numeral with unit symbol/abbreviation*)
>
> We walked 12 kilometres. (*numeral with unit name*)
>
> He ran eight miles. (*spelled-out number with unit name*)

The combination of spelled-out number and unit symbol or abbreviation ("twelve km," "eight mi.") is not acceptable with either SI or traditional measurements. See standard references for other considerations that may influence the choice between a numeral and a spelled-out number.

Spaces in numerals

9.34   In traditional English-language usage, a comma is used between sets of three digits in large numbers. A space, not a comma, is used in SI for this purpose – ideally, a thin space.

> 300 000
>
> 20 000

A space is optional in SI if there are only four digits:

> 1 000   *or*   1000

When figures are in columns (as in tables), a space must be used if any number in the column contains five or more digits:

5000	*but*	5 500
4050		4 050
826		826
9876		10 376

Fractions

9.35   In SI measurement, decimal fractions must be used, rather than fractions with a numerator and denominator. Decimal fractions are also acceptable with traditional measurements.

> 0.5 cm in diameter (*not* ½ cm in diameter)
>
> 1.5 in. *or* 1½ in.

9.36   A zero precedes the decimal marker if the number is less than 1:

> 0.25 mL
>
> 0.8%

The zero before the decimal point is often omitted in ammunition calibres (.22 rifle) and probabilities ($p < .001$).

Adjectival uses

9.37   Contrary to editorial myth of unknown origin, a hyphen may be used between a number and an SI unit symbol or name when they modify a noun, just as it may be used with traditional measurements (but see 9.38). If the meaning is clear in its context, the hyphen may be omitted:

> 35-mm film/35 mm film
>
> five-pound package/five pound package
>
> 100-watt bulb/100 watt bulb
>
> 2500-acre provincial park/2500 acre provincial park
>
> 100-km/h speed limit/100 km/h speed limit
>
> 100-yd. dash/100 yd. dash

Do not use either a hyphen or a space with non-letter symbols (see 9.32).

9.38   In SI style, a hyphen is *not* generally used between a numeral and a symbol in an adjectival phrase where more than one measure is given. The hyphen is more common with traditional measurements.

> a 4 m x 6 m rug
>
> a 9-by-12-inch envelope

9.39   Use hyphens to avoid confusion in compounds with two sets of numbers:

> 14 two-kilogram packages
>
> two 26-inch televisions
>
> two 14-kg packages
>
> twenty-two 1-qt. bottles
>
> 18 one-litre flasks
>
> 224 15-lb. boxes

The hyphen may be omitted if the meaning is clear.

CONVERSION

Table 9.4   Approximate SI/traditional conversions

For more precise conversions, consult official sources and references, some of which are listed at the end of this chapter.

		Length			
2.54 cm*	=	1 in.	1 cm	=	0.394 in.
0.305 m or 30.48 cm*	=	1 ft.	1 m	=	3.281 ft.
0.914 m	=	1 yd.	1 m	=	1.094 yd.
1.609 km	=	1 mi.	1 km	=	0.621 mi.

		Area			
6.452 cm²	=	1 sq. in.	1 cm²	=	0.155 sq. in.
0.093 m²	=	1 sq. ft.	1 m²	=	10.76 sq. ft.
0.836 m²	=	1 sq. yd.	1 m²	=	1.196 sq. yd.
0.405 ha	=	1 acre	1 ha	=	2.471 acres
2.59 km² or 259 ha	=	1 sq. mi.	1 km²	=	0.386 sq. mi.

		Capacity/volume			
28.41 cm³ or mL	=	1 imp. fl. oz.	1 cm³ or mL	=	0.035 imp. fl. oz.
29.57 cm³ or mL	=	1 U.S. fl. oz.	1 cm³ or mL	=	0.034 U.S. fl. oz.
1.136 L	=	1 imp. qt.	1 L	=	0.880 imp. qt.
0.946 L	=	1 U.S. qt.	1 L	=	1.057 U.S. qt.
4.546 L	=	1 imp. gal.	1 L	=	0.220 imp. gal.
3.785 L	=	1 U.S. gal.	1 L	=	0.264 U.S. gal.
16.39 cm³ or mL	=	1 cu. in.	1 cm³ or mL	=	0.061 cu. in.
28.32 L or 0.028 m³	=	1 cu. ft.	1 L	=	0.035 cu. ft.
0.765 m³	=	1 cu. yd.	1 m³	=	1.308 cu. yd.

		Weight (mass)			
28.35 g	=	1 oz.	1 g	=	0.035 oz.
0.454 kg	=	1 lb.	1 kg	=	2.205 lb.
0.907 t or 907.2 kg	= 1 (2000-lb.) ton	1 t	=	1.102 (2000-lb.) tons

---

* These factors are exact.

Sources: *CMPG* and conversion tables in various dictionaries.

Precision in conversion

9.40   When traditional measurements are converted to SI measurements, and vice versa, the precision of a converted value should reflect the precision of the original. Do not make the mistake of converting the imprecision of "We walked almost 3 miles before the storm overtook us" to "We walked almost 4.8 kilometres." It would be sensible here to use "almost 5 kilometres."

It is not always obvious how precise the original measurement was intended to be. When converting a floor area given as "63 m²," for instance, the editor will probably need to query in order to determine whether the writer wishes to indicate a precise quantity (678 sq. ft.) or a round figure (680 sq. ft.).

Still getting good mileage

9.41 Canadians have held on to the word **mileage** to refer to the fuel consumption of vehicles, although it is now measured in SI terms. **Kilometrage** never really got going in this sense, but it is sometimes used to mean the total number of kilometres travelled by a particular vehicle. **Hectarage** also ran out of gas.

Soft and hard conversion

9.42 *Soft conversion* means giving the precise equivalent of an established quantity in the other system of measurement. In packaging, for example, a juice can containing 48 ounces that is labelled "1.36 L" has undergone soft conversion. *Hard conversion* means switching to round quantities: toothpaste makers have chosen hard conversion and sell their product in 50 mL, 100 mL, and 150 mL tubes.

In editorial work, the choice between soft and hard conversion may depend on the practical application of the quantities in question. In converting an American crafts article calling for "3-inch" ribbon, it is not helpful to tell a Canadian reader that the SI equivalent is 7.62 cm (soft conversion). The Canadian reader needs to know which standard SI width of ribbon will work (hard conversion), and other components of the crafts project may have to be adjusted to fit the materials available in Canada.

Compound units

9.43 When converting a compound unit, such as a rate, convert to the corresponding standard expression; that is, the second element in the compound must be in the form "per unit" or a multiple of 10, such as **per 100 units.** Do not merely "translate" the quantities:

Traditional	SI
15 lb/acre	16.8 kg/ha (*not* 6.81 kg/0.404 ha)
45 mpg	6.3 L/100 km (*not* 72 km/4.546 L)

Note that for some conversions, more than just the units must be changed. In measurements of fuel consumption, for instance (the second example above), the formula must be reversed from distance per quantity of fuel in the traditional system to quantity of fuel per distance in SI.

Dual measurements

9.44   Giving both SI and traditional measurements for expressions of quantity is not acceptable in scientific and technical usage. In general usage the full range of variations is seen.

Recipes in Canadian cookbooks and magazines commonly use dual measurements; the SI measurements are necessarily hard conversions (see 9.42). The challenge in providing accurate conversion is not so much in performing the necessary arithmetic but in determining truly standard values for imperial or traditional measurements. Measurements of volume vary "officially" among Canada, Europe, and the United States, and manufacturers of kitchen utensils in traditional measurements do not seem attentive to any known standards. *Gourmet* magazine reported in September 1999 that seven tablespoon measures found in its staff's home kitchens varied in quantity by more than 100 percent.

Table 9.5 gives the principal conversions used by national Canadian food magazines and in Canadian cookbooks. Not all the conversions follow arithmetical logic, but they have become widely accepted in this field.

Table 9.5   Traditional/SI equivalents for recipes

Volume		Length		Weight	
¼ tsp.	= 1 mL	¼ in.	= 5 mm	1 oz.	= 25 g
½ tsp.	= 2 mL	½ in.	= 1 cm	2 oz.	= 50 g
1 tsp.	= 5 mL	1 in.	= 2.5 cm	4 oz.	= 125 g
1 tbsp.	= 15 mL	2 in.	= 5 cm	⅓ lb.	= 170 or 175 g
2 tbsp.	= 25 mL	5 in.	= 12 cm	½ lb.	= 250 g
3 tbsp.	= 45 or 50 mL	10 in.	= 25 cm	1 lb.	= 500 g
¼ cup	= 50 mL	12 in.	= 30 cm	2 lb.	= 1 kg
⅓ cup	= 75 mL			5 lb.	= 2.2 kg
½ cup	= 125 mL				
⅔ cup	= 150 mL				
¾ cup	= 175 mL				
1 cup	= 250 mL				
4 cups	= 1 L				

SOURCES

"Calculators On-Line Center." In Jim Martindale with Frank Potter, *Martindale's "The Reference Desk"* [online]. UCI Science Library. Revised February 17, 2000. [Cited February 17, 2000.] Especially useful pages are found in Part II – Mathematics, Unit Conversion. <www-sci.lib.uci.edu/HSG/RefCalculators.html>.

Canadian Metric Practice Guide. Prepared by the Canadian Standards Association. Rexdale, Ont.: CSA, 1989. National Standard of Canada CAN/CSA-Z234.1-89; reaffirmed 1995. Order in print, diskette, or CD-ROM from CSA, 178 Rexdale Blvd., Toronto, ON M9W 1R3; <www.csa-international.org>. In 1999 the association changed its name to CSA International. A new edition is expected in 2000.

Cardinal's Handbook of Recipe Development. By Evelyn Hullah. Don Mills, Ont.: Cardinal Kitchens, 1984.

"International System of Units (SI)." *NIST Reference on Constants, Units, and Uncertainty* [online]. [United States.] National Institute of Standards and Technology. [Cited December 14, 1999.] Gives clear, brief descriptions of SI with useful lists and tables. <physics.nist.gov/cuu/Units/index.html>.

Metric Editorial Handbook. Rexdale, Ont.: Canadian Standards Association, 1980. Special Publication Z372-1980. Out of print.

Documentation

Chapter 10 – Documentation

10.1   Authors provide documentation such as notes and bibliographies for two reasons: to acknowledge the work of others, and to give readers the information needed to locate and consult these sources themselves. Readers may want to check an author's conclusions against his or her sources or simply look for further information on a given topic. In addition, a sterling list of sources can enhance an author's credibility (and a less than sterling one may have the opposite effect).

Not all material that writers look at during their research needs to be acknowledged. It is their responsibility to determine which sources should be documented and to provide all the bibliographic details. Writers often seek an editor's advice on both matters. On the question of when to document, editor and author can refer to most standard references and to the conventions of various disciplines. As for providing full details, see "A Modest Proposal," 10.151.

In tackling documentation, editors have an array of standard approaches to choose from, as well as style guides devoted to each. In academic and technical fields, these guides are generally useful and complete. Editors working with more general material or with interdisciplinary works, however, may not find the single-discipline guides sufficient. These guides may also be overly complex for a given job, and none offers much, if any, help in handling specifically Canadian works, such as certain government documents. In addition, documentation since the 1990s has included a new and idiosyncratic kind of reference: the electronic document.

10.2   This chapter aims to make things simpler for editors on all these fronts. It provides a set of basic, fill-in-the-blanks matrixes for creating complete, consistent references to fit virtually any documentation situation. They were developed in consultation with a team at the National Library of Canada, who established bibliographic standards for the NL's *Bibliographic Style Manual* (1990), and have been adapted for editors. These matrixes may be used for almost every conceivable type of source, from simple books and periodicals to microforms, CDs, musical scores, maps, and correspondence. Matrixes for electronic sources, such as CD-ROMs and online magazines, have been added to this edition of *Editing Canadian English*.

This chapter is not intended to answer every question of documentation. It does not, for example, dictate style (punctuation, capitalization, and so forth) but instead focuses on content – the information that must be included and how it should be ordered for various sources and types of documentation. If the required information is present in a group of citations, editors may use any reasonable style as long as they are consistent.

For a brief discussion of style, in particular the style used for the examples in this chapter, see 10.128–45.

Context, context, context

10.3   As in every other stage of their work, editors must consider context – the nature of the manuscript and its intended readership – in putting together each set of documentation. For instance, in a popular magazine, a reference to a novel might be cut to the bone, including only the author and title. The same work cited in a doctoral thesis would likely include all the standard elements and possibly a long commentary in the etcetera element (see 10.29). Similarly, citations to electronic sources in most cases should be as complete as those for print sources, but a passing reference in a newspaper might include only the site name and Internet address.

The nature of the works cited may suggest other variations. For instance, if most of the citations in a set of proceedings refer to maps, it would be sensible to omit the descriptive identifier **[map]** (see 10.47) from those citations, adding instead an appropriate identifier to any exceptions (e.g., **[newspaper article], [monograph]**).

Finally, the arrangement of type and other graphic elements on the covers, mastheads, title pages, and other identifying matter of some works is so unclear or incomplete that the editor, even with the original work in hand, cannot create a definitive citation for it. As long as a reasonable consistency is maintained within each set of documentation, and all works are cited in enough detail so that readers can locate them, the crucial editorial requirements have been fulfilled.

BASIC MATRIXES FOR FULL CITATIONS

10.4   Style guides traditionally distinguish between two main kinds of references: bibliographies (lists of full citations at the end of the text) and notes (shorter, partial citations inserted within text, at the bottom of the page, or at the ends of chapters), each with their own format and style rules. However, in practice these categories are becoming blurred, with bibliographies often omitted and full citations given within text or in notes instead.

The full citation is the basic unit of documentation. It includes all the information readers need to find the work referred to. A short citation contains only some of this information and merely refers readers to a full citation. Short citations, which may appear in footnotes, as references within the text, or in endnotes, do not provide enough information to be the only documentation given. Therefore, a full citation for each source cited ordinarily must appear somewhere within a work. (For exceptions, see 10.3.)

Below are four basic matrixes for full citations: for a book, a book part, a serial run, and a serial part. (Books include one-time publications such as reports and handbooks. Serials include newspapers, journals, magazines, newsletters, annual reports, and other periodicals, whether they appear regularly or irregularly.) Following these is a series of matrixes based on the main four but adapted for other sources, including artworks, television programs, parliamentary records, and various kinds of electronic documents. Once editors have assembled the information elements for a full citation, they can then create any type of reference – bibliography entry, note, or short citation. For examples of short citations, see 10.146–50.

Note: These matrixes list all the elements a full citation might contain – not every full citation will include them all. (For example, many works have no secondary responsibility element – see 10.18–21.) **Elements marked * are not essential for locating the work but may be of significant interest to the reader.**

BOOK: BASIC FULL CITATION

10.5   The information elements are ordered as follows:

Author

Title

Secondary responsibility (e.g., editor, translator, illustrator)

Edition

Publication information: place*

　　　　　　　　　　　　publisher*

　　　　　　　　　　　　year

Length (e.g., number of pages, volumes)*

Series*

Etcetera*

* Not essential for locating but may be of interest

10.6   Some style manuals omit publisher and often place of publication in the basic full citation. We strongly recommend retaining all three components of publication information in all types of citations because (a) the full information may be useful for judging a work's credibility, tracing publication rights, or assessing a work's availability; and (b) it is not in the best interests of the publishing community to ignore the role of the publisher.

Author

10.7   The person, persons, or corporate body primarily responsible for the work is listed here. When the author is named on the title page of a work, the citation usually begins with the author element. (For exceptions, see 10.15 and 10.19.)

> Zuehlke, Mark. *The Gallant Cause: Canadians in the Spanish Civil War 1936–1939.* Vancouver: Whitecap Books, 1996.
>
> Dewitt, David B., and John J. Kirton. *Canada as a Principal Power: A Study in Foreign Policy and International Relations.* Toronto: John Wiley & Sons, 1983.
>
> Lerner, Sally, Charles Clarke, and Robert Needham. *Basic Income: Economic Security for All Canadians.* Toronto: Between the Lines, 1999.

10.8   An editor, compiler, or illustrator can have primary responsibility for a work or can share it with a writer. The respective roles of joint authors may be given after their names:

> Manguel, Alberto, ed. *God's Spies: Stories in Defiance of Oppression.* Toronto: Macfarlane Walter & Ross, 1999.
>
> Ye, Ting-xing, author; and Suzane Langlois, illustrator. *Share the Sky.* Toronto: Annick Press, 1999.

10.9   A corporate body (such as an organization or a government department) is considered an author when the work is of an administrative nature (e.g., a company's handbook on sexual harassment) or reflects the collective thought or activity of the group (such as a brief, a policy statement, or an annual report).

> Canadian Environmental Law Association. *The Environmental Implications of Trade Agreements.* Report prepared for the Ontario Ministry of Environment and Energy. Toronto: CELA, 1993.
>
> Vancouver Public Library. *Great Canadian Books of the Century.* Vancouver and Toronto: Douglas & McIntyre, 1999. Selected by VPL staff.

10.10   For government documents, it is often necessary to add the name of the originating country, province, municipality, or other jurisdiction at the beginning of the author element (see 10.72):

> Newfoundland. Royal Commission on Electrical Energy. *Report of the Royal Commission on Electrical Energy.* [St. John's: the Commission], 1966. With maps and graphs.

10.11   A corporate body can sponsor or facilitate a work without being its "author." Although the corporate name may appear on the title page, the body should not be listed as the author if the work does not reflect the group's collective thought or activity; in such works the corporate body is usually listed as the publisher or placed in the secondary responsibility element (see 10.21).

10.12 Sometimes, as in the example below, a disclaimer makes it clear that the work reflects a personal author's views and not those of the sponsoring corporate body. The disclaimer reads:

> The findings of this Discussion Paper are the personal responsibility of the author and, as such, have not been endorsed by members of the Economic Council of Canada.

Here the citation would begin with the name of the personal author because his name is on the title page:

> Campbell, Harry F. *Exhaustible Resources and Economic Growth: The Case of Uranium Mining in Saskatchewan.* Ottawa: Economic Council of Canada, 1984.

10.13 More often, the degree to which a work reflects the collective activity or thought of its sponsor is a matter of judgment. For clues, the editor can examine the graphic design of the cover and title page and scan material such as the foreword or preface. If the corporate body is deemed not to be the "author" and no personal author is listed on the title page, the citation begins with the work's title (see 10.15–16). For cases where a corporate body cannot be listed in either the author element or the publisher element, see 10.21 and 10.29.

Title

10.14 Include the subtitle in the citation if it appears on the title page of the work.

10.15 A citation should begin with the title rather than the author when:

- the author (see 10.7–13 for definitions) is not named on the title page. In this case, the author's name follows the title in the citation:

  > *A Day in the Life of Canada.* Compiled by Rick Smolan and David Cohen. Toronto: Collins, 1984.

- the role of the author is clearly subordinate to the contents of the work, as in most reference books:

  > *The Oxford Companion to Canadian History and Literature.* Edited by Norah Story. Toronto: Oxford University Press, 1967.

  > *The Gazette Style.* By Joseph N. Gelmon. Technical assistance by Bobb Ross. Montreal: Gazette, 1999. Electronic edition available at <www.montrealgazette.com/STYLE/>.

- the work is the product of a corporate body but is not administrative and not reflective of the group's collective thought or activity, and no personal author is listed on the title page (see 10.7–13):

> *Elements of the Drama.* Vancouver: British Columbia Teacher's Federation, [197?].

Who's on first?

10.16   It's not always easy to determine the roles of the various participants in a work. The following is one way an editor might arrange this citation:

> *Plants.* Produced by the Ontario Science Centre. Photographs by Ray Boudreau. Toronto: Kids Can Press, 1994. Starting with Science Series.

In this book, the phrase "By the Ontario Science Centre" appears on the cover and title page, but should the centre be deemed the author – does the book reflect its collective thought or activity? The editor in this case has decided that it does not. And although authors' names are given, they appear on the copyright page, not the title page. The CIP data indicate that libraries list the book under its title, which is a sensible solution. Since the centre is clearly not the publisher, it has been positioned as having secondary responsibility.

Often the problem of whether to begin a citation with author or with title is a matter of editorial discretion, and it need not be resolved the same way in every set of documentation: a title entry may be suitable for one manuscript, an author entry for the next.

10.17   Ambiguous elements of a citation can sometimes be handled in the etcetera element (see 10.29).

Secondary responsibility (where applicable)

10.18   A contributor such as an editor, compiler, translator, or illustrator who is named on the title page but was not primarily responsible for the work is listed here:

> Harris, Marjorie. *Seasons of My Garden.* Photographs by Andreas Trauttmansdorff. Vancouver: Raincoast Books, 1999.

10.19   A person assigned to prepare a corporate document for which the corporate body takes primary responsibility (see 10.9) can be listed in the secondary responsibility position:

> Association of Universities and Colleges of Canada. *The Role of the University with Respect to Enrolments and Career Opportunities, Admission Policies, Continuing Education and Community Colleges.* Prepared by Marion Porter, coordinator of the Task Force, et al. Ottawa: AUCC, 1977.

10.20　When the name of a writer of a preface, an introduction, or similar copy is of interest, it can be listed here:

> Darling, Christopher, and John Fraser. *Kain & Augustyn.* Foreword by Rudolf Nureyev. Toronto: Macmillan, 1977.

10.21　A corporate body is listed in the secondary responsibility element when it is neither the publisher nor the author (as defined in 10.9 and 10.11) of a work but has sponsored or facilitated it:

> Hickman, Pamela. *Birdwise.* Sponsored by the Federation of Ontario Naturalists. Illustrations by Judie Shore. Toronto: Kids Can Press, 1988.

Edition (where applicable)

10.22　List edition information when it is shown on the work's title page or copyright page. The terms **reprint, printing,** and **impression** do not designate editions and should not be included in a citation.

> Swaigen, John, ed. *Environment on Trial.* 3rd ed. Toronto: Canadian Institute for Environmental Law and Policy, 1991.

Publication information

10.23　If the title page lists two places of publication, give the first one or both. If it lists more than two, give the first Canadian place name, if there is one; otherwise give the first place listed. Editors who prefer to give the English forms of non-English place names should do so consistently.

10.24　List the publisher's name largely as it appears on the work, but omit **The, Inc., Ltd.,** etc.; retain **Press,** however. When a corporate author is also the publisher of the work, the name can be given in a shortened form in the publication information.

> Canadian Broadcasting Corporation. *Culture, Broadcasting, and the Canadian Identity: A Submission to the Cultural Policy Review Committee.* [Ottawa]: CBC, 1981.

10.25　When the copyright date and the date of publication differ, use the latter.

10.26　The abbreviations **n.p.** and **n.d.** mean "no place" or "no publisher" and "no date." (The Latin equivalents **s.l., s.n.,** and **s.d.,** which may occur in historical documents, are no longer used.)

Length

10.27　In citations for complete multi-volume works, include the number of volumes. The number of pages need not be included in most basic citations, but it may be of interest to indicate the scope of some works, particularly those of unexpected length. For instance, the title *History of French in Canada* may appear to lead the reader to a comprehensive survey; the length element **13 pp.** points out that the work is, in fact, little more than a pamphlet.

Series (where applicable)

10.28   It may interest the reader to know that a work was included in, for instance, the New Canadian Library Series. Or the reader might want to consult other works in a series. The series name can also be helpful in locating a book.

> Mistry, Rohinton. *Such a Long Journey*. Afterword by Alberto Manguel. Toronto: McClelland & Stewart, 1993. New Canadian Library Series.

In a citation for one volume of a multi-volume set, the series element contains the set title and the number of volumes in the set:

> Diefenbaker, John G. *The Tumultuous Years 1962–1967*. Toronto: Macmillan, 1977. Vol. 3 in *One Canada: Memoirs of the Right Honourable John G. Diefenbaker* (3 vols.).

Etcetera (where applicable)

10.29   This useful element can be used to list additional bibliographic data that do not fit into other elements. It may include an original title of a translated work, an earlier title, information about earlier editions or printings, a brief description of the work (e.g., **Ph.D. dissertation, University of Regina**), information about the source of the work (e.g., the address or Web site of a small or obscure publisher, or the notation **From a private collection**), or any other information that is relevant to the work and useful to the reader.

> Hébert, Anne. *Am I Disturbing You?* Translated by Sheila Fischman. Toronto: Anansi, 1999. Published in French under the title *Est-ce que je te dérange?*
>
> Canada. Treasury Board. *First Report of the Advisory Committee on Senior Level Retention and Compensation*. Ottawa: Treasury Board of Canada, 1998. Available online at <www.tbs-sct.gc.ca/>.
>
> Rex, Kay. *No Daughter of Mine: The Women and History of the Canadian Women's Press Club, 1904–1971*. Foreword by Betty Kennedy. Toronto: Cedar Cave Books, 1995. Published in partnership with the Women's Press Club of Toronto. Cedar Cave Books, Box 867, Station F, Toronto, ON M4Y 2N7.
>
> Centre for Trade Policy and Law. *Trade, Sustainable Development, and the Environment: A Bibliography*. Compiled by Maria Isolda P. Guevara. Ottawa: CTPL, 1995. Prepared in conjunction with the International Institute for Sustainable Development.

In the last example, the IISD is placed in the etcetera element because its role is unclear in the source document. The institute is listed on the cover but not the title page and is identified on the copyright page only as the joint copyright holder. The etcetera element is useful in such cases, although the editor has to create a plausible description (here, **Prepared in conjunction with**). Probably no harm done. But such ambiguities could be avoided if the design and text of every cover, title page, and copyright page were checked by an editor before publication. The documenter's job would be easier, and so would the librarian's.

BOOK PART: BASIC FULL CITATION

10.30   Add to the basic book citation:

Author of part
Title of part
Location of part within book*

The information elements are ordered as follows:

Author of part
Title of part
Author of book
Title of book
Secondary responsibility
Edition
Publication information: place*
                         publisher*
                         year
Location of part*
Series*
Etcetera*

---

* Not essential for locating but may be of interest

Author of part

10.31   Usually the author of the part will be different from the author of the book, who is often an editor or compiler:

> Donnelly, Michael. "Coping with Interdependence: Japan and the United States." In Wendy Dobson and Hideo Sato, eds., *Managing U.S.–Japanese Trade Disputes: Are There Better Ways?* Ottawa: Centre for Trade Policy and Law, 1996.

10.32   When the author of the part is the same as the author of the book, list the full name in this element and use a pronoun for the author of the book:

> Munro, Alice. "The Ottawa Valley." In her *Something I've Been Meaning to Tell You*. Toronto: McGraw-Hill Ryerson, 1974.

When the author's gender is unknown, repeat the surname:

> Robertson, A.N. "Raining Chats and Chiens." In Robertson's *Paris Memories*. Toronto: Vanity Press, 1997.

Title of part

10.33   Include the subtitle if it appears on the opening page of the part.

> Drew, Wayland. "Laughter in the Labyrinth: Wilderness and Soul." In Lori Labatt and Bruce Litteljohn, eds., *Islands of Hope: Ontario's Parks and Wilderness*. Toronto: Firefly Books, 1992, pp. 65–72.

Location of part

10.34   List the inclusive page numbers (and volume number, where applicable). Many editors omit the abbreviations **p.** and **pp.,** listing only the page numbers themselves. Join the location to the element preceding it with a comma. The location element may be eliminated altogether if the part can be found easily without it.

> Vanderhaeghe, Guy. "Dancing Bear." In *The Oxford Book of Canadian Short Stories in English*. Selected by Margaret Atwood and Robert Weaver. Paperback edition. Toronto: Oxford University Press, 1988, pp. 404–17.

SERIAL: BASIC FULL CITATION

10.35   Use this matrix for citations to single complete issues of a periodical and for serial runs of two or more consecutive issues.

Title

Sponsoring body

Edition

Issue designation

Etcetera*

* Not essential for locating but may be of interest

Title

10.36   Generic and non-distinctive titles (e.g., **Bulletin, Focus**) are often found in serials. When two serials with identical titles appear in the same set of documentation, make sure that distinguishing information appears in the sponsoring body element or in the etcetera element.

Contact. Periodical Writers Association of Canada. April 1999.

Contact. Friends of Alien Beings Society. North American edition. Vol. 22, no. 6 (November-December 1997).

Sponsoring body (where applicable)

10.37 Citations to general-interest magazines do not usually include the publisher. However, a citation to a serial sponsored by a group other than a commercial publisher – generally an academic, professional, or government body – should include the sponsoring body.

Elm Street. November/December 1997.

Physics Series. University of Toronto. 1935–1938/9. University of Toronto Studies. Continuation of *University Studies in Physics.*

Newsletter. Canadian Research Institute for the Advancement of Women. Vol. 1, no. 1 (October 1981–).

Potpourri. Gardiner Museum of Ceramic Art. Vol. 9 (Fall 1999). Membership newsletter.

Edition (where applicable)

10.38 Include the language (e.g., **English edition**) or market (**North American edition**) of serial editions.

Time. Canadian edition. November 8, 1999.

Issue designation

10.39 For a serial run, give the publication history of the work: the dates and numbers of the particular issues designated in the citation. Record the designation as it appears on the serial – using season, week, part, or whatever elements the serial shows – but standardize abbreviations and capitalization. (For general-interest magazines, the volume and number designations are customarily omitted.) Enclose the date in parentheses when both volume/number designations and dates are present.

August 1955

Vol. 51, no. 4 (April 1985)

No. 10 (April 1974)–no. 41 (February 1984)

Vol. 99, no. 12, whole number 3657 (Winter 1984–)

3rd ser., vol. 1 (May 1907)–3rd ser., vol. 56 (June 1926)

Etcetera (where applicable)

10.40   This element can be used to include previous titles of the serial, frequency (e.g., **monthly**), a corporate sponsor of a trade magazine, or other descriptive information.

> *The Canadian Journal of Information and Library Science/Revue canadienne des sciences de l'information et de bibliothéconomie.* Canadian Association for Information Science. Vol. 18, no. 1 (April 1993). In English and French. Former title was *The Canadian Journal of Information Science/Revue canadienne des sciences de l'information* (last issue December 1990).
>
> *Healthwatch.* Fall 1999. Distributed by Shoppers Drug Mart.

For serials in electronic formats, see 10.108 and 10.116.

SERIAL PART: BASIC FULL CITATION

10.41   Serial parts are articles or items within one issue (or within a discrete number of issues) of a serial publication.

Add to the basic serial citation:

Author of part
Title of part
Location of part within serial issue*

The information elements are ordered as follows:

Author of part

Title of part

Title of serial

Sponsoring body

Edition

Issue designation

Location of part*

Etcetera*

---

* Not essential for locating but may be of interest

> Foster, Peter. "The Money Pit." *Toronto Life.* June 1999, p. 82.
>
> Frechette, Louise. "Canada and the 1995 G7 Halifax Summit." *Canadian Foreign Policy/La Politique étrangère du Canada.* Norman Paterson School of International Affairs, Carleton University. Vol. 3, no. 1 (Spring 1995), pp. 1–4.
>
> Smith, Stephen. "Forty Great Works of Canadian Fiction." *Quill & Quire.* Vol. 65, no. 7 (July 1999), pp. 21–23.

For serial parts in electronic formats, see 10.109 and 10.117.

NEWSPAPERS

10.42 Use the matrixes for serial and serial-part citations, minus the sponsoring body and series elements. (For titles of newspapers, see 12.89–100, "newspapers," and 3.51.)

NEWSPAPER RUN:

Title

Edition

Issue designation

Etcetera*

---

* Not essential for locating but may be of interest

The Globe and Mail. 1936– . Published daily except Sundays.

NEWSPAPER PART:

Author of part

Title of part

Title of newspaper

Edition

Issue designation

Location of part

Etcetera*

---

*Not essential for locating but may be of interest

Landsberg, Michele. "Women Ambassadors Hailed as Rare, Rejuvenating for UN." *The Globe and Mail.* September 20, 1986, p. A2. Column.

Persky, Stan. "East Still Feels like a Poor Cousin in the New Germany." *The Vancouver Sun.* November 16, 1999, p. A17.

Identity crisis

10.43 Many newspapers publish several editions, in different markets or at different times of day. Some stories may appear in one edition and not another; or a story may change through various editions.

When an edition can be identified, add the information to the citation after the newspaper title. But unfortunately for editors and librarians, many newspapers provide no means of distinguishing one edition from another; nothing on the front page, masthead, or anywhere else identifies the edition.

CONFERENCE PROCEEDINGS

10.44   For conference proceedings published as monographs, use the matrixes for books and book parts, minus the edition and length elements. The author of published proceedings is assumed to be either the conference itself, when the conference name is specific, or the sponsoring body, when the conference name is generic.

The date and place of a once-only conference are included as part of the etcetera element; the date, place, and numerical designation of a recurring (e.g., annual) conference are included in the author element. The etcetera element can describe the sponsorship or purpose of the gathering or the contents of the published work.

PROCEEDINGS:

Author

Title

Secondary responsibility

Publication information: place*

                             publisher*

                             year

Series*

Etcetera*

* Not essential for locating but may be of interest

> Seminar on Canadian Universities. *Proceedings of the Seminar on Canadian Universities.* Ottawa: Association of Universities and Colleges of Canada, 1976.

> Symposium on Exact Philosophy (1st, 1971, Montreal). *Exact Philosophy: Problems, Tools, and Goals.* Edited by Mario Bunge. Dordrecht, Holland, and Boston: D. Reidel Publishing, 1973. Synthese Library. Symposium held to celebrate the sesquicentennial of McGill University and establish the Society for Exact Philosophy.

10.45   When the name of a conference is generic (**Conference, Annual Meeting**), use the name of the sponsoring body as the author, followed by the conference name and, where appropriate, numerical designation:

> Royal Society of Canada. Symposium (23rd, 1980, Yellowknife). *A Century of Canada's Arctic Islands, 1880–1980.* Edited by Morris Zaslow. Ottawa: RSC, 1981.

PROCEEDINGS PART:

Author of part

Title of part

Author

Title

Secondary responsibility

Publication information: place*

                       publisher*

                       year

Location of part*

Series*

Etcetera*

* Not essential for locating but may be of interest

> Valaskakis, Kimon. "The Information Revolution: Substantive Issues and Methodological Challenges." In UNESCO Symposium on the Fundamental Problems of, and Challenges for, the Social Sciences in North America. *Global Crises and the Social Sciences: North American Perspectives*. Edited by John Trent and Paul Lamy. [Ottawa]: University of Ottawa Press/UNESCO, 1984, pp. 211–39. Symposium held at Mont-Sainte-Marie, Quebec, May 3–7, 1983.

BOOK REVIEWS

10.46   Use either the book-part or the serial-part matrix, depending on where the review appeared. Include the author and title of the work reviewed in the etcetera element.

> Frye, Northrop. "Canada and Its Poetry." In his *The Bush Garden: Essays on the Canadian Imagination*. Toronto: Anansi, 1971. Review of A.J.M. Smith, ed., *The Book of Canadian Poetry*.

> Pyper, Andrew. "Wayne's World." *Quill & Quire*. Vol. 65, no. 11 (November 1999), p. 20. Review of Wayne Johnston, *Baltimore's Mansion*.

ALTERNATIVE FORMATS

10.47   Works published in alternative formats, such as Braille, large type, books on tape, and microfiche, are identified in citations by a descriptive element. Add to any of the basic matrixes an appropriate *descriptive identifier* in square brackets after the title. (Note that these formats are not considered editions.) Information about publication arrangements or distribution can be added in the etcetera element. (For electronic sources, see 10.104–23.)

> Laurence, Margaret. *The Stone Angel* [large print]. London, Ont.: Gatefold Books, 1980. Canadian Large Print Books. Published by arrangement with McClelland & Stewart, Alfred A. Knopf, and Macmillan London.

> *Saturday Night* [microform]. Vol. 88, no. 1, whole number 3535 (January 1973)–vol. 90, no. 7, whole number 3561 (December 1975). Originally published by New Leaf Publications.

UNPUBLISHED MATERIAL

10.48   A published work is defined as one that has been both *produced in multiple copies* and *made available to the public*. Unpublished material, therefore, is less likely to be found in libraries than in archives, files, and private collections.

10.49   Unpublished works such as manuscripts and typescripts, dissertations, internal documents of a government or company, letters and diaries, and notes are entered in documentation with a *repository* element instead of publication information. In the citation of a work not yet deposited in a formal collection, such as a draft manuscript being circulated privately before publication, the repository can be listed as **Private collection** or as an institution with which the work's author is affiliated: **Institute for Policy Analysis, University of Toronto.**

10.50   A descriptive identifier follows or replaces the title. Where the descriptive identifier and other information do not make clear the scope of the work, a length element may be informative.

UNPUBLISHED MATERIAL:

Author

Title

Descriptive identifier

Date

Length (e.g., number of pages, volumes)*

Repository

Etcetera*

* Not essential for locating but may be of interest

Benotto, Mary Lou. Ethics in Family Law: Is Family Law Advocacy a Contradiction in Terms? [photocopied typescript]. December 1995. Private collection. Speech to the Annual Convention of the Advocates' Society, Nassau, Bahamas.

Salverson, Laura Goodman. The Funny Side of Failure [typescript]. N.d. 67 sheets. Ottawa, National Library of Canada, Literary Manuscripts Collection, Laura Goodman Salverson Papers, unit III (a), file 27. Draft 2 (?) of autobiographic unpublished memoir.

Sward, Robert. [Diary.] 1969. Ottawa, National Library of Canada, Literary Manuscripts Collection, Robert Sward Papers, Journals/Diaries, II, B, I.

10.51 In a citation of an unpublished thesis or dissertation, the etcetera element replaces the descriptive identifier and the repository element:

Boyle, William J. Weakness of Will and Self-Control According to St. Thomas Aquinas. 1982. Ph.D. dissertation, University of Toronto.

EPHEMERA

10.52 Ephemera include documents that are published but not always easily accessible in ordinary libraries. Works like press releases, postcards, brochures and leaflets, and theatre programs may be available only in repositories such as archives and private collections.

Citations of ephemera usually begin with the title. Instead of an author, the citation lists a sponsoring agency after the title and descriptive identifier.

EPHEMERA:

Title

Descriptive identifier

Sponsoring agency

Publication information: place*

publisher*

date

Repository

Etcetera*

* Not essential for locating but may be of interest

Traveling Jacques Cartier Exhibition Prepared by National Library [press release]. National Library of Canada, Public Relations Office. Ottawa: NLC, January 24, 1984. Available in French under the title *Préparation d'une exposition itinérante sur Jacques Cartier par la Bibliothèque nationale.*

Étienne Brûlé: "Discoverer of Ontario" 1592–1632 [leaflet]. Brewers Warehousing. N.p.: n.p., c.1965. Ottawa, National Library of Canada, Literary Manuscripts Collection, Canadian Centennial in Oxford Committee, file 1.

10.53   Where the descriptive identifier does not make it sufficiently clear that the work is short, include a length element after the publication information.

AUDIOVISUAL AND ORAL WORKS

10.54   For works that exist in a non-print format – on film or tape, or only as "live" presentations – add a descriptive identifier after the title.

Sound recordings

10.55   Recordings of music or text are published on CDs, tapes, and other forms. Citations of these works must distinguish between responsibility for the original work and responsibility for the recording; hence the publication date is that of the recording, not the copyright date of the original work.

SOUND RECORDING:

Author or composer

Title

Descriptive identifier

Secondary responsibility (performer, where applicable)

Publication or release information: place*

  publisher*

  date

Identifying number (of published recording)

Etcetera*

---

* Not essential for locating but may be of interest

Bach, J.S. *The Well-Tempered Clavier, Book I* [sound recording]. Glenn Gould, piano. The Glenn Gould Edition. Sony Classical, 1993. SM2K 52500, 52602. 2 discs. Originally recorded 1962–65.

Ravel, Maurice. *Daphnis et Chloé* [sound recording]. Orchestre symphonique de Montréal and Choeur de l'orchestre symphonique de Montréal conducted by Charles Dutoit. [St-Laurent, Que.]: Decca, 1981. London LDR 71028. Complete ballet music and vocals.

Waddington, Miriam. *A Poetry Reading* [sound recording]. Read by Miriam Waddington. Toronto: League of Canadian Poets, [1982]. Modern Canadian Poets and Recorded Archives Taping Series.

10.56   A citation of an unpublished sound recording contains a repository element rather than publication information:

> Green, Howard. [Sound recording of interview.] Interviewed by Peter Stursberg. October 26, 1971. Ottawa, National Archives of Canada, National Film, Television and Sound Archives, Peter Stursberg Collection.

Films, videotapes, etc.

10.57   Citations of motion pictures, slide shows, music videos, and taped television programs usually begin with the title. There is an author element only when one person has sole responsibility for the work.

FILM AND VIDEO:

Title

Descriptive identifier

Artistic or administrative responsibility (director, producer, etc.)*

Production information: place*

                                          production company*

                                          date

Series*

Distributor/repository

Etcetera*

---

* Not essential for locating but may be of interest

> *Crowns and Bridges* [motion picture]. Directed by Graham Parker and produced by Paul Russell. Toronto: Scene II Production, 1979. Dentistry Today Series. Distributed by Take Three Video Education. In colour, 15 minutes running time.
>
> *The Halifax Explosion, 1917* [filmstrip]. N.p.: National Film Board of Canada, [1980]. Atlantic People's History Series. Distributed by the NFB. With tape cassette.
>
> *Small in the Family* [television program]. Directed by A. Bright and produced by C. Dull. Toronto: Drop Outs, 1975–77. Distributed by Who Wants to Know Bros. Series focusing on the effects of being 4'11" in a family where everyone else is at least 6'6".

Interviews

10.58 An interview conducted for research purposes but not recorded or transcribed is cited as follows:

INTERVIEW:

Author (interviewee)

Descriptive identifier

Secondary responsibility (interviewer)

Date

Etcetera*

---

* Not essential for locating but may be of interest

> Nagoya, Masayo. [Telephone interview.] Interviewed by Claire Charlebois. March 16, 1998.

> Klein, Gilda. [Interview.] Interviewed by Rick Cornish. August 11, 1997. Interview took place at the International Psychoanalytic Conference in Banff, Alberta.

10.59 For a published interview, use the book-part or serial-part matrix, depending on where the interview was published. The interviewee is considered the author of the book or serial part, and the interviewer is listed after the part title. Where the title of the part does not make it clear, the descriptive identifier **interview** should be added in square brackets.

> Saul, John Ralston. "An Interview with John Ralston Saul." Interviewed by Tony Makepeace. *Blood & Aphorisms*. No. 12 (Fall 1993), pp. 32–37.

> Singer, Isaac Bashevis. "A Celebration of Love" [interview]. Interviewed by Charles Greenfield. *Maclean's*. February 20, 1984, pp. 10, 12.

> Mitchell, W.O. "One Hour in High River, Alberta" [radio interview]. Interviewed by Peter Gzowski. In *Peter Gzowski's Book About This Country in the Morning*. Edmonton: Hurtig, 1974, pp. 18–25.

Speeches and broadcasts

10.60 A citation referring to a "live," unpublished speech or broadcast can be created. Often the title must be supplied (in square brackets). The absence of either a repository or publication information indicates that the work referred to existed in electronic or live form only.

Author (speaker)

Title

Secondary responsibility

Title of broadcast

Descriptive identifier

Date

Etcetera (description or producer)*

* Not essential for locating but may be of interest

> Beer, D.G. "*The Oresteia*" [lecture]. October 18, 1983. Delivered as an introduction to the world premiere performance of Robert Lowell's translation of *The Oresteia* at the National Arts Centre, Ottawa.
>
> Barton, Jack, et al. [Poetic language of Shakespeare.] *Playing Shakespeare* [television program]. June 26, 1985. Shown on TVOntario, Toronto.
>
> Suzuki, David. "Hidden Killer: Portrait of an Epidemic" [television program]. *The Nature of Things.* October 18, 1999. Produced by the Canadian Broadcasting Corporation, Toronto.
>
> MacIvor, Daniel. [Current projects.] Interviewed by Nora Young. *Definitely Not the Opera* [radio program]. October 30, 1999. Produced by the Canadian Broadcasting Corporation, Winnipeg.

10.61 A citation apparently referring to a speech or broadcast may actually refer to a published transcript of the presentation. In that case, the citation is edited according to one of the four basic matrixes.

10.62 A speech handed out in photocopies in small numbers but not officially published is treated as an unpublished document (see 10.48–51). For recordings of speeches and broadcasts, see 10.55–56.

Printed music

10.63 For citations of musical scores, use the book matrix, with the addition of a descriptive identifier.

> Anhalt, Istvan. *Foci* [music]. Scarborough, Ont.: Berandol Music, 1972. For instrumental ensemble, percussion, soprano, and tape recorders.

GRAPHIC WORKS

Maps

10.64   For citations of maps and globes as independent works, use the following matrix:

MAP:

Author
Title
Descriptive identifier
Edition
Publication information: place*
                         publisher*
                         date
Series*
Etcetera*

---

* Not essential for locating but may be of interest

> Canada. Department of National Defence. Mapping and Charting Establishment. *Military City Map – Fredericton* [map]. Edition 2. Ottawa: DND, Mapping and Charting Establishment, 1978. Series A902. Includes diagram showing relationship of the military city map to the national topographic system.

> Smith & Son. *C. Smith & Son's Education Globe* [globe]. London: Smith, 1893. Ottawa, National Archives of Canada, National Map Collection.

In the citation above, the repository is included after the publication information because the work, although published, is not easily available to the public.

10.65   The scale of the map can be added after the edition element.

> *Ottawa Hull City Map* [map]. 1:36,000 approx. Markham, Ont.: Allmaps Canada, n.d. Includes additional smaller maps.

10.66   A citation of a map published in a book or serial follows the pattern of book-part and serial-part citations, with the addition of a descriptive identifier.

> "Central Ottawa" [map]. In James Hale and Joanne Milner, *Ottawa with Kids*. Toronto: Macfarlane Walter & Ross, 1996, pp. 4–5. Indicates locations of interest to visitors.

> Air Canada. "Air Canada North American Routes" [map]. *enRoute*. Vol. 13, no. 3 (March 1985), p. 141.

Artworks

10.67   Citations can be created for original graphic works, such as drawings and paintings, and for three-dimensional objects such as sculptures. Reproductions of artworks can also be cited.

ORIGINAL ARTWORK:

Author (artist)

Title

Descriptive identifier

Date

Repository (including catalogue number, where applicable)

Etcetera*

* Not essential for locating but may be of interest

> Carr, Emily. *Autumn in France* [painting]. C.1912. Ottawa, National Gallery of Canada, no. 4882. Signed lower right: M. EMILY CARR.
>
> Karsh, Yousuf. *Lord Tweedsmuir, W.L. Mackenzie King, F.D. Roosevelt, and Elliott* [*sic*] *Roosevelt* [photograph]. July 31, 1936. Kingston, Ont., Queen's University, Douglas Library, John Buchan Collection. James Roosevelt has been incorrectly identified as Elliott Roosevelt.

10.68   The dimensions of the work can be included after the date:

> Moore, Henry. *Three Way Piece-Points* [sculpture]. 1964. 64 cm high. Ottawa, National Library of Canada. Bronze sculpture presented to Canada by Britain in 1967 in celebration of the Centenary of Confederation.

10.69   For published graphic works held in archives or private collections, such as limited-edition prints, add place and publisher to the date element.

> Askren, Alice. [No. 1: Falling Leaf Creatures.] In her *Creatures* [etchings]. Calgary: Lettuce Press, 1978. Ottawa, National Library of Canada, Rare Book Collection. Hand-coloured with Talens watercolours on BFK Rives paper. 12/20.

10.70   A citation of a photographic reproduction of an original work focuses on the reproduction, not on the original. Information concerning the original artwork can be included in the etcetera element.

> Kane, Paul. "Spearing Salmon by Torchlight at Fox River" [photographic reproduction]. In Sally Gibson, *More Than an Island: A History of the Toronto Island*. Toronto: Irwin Publishing, 1984, p. 6. Original painting (c.1845) is in the Royal Ontario Museum, Toronto.

GOVERNMENT DOCUMENTS

Reports and studies

10.71 Most government reports and studies can be shoehorned into one of the four basic matrixes. (Many corporate documents follow similar patterns.) Some minor adjustments should be made, as follows.

Author

10.72 When a government body is listed as a corporate author, it may be necessary to add a *jurisdiction* to a citation even if it does not appear on the work's title page. The author may not be properly identifiable without it:

> Canada. National Museum of Natural Sciences
>
> Canada. Parliament. House of Commons
>
> Ontario. Ministry of the Environment
>
> Newfoundland. Royal Commission on Electrical Energy

10.73 Resist the temptation to list a commission chair as the author, since this is rarely the case. More often the commission (or task force, committee, working group, etc.) is the corporate author. The chair is listed in the secondary responsibility element if his or her name is recorded on the title page or copyright page as having such responsibility (e.g., **Coordinated by**). If the name is not so listed, record it (when it is of interest) in the etcetera element.

> Canada. Federal Cultural Policy Review Committee. *Report of the Federal Cultural Policy Review Committee.* [Ottawa]: Department of Communications, Information Services, 1982. Committee co-chairs were Louis Applebaum and Jacques Hébert.
>
> Canada. Mackenzie Valley Pipeline Inquiry. *Northern Frontier, Northern Homeland: Report of the Mackenzie Valley Pipeline Inquiry,* vol. 1. [Ottawa]: Supply and Services Canada, 1977. Prepared by Mr. Justice Thomas Berger.

10.74 A government report can be listed as the work of a personal author rather than a corporate body if a personal author is listed on the title page; many reports are prepared for and published by government agencies but do not reflect the collective thought or collective activity of the agencies (see 10.11–13).

> Britton, John N.H., and James M. Gilmour. *The Weakest Link: A Technological Perspective on Canadian Industrial Underdevelopment.* Assisted by Mark G. Murphy. Ottawa: Science Council of Canada, 1978. Background Study, no. 43. Prepared as a contribution to a comprehensive review of Canadian industrial and technology policy undertaken by the Science Council Industrial Policies Committee.

Page, James E. *Reflections on the Symons Report: The State of Canadian Studies in 1980: A Report* ... Ottawa: Department of the Secretary of State, 1981. Comments on *To Know Ourselves: The Report of the Commission on Canadian Studies.*

A walk through the wild

10.75 Government and other group documents often present especially thorny problems of documentation. For example, the cover and title pages of one government report give this information:

> Advisory Committee
> on Senior Level Retention and Compensation
> First Report: January 1998
>
> Prepared for the President of the Treasury Board,
> the Honourable Marcel Massé

On the copyright page the title appears as:

> First Report of the Advisory Committee on Senior Level Retention and Compensation

The committee chair's name appears as author of the preface. Two bibliographic possibilities the editor might consider are:

> Canada. Advisory Committee on Senior Level Retention and Compensation. *First Report.* Ottawa: Treasury Board of Canada, 1998. Committee chair was Lawrence F. Strong.

> Canada. Treasury Board. *First Report of the Advisory Committee on Senior Level Retention and Compensation.* Ottawa: Treasury Board of Canada, 1998. Committee chair was Lawrence F. Strong.

In this case, the first solution presents each piece of information only once and is closer to what is recorded on the title page. However, the second version is perhaps the better choice, since it identifies the sponsoring body up front and has a more informative title. Whichever arrangement the editor chooses, there is no need to mention the Treasury Board president, whose role may be assumed.

Title

10.76 Government documents frequently carry on the title page long statements of responsibility that could be taken either as titles (or subtitles) or as information on sponsorship or secondary responsibility. The editor often wonders whether it is necessary to record the whole windy thing, especially if the information it gives will be repeated elsewhere in the citation – as author, secondary author, publisher, etc.

> As Feathers Fly: A National Report on the Canada Goose in Crisis Prepared by the Fowl Monitoring Bureau for the Marsh Inhabitants Branch, Ornithological Directorate, Zoology Canada.

When the statement of responsibility – in the above example, beginning at "Prepared by" – can be separated from the title and subtitle without damaging grammar or sense, it can be removed to the etcetera element.

> *As Feathers Fly: A National Report on the Canada Goose in Crisis* ... Ottawa: Zoology Canada, 1980. Prepared by the Fowl Monitoring Bureau for the Marsh Inhabitants Branch, Ornithological Directorate, Zoology Canada.

> *The Film Industry in Canada: A Report* ... [Ottawa]: Department of the Secretary of State, 1976. Prepared by the Bureau of Management Consulting for the Arts and Culture Branch, Secretary of State.

Publication information or issue designation

10.77 When no specific information is given on the work about its publisher, then the printer (Queen's Printer, Supply and Services, Government Publishing Centre, etc.), if given, is listed as the publisher. Month and day are sometimes included in the publication date of a government document; generally, they need not be included in book citations but should be part of the issue designation element of serial citations.

10.78 Statistics Canada and some other government agencies assign catalogue numbers to their publications. The catalogue numbers usually indicate the year in which the data were collected rather than the year in which the work was published; often the date of publication is not listed on the work.

10.79 In a serial citation, list the catalogue number as the issue designation element; the date of publication, when present, can be added in parentheses:

> Statistics Canada. *Financial Statistics of Education.* No. 81-208 (1983).

In a book citation, list the catalogue number in the etcetera element.

> Statistics Canada. *Environmental Perspectives, 1993: Studies and Statistics.* Ottawa: Minister of Industry, Science and Technology, 1993. No. 11-528E.

Etcetera

10.80 This element can list a French title for the report, a description of its contents (**Summary of recommendations**), an explanation of its provenance (**Prepared as part of a policy review, Submitted on the occasion of a conference**), a postal or Internet address, or other information.

Newfoundland. Royal Commission on Electrical Energy. *Report of the Royal Commission on Electrical Energy.* [St. John's: the Commission], 1966. With maps and graphs.

For brochures and press releases, see 10.52–53. For speech transcripts not included in published monograph or serial collections, see 10.48–51. For electronic documents, see 10.104–23.

Parliamentary records

10.81   Legislative documents of the federal, provincial, and territorial governments fit neither the book matrixes nor the serial matrixes, so a combined format may be used for them. Keep in mind that the titles of legislative papers vary from jurisdiction to jurisdiction and also change over the years.

The same format may be applied to *Debates* (in some jurisdictions the proper name for Hansard), *Minutes of Proceedings and Evidence* (committee records), *Journals* (Speaker's papers, Senate business), and *Order Papers* (agendas).

PARLIAMENTARY RECORDS:

Jurisdiction

Legislative assembly or body

Committee (where applicable)

Title of work

Numerical designation of legislature and session*

Volume and issue numbers (where applicable)

Issue date (for a daily issue, such as one day's *Debates* or *Order Paper*) or inclusive dates (for a collected volume)

Publication information: place*

publisher*

year

Etcetera*

* Not essential for locating but may be of interest

Manitoba. Legislative Assembly. *Debates and Proceedings (Hansard).* 32nd Legislature, 4th Session. Vol. 33, no. 88 (July 11, 1985). [Winnipeg]: Queen's Printer, 1985.

Canada. Parliament. House of Commons. Standing Committee on Justice and Legal Affairs. *Minutes of Proceedings and Evidence.* 30th Parliament, 1st Session. No. 3 (November 19, 1974)–no. 10 (December 12, 1974). Ottawa: Queen's Printer, 1974.

Canada. Parliament. House of Commons. Standing Committee on Environment. *Minutes of Proceedings and Evidence Respecting Future Business of the Committee.* 34th Parliament, 3rd Session. Vol. 132, no. 37 (May 7, 1992). Ottawa: Queen's Printer, 1992.

Canada. Parliament. House of Commons. *Order Paper and Notices.* 33rd Parliament, 1st Session. No. 134 (June 28, 1985). [Ottawa]: Queen's Printer, 1985. English and French in parallel columns.

10.82   For a part entry, add the author of the part, the title of the part, and the inclusive page numbers:

MacDonald, Flora, Hon. "Communications: Closure of CNCP Telegraph Office." In Canada. Parliament. House of Commons. *Debates.* 32nd Parliament, 1st Session. Vol. 21 (March 9, 1983–April 21, 1983). Ottawa: Queen's Printer, 1983, p. 23645. Statement was made on March 10.

[Motion by Mr. Deachman, seconded by Mr. Forest, that the name of Mr. Rock be substituted for Mr. Cyr on the Standing Committee on Public Accounts.] In Canada. Parliament. House of Commons. *Journals.* 28th Parliament, 1st Session. Vol. 115, nos. 1–198 (September 12, 1968–October 22, 1969). Ottawa: Queen's Printer, 1969, p. 426.

Here the part element is in square brackets because it is not a published title but the content of a motion.

Sessional papers

10.83   Sessional papers are documents tabled in Parliament but published by outside agencies. They are cited as individual documents – that is, in whatever book or serial format is appropriate. In historical texts, sessional papers may be cited as items in the serial *Sessional Papers;* use the same matrix as for other parliamentary records (see 10.81).

Gazettes

10.84   All parliamentary and legal notices, regulations, and acts in Canada are published in the gazettes of the federal and provincial governments. Be sure to include in a citation the part number of gazettes such as *The Canada Gazette* that appear in more than one part.

The Canada Gazette. Part I. Vol. 104, no. 1 (January 3, 1970)–vol. 104, no. 26 (June 27, 1970). In English and French.

LEGAL DOCUMENTS

10.85 Legal editing is a specialized field. Legal publishers have well-developed house styles, and many guides have been written to handle the formalities and intricacies of publishing legal information. Many editors use the *Canadian Guide to Uniform Legal Citation*, 3rd ed., produced by the *McGill Law Journal.*

Some basic rules are outlined here for the use of the general editor who finds an occasional legal citation in a non-legal text. For more complex questions, editors should consult legal publishers or librarians at the libraries attached to law schools, legislatures, and law firms. Only the largest of public reference libraries will have the reference works needed to check legal citations.

Legal periodicals

10.86 Use the matrixes for serial run and serial part. When the material is intended for readers in the legal field, periodical titles can be abbreviated; standard abbreviations are found in *The Canadian Abridgment Key & Research Guide* and other standard legal references.

Case citations

10.87 Tradition weighs heavily in the style of case citations, imposing several conventions of punctuation and abbreviation that may seem peculiar to the general reader or the general editor. Nonetheless, editors should not attempt to translate a citation from traditional style to one that conforms more closely to bibliographic rules for other documents, as this may introduce inaccuracies.

Following is an explanation of the traditional style.

10.88 Full citations of cases are of two types: "square-bracket" and "round-bracket" citations. The choice between them depends upon which reporting series the case appears in; some series use one style, some the other.

SQUARE-BRACKET CITATION:

Title of case (often called "style of cause" – the names of the parties involved)

Date of publication

Report: volume, title (abbreviated), first page number or page referred to

Dagenais v. Canadian Broadcasting Corporation, [1994] 3 S.C.R. 835. (*Meaning page 835 of volume 3 of the 1994* Supreme Court Reports.)

Title of case

Date of decision

Report: volume, title (abbreviated), first page number or
page referred to

> *Pearcy v. Foster* (1921), 51 O.L.R. 354.
> (*Meaning page 354 of volume 51 of the* Ontario Law Reports.)

10.89 Note that the title of the case, but not the abbreviated title of the report, is italicized. Some publishers leave the **v.** in roman type. The periods after **v.** and in the report abbreviations may be omitted, but legal publishers tend to retain them.

Note also that square-bracket dates always *follow* the comma, and round-bracket dates always *precede* the comma. Do not, for any reason, change round brackets to square ones nor square brackets to round.

10.90 In addition, the "court level" – an abbreviation identifying the court where the case was heard – is included at the end of a citation if the title of the reporting series does not name the court.

> *Pearcy v. Foster* (1921), 51 O.L.R. 354 (H.C.).
> (*Meaning High Court; Ontario is given in the report title.*)

> *R. v. Paveley*, [1976] C.T.C. 477, 76 D.T.C. 6415 (Sask. C.A.).
> (*This case appears in two reporting series,* Canadian Tax Cases *and* Dominion Tax Cases, *but neither title identifies the court – Saskatchewan Court of Appeal.*)

Statutes

10.91 Statutes are published first in sessional volumes (one volume for each legislative session), then in revised, consolidated volumes compiled about every 10 years. In the revised volumes, statutes are renumbered. Once a statute has been collected into a revised volume, it should be cited in that form.

Title of act (where both a long and a short title exist, use
the short title)

Title of statute volume (abbreviated), with year

Chapter number (each statute is a separate chapter)

> Newfoundland Privacy Act, R.S.N. 1990, c. P–22.
> (*Meaning from* Revised Statutes of Newfoundland 1990.)

Human Rights Act, S.B.C. 1984, c. 22.
(*Meaning from* Statutes of British Columbia 1984.)

10.92   Note that full titles of statute volumes are italicized but abbreviations are not. The article **the** at the beginning of some titles of acts can be omitted. Periods can be omitted from the abbreviated titles of statute volumes. Note also that although statute titles are not italicized in these examples, some style guides italicize them (see also 10.132).

10.93   In historical material, references to statutes may appear in an older style, with the volumes dated by regnal year rather than calendar year. When these older volumes do not include the name of the jurisdiction in their titles, list it at the beginning of the citation, as the author element.

Canada. *Statutes,* 42 Vict., c. 15.
(*Meaning in the 42nd year of Queen Victoria's reign.*)

Statutes of New Brunswick, 18 Vict., c. 38.

The Constitution and the Charter of Rights

10.94   The correct names of Canada's constitutional documents are a complex matter. *The Canadian Encyclopedia* is one good source for a brief history of the changes in names.

Until April 1982, Canada's constitution consisted of the British North America Act, 1867 (a statute of the British Parliament), plus several later BNA Acts. In 1982 the BNA Act, 1867, was renamed the Constitution Act, 1867.

On April 17, 1982, the Constitution Act, 1982, became Canada's constitution. It may be cited as:

Constitution Act, 1982 [en. by the Canada Act 1982 (U.K.), c. 11, s. 1].

10.95   The Canadian Charter of Rights and Freedoms consists of Part I (sections 1–34 only) of the Constitution Act, 1982. It may be cited as:

Constitution Act, 1982 [en. by the Canada Act 1982 (U.K.), c. 11, s. 1], pt. I (Canadian Charter of Rights and Freedoms).

ARCHIVAL MATERIAL

10.96   Archives can contain any of the types of material, published or unpublished, referred to in this chapter. In general, material held in archives is there because it exists in only one copy, such as personal correspondence, or because, although it was created in multiple copies, only a small number of copies remain. Material such as government records is collected in archives because governments wish to make it available to historians and to the public but do not wish to publish it formally.

10.97   Citations of published works held in archives should list both the publication information and the repository.

10.98   The Public Archives of Canada (now the National Archives of Canada) published a guide in 1983 called *Archival Citations*, which provides standardized formats for various archival citations. In general, the formats presented there differ from those given in this chapter in the *order* of elements only; the information included in the citations is similar.

The guide suggests including the archives' catalogue numbers, accession numbers, and call numbers, where applicable, in citations. These identifying numbers may simplify locating the work for readers who follow up archival citations, although they are not strictly necessary. When including these numbers in citations, add them to the repository element.

BILINGUAL PUBLICATIONS

10.99   In a work intended for a primarily English-speaking audience, it is rarely necessary to give full bibliographic details of the French version of a given publication, especially if the work's author has referred only to the English version. But the existence of a French edition or version should be acknowledged. The amount of detail to include in this acknowledgment depends on the author's and editor's judgment of the intended reader's interest in the French version.

10.100 In a citation referring to a work with a bilingual title – that is, a title given in both languages on the same title page – record both titles in the title element, with the version that appears first recorded first.

> *Mystery and Adventure in Canadian Books for Children and Young People/ Romans policiers et histoires d'aventures canadiens pour la jeunesse.* List prepared by Irene E. Aubrey. Ottawa: National Library of Canada, 1983. English and French annotations in parallel columns.
>
> *ACS Newsletter/Bulletin de l'AEC.* Association for Canadian Studies. Vol. 6, no. 4 (Winter 1984). Text in English and French.

10.101 In a citation of a work with a French title on one title page and an English title on a separate title page – either side by side or in "tumble" format (head to foot) – give the citation in English and list the French title in the etcetera element.

> Eichler, Margrit, and Jeanne Lapointe. *On the Treatment of the Sexes in Research.* [Ottawa]: Social Sciences and Humanities Research Council of Canada, 1985. English and French text in tumble format; French title is *Le traitement objectif des sexes dans la recherche.*

> *At the Centre.* Canadian Centre for Occupational Health and Safety. Vol. 8, no. 1 (March 1985–). English and French text; French title is *Au Centre.*

10.102 In a serial-part entry, include the French title of the part. The French title of the serial should appear only if the two serial titles are on the same title page.

> Moore, Mavor. "Who's Got the Money and How Can We Get Our Hands on It?" *The Canadian Composer.* No. 54 (November 1970), pp. 18, 20. French title is "Qui a l'argent et comment mettre la main dessus?"

10.103 When a French version of a work is published as a physically separate book or serial, the French title can be included in the etcetera element: **Published in French under the title ...**

ELECTRONIC DOCUMENTS

10.104 The complex and fluid nature of electronic publishing makes attempts to establish rules for documentation a risky business, however essential. Authors may now refer to an ever-expanding array of electronic sources, including Web sites, email, discussion lists and newsgroups, information available using Gopher, Telnet, or File Transfer Protocol (FTP), online databases, software programs, CD-ROMs, DVDs, and video games. Much of this material is subject to ongoing revision or can vanish altogether.

Conventions for citing electronic sources are continually evolving to meet the demands of new technology. If a work refers to many or complex electronic sources, editors should consult standard or specialized guides, some of which are available online (see Sources). However, for occasional citations, the matrixes given here may be useful.

The essential information elements for most electronic works are similar to those for other forms of publishing, and the editorial aim of citations to them is the same: give enough information to identify the source and allow readers to locate it (to which must be added "if possible").

10.105 Three broad categories of documents are considered in this section: CD-ROMs and diskettes (stand-alone sources that store information accessible by computer); online documents; and discussion lists and email (sent by the Internet but often not available online). The matrixes below may be used for some common examples within these categories.

CD-ROMs and diskettes

10.106 Matrixes for these documents are similar to those for books and serials:

CD-ROMS AND DISKETTES – DOCUMENT:

Author

Title

Descriptive identifier

Secondary responsibility*

Edition/version

Publication information: place*

                            publisher

                            year

Length (e.g., number of disks)*

Series*

Etcetera*

---

* Not essential for locating but may be of interest

Look for documentation information on the first screen and on the packaging. If the nature of the work suggests that readers should know the hardware required to use the CD-ROM or diskette, this information may be included in the etcetera element.

> *Canadian & World Encyclopedia* [CD-ROM]. 1998 ed. Toronto: McClelland & Stewart, 1997. Includes a second disk, *Life & Times of the Prime Ministers.* System requirements: IBM PC or compatible, Windows 3.1 or Windows 95; or Macintosh 68040 or PowerPC.

> *Monty Python's Complete Waste of Time* [CD-ROM]. Richardson, Tex.: 7th Level, 1994–95. Includes games and installations. Accompanied by a user manual.

> *Avagio Publishing System* [diskettes]. Ver. 1.0. Alameda, Cal.: Unison World, 1990. Four 3.5-inch diskettes and seven 5.25-inch diskettes. Accompanied by a user manual.

CD-ROMS AND DISKETTES – PART:

10.107 Author of part

Title of part

Author of document (if different)

Document title

Descriptive identifier

Secondary responsibility*

Edition/version

Publication information: place*

                                 publisher

                                 year

Location (e.g., which disk)

Series*

Etcetera*

*Not essential for locating but may be of interest

Bell, Catherine, and William B. Henderson. "Aboriginal Rights." In *Canadian & World Encyclopedia* [CD-ROM]. 1998 ed. Toronto: McClelland & Stewart, 1997. Disk 1.

CD-ROMS AND DISKETTES – SERIAL:

10.108   Title

       Descriptive identifier

       Sponsoring body

       Edition/version

       Issue designation

       Etcetera*

* Not essential for locating but may be of interest

Canadian Regional NewsDisc [CD-ROM]. Atlantic Region edition. No. 1 (December 1999). Issued monthly. Includes text of five newspapers.

CD-ROMS AND DISKETTES – SERIAL PART:

10.109   Author of part

       Title of part

       Title of serial

       Descriptive identifier

       Sponsoring body

       Edition/version

       Issue designation

       Etcetera*

* Not essential for locating but may be of interest

Kronski, Kyle. "No Bull – Canadians Are Eating Less Beef." *Prairie Newsdisc* [CD-ROM]. May 1995–April 1996. Originally published in *Calgary Sentinel,* February 17, 1996, Final edition, p. A22.

Online documents

10.110 Citations to online sources add two unique elements to basic print ma-trixes: the Internet address (how to get to the document – for Web sites, the URL) and the access date (the date the source was consulted). This date establishes a time when the information cited was available.

10.111 Search engines and browsers have created an environment for documen-tation of online sources that differs considerably from the print environ-ment. These tools can often locate documents on the basis of just a few words, making detailed citations – and even Internet addresses – apparently superfluous.

However, despite the capability of search engines, documentation should provide as much help as possible to those who are trying to locate a document and judge its usefulness. Information such as the author's full name and the identity of the site allows a reader to assess a work's cred-ibility. Publication and revision dates are necessary (though often not available, unfortunately) if readers are to judge the currency and reliabil-ity of information.

10.112 The four matrixes below include all possible elements for full citations of online documents (including World Wide Web, Gopher, and FTP proto-cols), serials, and parts. Although very little of the information may be needed to track down a particular text, we recommend including other elements when they have bibliographic value.

ONLINE DOCUMENT:

Author
Title or filename
Descriptive identifier
Secondary responsibility (e.g., editor, agency)*
Edition/version/file
Publication information: name of site or host
                                  publication date
                                    revision date
Access date
Series*
Etcetera*
Address (URL, path, or directories)

* Not essential but may be of interest

Canada. *Copyright Act* [online]. Department of Justice. Revised 1999. [Cited December 4, 1999.] Also available in French. <Canada.justice.gc. ca/STABLE/EN/Laws/Chap/C/C-42.html>.

National Library of Canada. *Citing Electronic Sources: A Bibliography* [online]. Revised March 31, 1998. [Cited May 26, 1999.] Also available in French. <www.nlc-bnc.ca/services/eciting.htm>.

Association for Progressive Communication. *Women's Issues Conferences on IGC/APC and Partner Networks* [online]. Revised March 8, 1995. [Cited November 12, 1999.] <gopher://gopher.ipc.apc.org/Women/ Women's information available on WomensNet>.

ONLINE DOCUMENT – PART:

10.113 Author of part

Title of part

Author of document (if different)

Title or filename of document

Descriptive identifier

Secondary responsibility (e.g., editor)*

Edition/version/file

Publication information: name of site or host

publication date

revision date

Access date

Series*

Etcetera*

Address

* Not essential but may be of interest

Fowler, H.W. "Neologisms." In his *The King's English* [online]. 2nd ed. Bartleby Library: Great Books Online, 1999. [Cited October 24, 1999.] <www.bartleby.com/116/103.html>.

10.114 The distinction between a "complete" online document and a "part" is most easily discerned in works created originally in a print environment and transferred to the Internet. In sources originating in an electronic environment, the borderline may be unclear. Choose the matrix that will provide the most relevant information in the context of the work.

10.115 Note that the location element used in print matrixes would have little meaning in electronic publishing, since most document formats do not provide content in numbered pages or volumes. Section titles within the document, when available, may be given after the publication information:

> "Basic CGOS Style." In *The Columbia Guide to Online Style* [online]. By Janice R. Walker and Todd Taylor. Columbia University Press. Revised September 1, 1998. [Cited October 15, 1999.] At "The Elements of Citation." <www. columbia.edu/cu/cup/cgos/idx_basic.html>.

ONLINE DOCUMENT – SERIAL:

10.116 Title

Descriptive identifier

Sponsoring body

Edition/version/file

Issue designation

Date of revision

Access date

Etcetera*

Address

* Not essential but may be of interest

> *Canadian Journal of Neurological Sciences* [online]. Vol. 26, no. 3 (August 1999). Revised July 30, 1999. [Cited October 25, 1999.] Table of contents and abstracts from the print journal. <www.canjneurolsci.org/26aug.html>.

ONLINE DOCUMENT – SERIAL PART:

10.117 Author

Title of part

Title of serial

Descriptive identifier

Sponsoring body

Edition/version/file

Issue designation

Date of revision

Access date

Etcetera*

Address

* Not essential but may be of interest

Tovell, Vincent. "Interview with Phyllis Grosskurth." *Wordsworthy* [online]. Sponsored by the Canadian National Institute for the Blind. Vol. 7, no. 1 (Spring 1999). Revised May 28, 1999. [Cited October 25, 1999.] <www.cnib.ca/library/publications/wordsworthy/spring99/index.htm>.

Molnar, Jim. "Apocalypse Now." *Salon* [online]. December 3, 1999. [Cited December 3, 1999.] <www.salon.com/>.

Chain links

10.118   Online documents often provide links to other sites. When a link is of bibliographic interest within the context of the work, this information may be included in the etcetera element:

Nepal Community Development Foundation [online]. NCDF, 1999. Revised August 20, 1999. [Cited December 5, 1999.] Includes link to *ARMP Fog/Cloud Water Collection Page.* <www.nepalfriends.org/>.

Discussion lists and email

DISCUSSION LIST MESSAGE:

10.119   Author of message

Subject line of message

Name of discussion list

Descriptive identifier

Publication information: place of host system*

host name

date message was sent (day, month, year, hour)

Access date*

Etcetera*

Address

* Not essential but may be of interest

10.120   Discussion list messages may be archived, although some archives are available only to list members. Include an archive's public email or Internet address, when available, at the end of the citation.

Letterman, Josh. "Nailing the Slippery Solidus." *MIND-L* [discussion list]. Toronto: Harbourfront University, July 18, 1998, 2:24. [Cited May 23, 1999.] <MIND-L@listserv.har.edu>. Via <www.mindlist.archive.com>.

10.121 If the citation is to an entire list, omit the first two elements and insert the inaugural date in the publication information.

> *MIND-L* [discussion list]. Toronto: Harbourfront University, August 1997– . [Cited October 27, 1999.] <MIND-L@listserv.har.edu>.

EMAIL MESSAGE:

10.122 Author

Subject line of message

Descriptive identifier

Name of recipient (if appropriate)

Date sent

Access date*

Email address of sender (if appropriate)

Etcetera*

* Not essential but may be of interest

> Office of the Prime Minister. Safety First [email]. Message to RCMP Vancouver. September 31, 1997. [Cited February 30, 1999.] Confidential communication.

10.123 When an email message is in the nature of private correspondence, the addresses should normally be omitted. Check with the author of the work to determine whether the email cited is of a private or public nature.

AUTHOR/DATE SYSTEM

10.124 The so-called author/date system is an increasingly popular variation in the order of citation elements and is the system the *Chicago Manual* recommends. In author/date references, the date (year) of publication is listed directly after the author's name.

For example, a conventional ordering of elements for a full citation of a book might be:

> Choy, Wayson. *The Jade Peony*. Vancouver: Douglas & McIntyre, 1995.

In the author/date system, it would be:

> Choy, Wayson. 1995. *The Jade Peony*. Vancouver: Douglas & McIntyre.

10.125 Short citations in this system contain only the author and date elements, plus location (such as page or volume number) if necessary. For example, depending on the information contained in the surrounding text, an in-text reference to the full citation above might appear in any of the following forms:

> … One of several recent novels drawing on the authors' personal experiences of Vancouver's Chinese community is *The Jade Peony* (Choy, 1995) …

> … Choy (1995) draws on his own experiences of growing up in Vancouver's Chinatown …

> … The term "Gold Mountain" was common in the Chinese community before 1923 (Choy, 1995, 17) …

10.126   If the author/date system is used in a work, all references – bibliography entries, footnotes, in-text notes – should have this format.

The following examples are for an electronic source styled as a full and a short citation:

> Rousseau, Jacques. Revised March 20, 1995. "Save the Tigers." In *Endangered Animals of the World* [online]. World Wildlife Watch. [Cited July 24, 1999.] <www.worldwild.org>.

> Rousseau, 1995.

10.127   Note that for online sources, the date in the short citation should be the publication date or last revision date, or (if neither of these is available) the access date. In the corresponding full citation, identify the dates.

For more examples of the author/date system used in short citations, see 10.146–50.

STYLE

10.128   Once editors have completed the first step in preparing a citation – determining and arranging the information elements – they must tackle the second step: arranging the elements in a consistent style of punctuation, capitalization, abbreviation, and italicization. Any of the traditional styles for documentation – for instance, those in the *Chicago Manual* and the *MLA Handbook* – can easily be applied when using the matrixes in this chapter. The style used for the examples in this chapter is explained below. For the style of notes, see 10.137–45. For the style of short citations, see 10.146–50.

Basic style and variations

10.129   Certain basic assumptions of style apply to all kinds of documentation – full and short citations, bibliographies, and notes.

Italics and quotation marks

10.130 In the examples in this chapter, italics are used for titles and subtitles of books and other published works, such as serials, newspapers, and brochures; for graphic works published or produced as single works, such as maps, paintings, or individual photographs; for audiovisual works, such as television series, films, and sound recordings; and for titles of electronic documents.

10.131 Quotation marks are used for titles of parts of published works – for instance, a chapter of a book or an article in a serial; a map in an atlas or a single serigraph within a series; an episode of a television series or a recording of one poem from a tape of an entire poetry reading; a section of an electronic document.

10.132 For titles of statutes and unpublished works, neither italics nor quotation marks are used. (This practice contrasts with that of many standard reference books, which use quotation marks for unpublished works.) For a definition of published works, see 10.48.

Capitalization

10.133 For titles and subtitles, capitalize all words except articles, conjunctions, and prepositions of fewer than five letters; cap any word that begins a title or subtitle. For other elements, the simplest approach is to treat the citation as ordinary prose: use capital letters for proper nouns and for any word that follows a full stop (period, question mark, or exclamation point); otherwise use lowercase. It is not necessary to follow the capitalization given on the work; **volume** or **number,** for example, may be lowercase in a citation even if uppercase on a serial's cover.

Abbreviation

10.134 Choose patterns of abbreviation for citations that are consistent with the abbreviation style of the rest of the manuscript.

Punctuation

10. 135 Periods are used most often between elements in citations prepared for bibliographies. (See 10.137–45 for note style.) However, the location element, such as the page number, is usually linked to the preceding element by a comma.

10.136 Square brackets are useful in citations to enclose important information that does not appear on the cover, the title page, or the copyright page of the cited work. They indicate that the author or editor has done some detective work or is making an educated guess. Brackets are also used to enclose a descriptive identifier (e.g., **[map]**, **[B.A. thesis]**, **[online]**).

For punctuation of the issue designation element of serials, see 10.39.

Note style

10.137 Editors who have used the matrixes in this chapter to assemble a set of full citations – say, for a bibliography – can extrapolate from them any kind of note (in-text, footnote, or endnote). Notes may be either full or short citations. Note style for full citations follows; for styling short citations, see 10.146–50.

Punctuation

10.138 The principal difference between the "bibliography" style described above and a style appropriate to notes is in punctuation: the periods in bibliography style are changed to commas or other punctuation in note style, so that the entire citation is set up as one "sentence." Some uppercase letters must be changed to lowercase to accommodate the new punctuation. Standard references such as the *Chicago Manual* and the *MLA Handbook* provide other possible styles for notes.

Changes are needed within the elements listed below; other elements remain unchanged except for linking punctuation.

Author

10.139 For personal authors, give first name or initial(s) followed by last name. If there is more than one author, list them in a series separated by commas and a final **and:**

BIBLIOGRAPHY STYLE:

Suzuki, David, with Amanda McConnell. *The Sacred Balance: Rediscovering Our Place in Nature* (Vancouver/Toronto: Greystone Books, 1997).

Ross, Val. "'I Am So Offended by That Crap.'" *The Globe and Mail.* November 6, 1999, p. D5. Interview with 1999 Giller Prize winner Bonnie Burnard.

Tovell, Vincent. "Interview with Phyllis Grosskurth." *Wordsworthy* [online]. Sponsored by the Canadian National Institute for the Blind. Vol. 7, no. 1 (Spring 1999). Revised May 28, 1999. [Cited October 25, 1999.] <www.cnib.ca/library/publications/wordsworthy/spring99/index.htm>.

Canadian Journal of Neurological Sciences [online]. Vol. 26, no. 3 (August 1999). Revised July 30, 1999. [Cited October 25, 1999.] Table of contents and abstracts from the print journal. <www.canjneurolsci.org/26aug.html>.

NOTE STYLE:

David Suzuki with Amanda McConnell, *The Sacred Balance: Rediscovering Our Place in Nature* (Vancouver/Toronto: Greystone Books, 1997).

Val Ross, "'I Am So Offended by That Crap,'" *The Globe and Mail*, November 6, 1999, p. D5 [interview with 1999 Giller Prize winner Bonnie Burnard].

Vincent Tovell, "Interview with Phyllis Grosskurth," *Wordsworthy* [online], sponsored by the Canadian National Institute for the Blind, vol. 7, no. 1 (Spring 1999), revised May 28, 1999 [cited October 25, 1999], <www.cnib.ca/library/publications/wordsworthy/spring99/index.htm>.

Canadian Journal of Neurological Sciences [online], vol. 26, no. 3 (August 1999), revised July 30, 1999 [cited October 25, 1999], [table of contents and abstracts from the print journal], <www.canjneurolsci.org/26aug.html>.

Title

10.140 With titles that are supplied in square brackets, change the period to a comma within the brackets.

BIBLIOGRAPHY STYLE:

Barton, Jack, et al. [Poetic language of Shakespeare.] *Playing Shakespeare* [television program]. June 26, 1985. Shown on TVOntario, Toronto.

NOTE STYLE:

Jack Barton et al., [Poetic language of Shakespeare,] *Playing Shakespeare* [television program], June 26, 1985 [shown on TVOntario, Toronto].

10.141 If the title is a quote, use single quotes enclosed within double quotes:

Blake Gopnik, "'The Works Are Slovenly, and So Am I,'" *The Globe and Mail*, September 22, 1999, p. C2 [review of an exhibition of works by artist John Scott].

Publication information

10.142 The three parts of this element are traditionally enclosed in parentheses in note style.

BIBLIOGRAPHY STYLE:

> Klinck, Carl F., ed. *Literary History of Canada: Canadian Literature in English*. Toronto: University of Toronto Press, 1965.

> Symposium on Exact Philosophy (1st, 1971, Montreal). *Exact Philosophy: Problems, Tools, and Goals*. Edited by Mario Bunge. Dordrecht, Holland, and Boston: D. Reidel Publishing, 1973. Synthese Library. Symposium held to celebrate the sesquicentennial of McGill University and establish the Society for Exact Philosophy.

> *The Halifax Explosion, 1917* [filmstrip]. N.p.: National Film Board of Canada, [1980]. Atlantic People's History Series. Distributed by the NFB. With tape cassette.

NOTE STYLE:

> Carl F. Klinck, ed., *Literary History of Canada: Canadian Literature in English* (Toronto: University of Toronto Press, 1965).

> Symposium on Exact Philosophy (1st, 1971, Montreal), *Exact Philosophy: Problems, Tools, and Goals*, edited by Mario Bunge (Dordrecht, Holland, and Boston: D. Reidel Publishing, 1973), Synthese Library [symposium held to celebrate the sesquicentennial of McGill University and establish the Society for Exact Philosophy].

> *The Halifax Explosion, 1917* [filmstrip] (n.p.: National Film Board of Canada, 1980), Atlantic People's History Series, distributed by the NFB [with tape cassette].

Etcetera

10.143 Use square brackets around the etcetera element.

BIBLIOGRAPHY STYLE:

> Carr, Emily. *Autumn in France* [painting]. C.1912. Ottawa, National Gallery of Canada, no. 4882. Signed lower right: M. EMILY CARR.

NOTE STYLE:

> Emily Carr, *Autumn in France* [painting], c.1912, Ottawa, National Gallery of Canada, no. 4882 [signed lower right: M. EMILY CARR].

Multiple citations

10.144 In notes that contain more than one citation, separate the citations with semicolons, adding **and** between the last two in a series. In notes citing more than one work by the same author, repeat the author's surname for each work.

> Canadian Broadcasting Corporation, *Culture, Broadcasting, and the Canadian Identity: A Submission to the Cultural Policy Review Committee* ([Ottawa]: CBC, 1981); John G. Diefenbaker, *The Tumultuous Years 1962–1967* (Toronto: Macmillan, 1977), *One Canada: Memoirs of the Right Honourable John G. Diefenbaker,* vol. 3; and Alice Munro, "The Ottawa Valley," in her *Something I've Been Meaning to Tell You* (Toronto: McGraw-Hill Ryerson, 1974).

> For further information, see Mavor Moore, "Who's Got the Money and How Can We Get Our Hands on It?" *The Canadian Composer,* no. 54 (November 1970), pp. 18, 20 [French title is "Qui a l'argent et comment mettre la main dessus?"]; and *The Film Industry in Canada: A Report ...* ([Ottawa]: Department of the Secretary of State, 1976), pp. 24–28 [prepared by the Bureau of Management Consulting for the Arts and Culture Branch, Secretary of State].

Ibid., idem, op. cit., loc. cit.

10.145 The use of **op. cit., loc. cit.,** and **idem** is out of fashion; **ibid.** is still seen, especially in academic material. Modern practice is to replace all these terms with appropriate short citations.

SHORT CITATIONS

10.146 A note (usually in-text note or footnote) may be a short citation if a full citation for the work is given elsewhere (e.g., in a bibliography or in endnotes). One form is the author/date style:

AUTHOR/DATE:

> Moore, 1970 (*for full citation, see 10.102*)
>
> Klinck, 1965 (*see 10.142*)
>
> Barton, 1985 (*see 10.140*)
>
> Canadian Broadcasting Corporation, 1981 (*see 10.24*)
>
> Suzuki with McConnell, 1997 (*see 10.139*)

In some styles, the separating comma is omitted.

10.147 Another common form gives the author and a short title that includes at least the first key word of the full title.

AUTHOR/SHORT TITLE:

> Moore, "Who's Got the Money?"
>
> Klinck, *Literary History*
>
> Barton, [Poetic language]
>
> Canadian Broadcasting Corporation, *Culture*
>
> Suzuki with McConnell, *Sacred Balance*

10.148 In the case of a book part or serial part, such as the Moore article, use the title of the part, not of the book or serial in which it appeared.

10.149 Add an author's initial if two or more authors with the same last name are cited in the work.

10.150 A short citation may include a page location:

> Moore, 1978, 18
>
> Suzuki with McConnell, *Sacred Balance*, 45

A MODEST PROPOSAL

This cri de coeur, which appeared in the first edition of Editing Canadian English, *failed to spark a wholesale revolution in documentation practices. We repeat it here with renewed hope for success in the new millennium.*

10.151 This proposal is not directed at those careful and meticulous authors who supply editors with complete and accurate citations when they submit manuscripts. For these rare paragons, editors have the greatest respect and unending gratitude.

But as editors are only too well aware, arranging and styling complete, consistent citations is only half the battle. The other half is *getting* the essential information to arrange and style when authors have not supplied it. Although it is unquestionably the author's responsibility to provide all the necessary elements for each note or reference – barring a contract that states otherwise – failure to do so is common, and the editor is usually left to fill in the blanks.

By the time the editor begins work on a manuscript, the author may well have gone on to other projects and may be unwilling or unable to supply the missing information in response to a long query list from the editor. Often, too, the author no longer has access to the sources in question; she or he may have difficulty checking the publication information of an obscure Latvian biography encountered three years earlier in an obscure Latvian library.

We would like to suggest a means of ending this scourge of the publishing process, a sort of vaccinating measure that could eradicate the pox of missing bibliographic information in our lifetime. Technology has brought us the photocopier, and this is a task it was born to: authors could photocopy, *during their research,* the title and copyright pages (or comparable sources of information – mastheads, publication notices, album covers, etc.) of every source from which they copy a quotation. They could then submit these photocopies to the editor, attached to the manuscripts of notes and references that they have compiled. For electronic documents, authors could submit printouts of relevant screens.

An author providing a complete set of such copies would never again be pestered by tedious editorial queries; an editor working with such source material would be spared hours of library research and correspondence; a publishing house that made this procedure part of its manuscript submission guidelines would receive no more outraged letters from authors of cited material complaining of insufficient or inaccurate identification of their works. (Authors notorious for sloppy copying of excerpts might also be asked to submit photocopies of quoted passages, in order to forestall outraged letters complaining of misquotation.)

The full-scale implementation of such a policy may seem like a utopian dream. But we believe that if publishers and editors began urging it upon their authors now, in a few years it would be second nature to all concerned.

SOURCES

The Canadian Abridgment Key & Research Guide. Toronto: Carswell, 1982– . Loose-leaf supplement to *The Canadian Abridgment;* published quarterly.

Canadian Guide to Uniform Legal Citation. 3rd ed. Toronto: Carswell, 1992. Produced by the *McGill Law Journal/Revue de droit de McGill.* English and French text in tumble format.

Columbia Guide to Online Style [online]. By Janice R. Walker and Todd Taylor. Columbia University Press. Revised September 1, 1998. [Cited October 12, 1999.] Excerpts from the print publication. <www.columbia.edu/cu/cup/cgos/idx_basic.html>.

MLA Handbook for Writers of Research Papers. By Joseph Gibaldi. 4th ed. New York: Modern Language Association of America, 1995. Some guidelines for citing electronic documents available at <www.mla.org/style/sources.htm>.

National Library of Canada. *Bibliographic Style Manual.* By Danielle Thibault. Ottawa: Supply and Services Canada, 1990.

———. *Bibliographic Style Manual: Section 3, Electronic Documents.* By Danielle Thibault. Ottawa: NLC, 1998. 7 pp. Loose-leaf supplement to *Bibliographic Style Manual.*

———. *Citing Electronic Sources: A Bibliography* [online]. Revised March 31, 1998. [Cited November 30, 1999.] Provides links to several guides to electronic citations. Also available in French. <www.nlc-bnc.ca/services/eciting.htm>.

———. National Library of Canada Bibliographic Style Manual [typescript]. By Willadean Leo. 1986. Editors' Association of Canada collection. Draft copy.

Online! A Reference Guide to Using Internet Sources [online]. By Andrew Harnock and Eugene Kleppinger. 1998 edition. N.p.: Bedford/St. Martin's, 1998. [Cited November 15, 1999.] Compares MLA, APA, CBE, and *Chicago* styles for citations to electronic sources. <www.bedfordstmartins.com/online/index.html>.

Public Archives of Canada. *Archival Citations: Suggestions for the Citation of Documents at the Public Archives of Canada.* Edited by Terry Cook. Ottawa: PAC, 1983. 30 pp. English and 30 pp. French in tumble format. French title is *Références aux documents d'archives.*

Publications Manual of the American Psychological Association. 4th ed. Washington: APA, 1994. Excerpts from the print publication at <www.apa.org/journals/webref.html>.

CHAPTER 11

Editors and the Law

Chapter 11 – Editors and the Law

11.1   In Canada, an editor is unlikely to be the target of litigation: it is rather the author and publisher who are in the line of fire. Nevertheless, an editor has some responsibility to ensure that a work does not present a legal risk, for the editor is, after all, the only person besides the author who reads the final manuscript closely.

It is not up to an editor to foretell how a court will treat a particular problem; even specialist lawyers cannot do so with certainty. (For that reason, many of the recommendations in this chapter must necessarily fall frustratingly short of being clear-cut rules.) What the editor can do is be aware of where the law influences what may be published and draw to the attention of author and publisher any material that might benefit from a lawyer's scrutiny.

This chapter outlines some of the basic principles of laws related to intellectual property and media. The aspects of law most relevant to editors are copyright, trademarks, libel, publication bans, breach of confidence, breach of trade secrets, and invasion of privacy.

COPYRIGHT

11.2   Copyright is a system of legal rights that evolved after the invention of the Gutenberg printing press to protect the *economic rights* of authors and publishers and the *moral rights* of authors.

In addition to copyright law, other forms of intellectual property legislation protect several other categories of creative works. For instance, inventions are protected by patent laws, and the design of manufactured articles can be protected by industrial design registration.

This section focuses primarily on the needs of print publishers; information on many other provisions of copyright law specific to the fine arts and the performing arts can be found in sources listed at the end of the chapter.

Economic rights and moral rights

11.3   Economic rights are those that the copyright owner may exchange for money (e.g., royalties): rights of publication, reproduction, adaptation, translation, public performance or broadcast, and electronic and digital rights. The copyright owner may sell (assign), license, or waive these rights under a contract or pass them on to heirs.

11.4   Creators have the moral right to be identified as authors of their works (or to remain anonymous); to protect their reputations as the creators of their works; and to preserve the integrity of those works. Moral rights may be infringed by, for example, the association of a work with a particular cause or the modification of a work in a way that the creator finds prejudicial to his or her honour or reputation. In a celebrated case, Canadian courts found that the moral rights of the artist Michael Snow were infringed when the management of a shopping centre that housed his work tied ribbons around the necks of Snow's sculptures of Canada geese. Moral rights may not be given away or exchanged for money (although they may be waived or passed on to heirs).

11.5   Copyright law in the United States generally includes protection for the moral rights of visual artists only.

Canadian copyright law

11.6   Canada's Copyright Act, originally enacted in 1924, underwent major revision in the Phase I amendments introduced in 1988 and the Phase II amendments (Bill C-32) introduced in 1996. The features of Phase I of most interest to print publishers were the strengthening and expansion of moral rights and provisions allowing the establishment of copyright collectives for print works (see 11.54–55). Phase II, implemented from 1996 to 1999, expanded exemptions from copyright law for various non-profit institutions (see 11.47) and altered the copyright protection of unpublished works (see 11.30). It also strengthened remedies for copyright infringement.

11.7   A third phase of amendments – to address issues raised by electronic publishing and the Internet – has been under discussion since the early 1990s. For now, electronic or digital texts (such as CD-ROMs, databases, Internet sites, or texts transmitted online) are protected by the same copyright provisions as other works, but technology makes those provisions more difficult to enforce.

11.8   The continuing change in copyright law means that editors must ensure they are consulting up-to-date references for advice. Contact the Canadian Intellectual Property Office (CIPO) and Canadian Heritage (see Sources) for the latest information.

International conventions and agreements

11.9   Canada belongs to the two major international copyright conventions, the Berne Convention and the Universal Copyright Convention (UCC), and to various international agreements on intellectual property, including one under the World Trade Organization (WTO). Most nations belong to one or another of these copyright conventions. Canada will continue to revise its copyright laws to keep up with changing international standards and agreements.

The major principle of these agreements is "national treatment": For example, the work of a Canadian copyright owner that is published in another Berne, UCC, or WTO signatory country receives the protection of the copyright laws of that country. In return, the work of a copyright owner in another signatory country receives the protection of Canada's copyright laws in Canada.

11.10　A small and shrinking number of countries have signed the UCC only (about 20, mostly in Central America and the former Soviet Union). To ensure copyright protection in those countries, a Canadian work must be filed or registered in those countries or must carry a copyright notice; see 11.11. As countries sign the Berne Convention, they are listed on the Web site of the World Intellectual Property Organization (WIPO); see *Contracting Parties ...* in Sources.

Registration and notice

11.11　In Canada, copyright protection exists automatically upon the creation of an original work. (For the types of works covered by copyright, see 11.15–17.) The copyright owner does not need to put any mark on the work to indicate ownership, nor register or deposit it with any agency.

However, marking or registering a work establishes the date of creation and may help the owner enforce his or her rights in the work if a dispute arises. In addition, these measures reinforce the importance of copyright, and they may help people who want to use the work to locate the copyright owner in order to seek permission.

Thus a copyright notice, although not obligatory for protection in most countries (see 11.10 for exceptions), is customary. The three elements of a notice are the copyright symbol © or the word **copyright,** the year of publication, and the name of the copyright owner. The word **by** should not be used.

> © 2000 Editors' Association of Canada/Association canadienne des réviseurs

The phrase "All rights reserved" is not required for protection in Canada or the United States.

11.12　Registering copyright in Canada involves filing certain forms with the Copyright Office (see Sources for the address) and paying a fee. No copy of the work is to be deposited. (Legal deposit with the National Library or deposit in a copyright collective is not related to copyright registration.)

11.13 An informal process known as "poor man's copyright" can help to prove copyright at a lower cost than registration with the Copyright Office. The copyright holder sends a copy of the work to himself or herself (or to another prearranged address) by registered mail. The registration receipt plus the parcel, if left *unopened,* can establish date of creation. However, if an ownership dispute goes to court, poor man's copyright gives an owner less protection than formal registration would have provided.

11.14 A work published in Canada is normally given copyright protection in the United States automatically. However, when a work is published simultaneously in Canada and the United States, publishers must register copyright in the United States if they wish to be able to sue for infringement, should the need arise. For more on American copyright registration, see chapter 15 of Lesley Ellen Harris's *Canadian Copyright Law,* chapter 4 of the *Chicago Manual,* and other sources listed at the end of this chapter.

What copyright protects

11.15 Copyright law protects only the *expression* of information or ideas; it does not protect the information or ideas themselves. By using substantially different words or forms of expression, an author or editor can convey the same ideas or information as in someone else's copyright work (see 11.42).

11.16 To be protected by copyright, a work must be *original:* that is, it must not be copied from another work but should originate from the author's independent creative effort, rather than a mechanical or automatic arrangement. It must also be *fixed* in a material form. (Electronic works are "material" once they are saved in any storage medium.)

11.17 These types of works are covered by copyright law, whether published or not, whether produced for profit or not, whether in draft or final form, and whether in handwriting, typescript, or electronic form:
- text: books, articles, brochures, letters, poems, lyrics, translations, indexes, student projects, speech notes or transcriptions, scripts
- illustrations: charts, tables, or diagrams (when the format is original), maps, drawings, design plans, photographs
- works of fine art: paintings, sculptures, etc.
- musical scores
- films, audio- and videotapes, CD-ROMs
- computer programs*

---

* "Public domain software," or "shareware," is protected by copyright but may be downloaded or copied without obtaining permission from the copyright owner.

- electronic texts and databases
- government publications*

What copyright does not protect

11.18   The list of what is *not* covered by copyright law is much smaller:

- names
- slogans
- titles (although original and highly distinctive ones may be covered)
- plots or characters
- ideas
- factual information
- works in which copyright has expired

11.19   Parodies are often successfully challenged in Canadian courts as breaches of copyright, especially when they reproduce too much of the work being parodied. In the United States, by contrast, parody is often protected as "fair use" (see 11.40).

Copyright ownership and duration in Canada

11.20   The starting point for most works protected by Canadian copyright law is that the copyright (including moral rights) in a published work is owned by its creator and, until 50 years after the creator's death, by his or her heirs.

11.21   The creator (or the heirs) can sign a contract to license the economic rights for any specified period, geographical area, or purpose. Less commonly, the rights can be sold (assigned) or given away.

11.22   A copyright that has been assigned by contract reverts to the author's estate 25 years after the author's death. A publisher's licence to use a copyright work automatically becomes invalid at that point unless the author has bequeathed the remaining 25 years of copyright to the publisher in a will. For details and exceptions, see Harris, *Canadian Copyright Law,* and David Vaver, *Copyright Law.*

11.23   Duration of copyright in published works is measured from the *end of the calendar year* of the relevant legal benchmark event, in most but not all cases the author's death. Fifty years later, the copyright expires; the work is then in the "public domain" and anyone can use it. Copyright cannot be renewed in Canada.

---

* Federal statutes and regulations and the decisions of federal courts and tribunals are protected by copyright but may be copied without seeking permission.

11.24 Various exceptions and difficulties under Canadian law are dealt with in this section. *In the absence of a contract to the contrary,* the following general rules apply.

Work created for an employer or client

11.25 Copyright in work created by an employee belongs to the employer. However, the employee remains the "author"* for the purpose of determining the duration of copyright, and the employee retains moral rights. The rule is different for work created by freelancers or consultants: these are independent contractors who retain copyright (but see 11.27).

Copyright disputes often turn on the distinction, not always obvious, between employee and freelancer. Clarifying copyright ownership through a contract *before* the work begins can be helpful to both parties.

Commissioned works

11.26 In three specific categories only – photography, portraits, and what the law calls "engravings" (a term that covers a broad range of artistic works) – the person or corporation who pays for the work owns the copyright. Copyright in other commissioned works is owned by their creators.

Government materials

11.27 Any federal or provincial government or Crown corporation retains copyright ownership of work prepared or published under its direction, including the work of freelancers. Copyright lasts for 50 years after first publication. But like other employees, government employees and freelancers retain moral rights.

Correspondence

11.28 The author of a letter normally holds copyright in its text, even though the recipient possesses the physical object. In the case of a business letter written by an employee, the copyright belongs to the employer.

Translations

11.29 A translator holds copyright in a translation. However, the author of the original work has the right to authorize (or forbid) translation or use of a translation; unauthorized translations infringe the author's copyright.

---

* "Author" is the term used in legislation to refer to all creators in all media, including photographers, musicians, advertising copywriters, and so on, as long as they are natural persons. Corporations can be "owners" but not "authors," except of photography (see 11.32).

Unpublished and posthumous written works

11.30   Before the Phase II amendments, copyright in unpublished written works lasted in perpetuity, and posthumously published works were protected for 50 years after first publication.

Under provisions that came into effect on December 31, 1998, works published posthumously and works unpublished at the author's death have the same terms of copyright as most other works: 50 years after the author's death.

The new provisions apply to the works of authors who died since 1998. For the works of authors who died before 1998, transitional provisions apply:

Author's death	First publication	Copyright expires
1948 or before	after author's death but before 1999	50 years after first publication
	1999 or after	December 31, 2003
	never published	December 31, 2003
1949–98	after author's death but before 1999	50 years after first publication
	1999 or after	December 31, 2048
	never published	December 31, 2048

Works of unknown authors

11.31   The difficulty or even impossibility of finding an unknown author does not change the fact of the copyright. Copyright protection lasts for 50 years after first publication or 75 years after a work's creation, whichever is the earlier. If no dates are known and the author cannot be identified, the provisions for seeking permission from unlocatable owners apply (see 11.51).

Photographs

11.32   As with other works, the author of a photograph is the first owner of copyright in it. But "author" has a particular definition in regard to photographs.

The author of a photograph is defined for copyright purposes not as the photographer but as the owner of the negative (or original photograph when there is no negative) at the time the photo was taken. Often that owner is indeed the photographer, but in many common situations the author is another party:

- When a photograph is commissioned, the person or corporation paying the commission is the author and owns the copyright.

- When the photographer is an employee, the employer is the author and normally owns the copyright.

The author, whether a person or a corporation, retains moral rights.

The duration of copyright is determined by whether the author is an individual or a corporation:

- When the author is an individual (or a corporation with the author as its majority shareowner), the copyright of the photograph lasts for 50 years after the author's death.

- When the author is a corporation (one where the author is not the majority shareowner), the copyright of the photograph lasts for 50 years after it was taken.

Copyright ownership and duration in the United States, United Kingdom, and Europe

11.33 U.S. copyright law differs from Canadian law in some important aspects of ownership and duration:

- In the United States, federal government documents are in the public domain.

- The employer rather than the employee is deemed to be the author (as well as the owner) of works created in the course of employment and therefore retains moral rights.

- The duration of copyright under American law differs in many circumstances from parallel situations under Canadian law; often it is longer. Major changes in American copyright law that took effect in 1978 make any further generalizations difficult. In 1998 most 50-year copyrights in the United States were extended by law to 70 years. See the *Chicago Manual* and Sources to find detailed information on American copyrights.

11.34 European countries and the United Kingdom also have different durations of copyright than Canada. Most commonly, copyright in those countries lasts 70 years beyond the author's death.

USING COPYRIGHT MATERIAL

When permission is essential

11.35 A wide gap exists between what is considered legal copyright practice in the courts and what is thought to be acceptable in everyday use. This section presents information that may differ from the guidelines followed by individual editors and publishers.

11.36 In Canada, copying a work or a "substantial" part of a work without the consent of the copyright owner is an infringement. The limited exceptions are discussed at 11.40.

There is a widespread belief in Canadian publishing that quotes consisting of fewer than 50 words may be reproduced without the permission of the copyright owner. This belief is not supported by Canadian law, nor is any rule of thumb that depends upon a specific number of words or percentage of the text. The crucial factor is not the number of words but the significance of the words or the proportion of the work the quotation represents *in the context of the particular work quoted.* A quote of 20 words could be "substantial" if, for example, it is an entire poem or represents the core of a Ph.D. thesis. Even an original and highly distinctive book title could be protected because of this concept of substantiality. The only safe generalization is: When in doubt, request permission.

11.37 Permission to use copyright material must be obtained regardless of whether any revenue is expected or derived from the use.

Fees and acknowledgment

11.38 Giving credit to the copyright owner does not constitute licence to reproduce material without written permission.

11.39 The fee or royalty for reproducing copyright material is set by the copyright owner. The copyright owner may also specify the wording of the acknowledgment of the copyright.

When permission is not needed

Fair dealing

11.40 The "fair dealing" provision allows copyright work to be quoted briefly for purposes of private study, research, criticism, review, or news reporting. Permission need not be sought, but the author and source must be identified. Most authorities consider fair dealing doctrine applicable to published works only. The law in this area is extremely imprecise, creating a level of uncertainty that, remarks David Vaver, "favours only those with deep pockets."

It is important to note that fair dealing is not the same as "fair use," which is an American doctrine. Although there are some similarities, the American fair use provision is worded more loosely and interpreted more broadly than fair dealing, so it allows more and different uses of copyright material than does fair dealing. For instance, "fair use" in American law allows multiple copying for classroom use in some cases, whereas Canadian "fair dealing" does not.

The copycat plague

11.41 Plagiarism is more an ethical than a legal concept. A university or a business may prohibit plagiarism through a policy or code of ethics, defining it as, for example, not only substantial copying but excessive reliance on the work of others. Although using someone else's ideas does not violate copyright, it could be plagiarism under such a policy.

Paraphrasing

11.42 As noted in 11.18, because information and ideas themselves are not subject to copyright, it is legitimate for authors and editors to paraphrase passages from copyright work in order to eliminate the need to seek permission. A *substantially* different expression of the same information does not require permission (although acknowledgment of the source may be expected on ethical grounds).

Audiotapes for private use

11.43 As of March 1998, a person may make a single copy of an audiotape for private use. Multiple copying without a licence remains prohibited.

Non-material forms

11.44 To be regarded as an infringement, reproduction of a work must be fixed in material form. Thus singing a copyright song in the shower does not violate copyright law, but making a photocopy of the score does.

Public domain

11.45 It is not necessary to obtain permission to reproduce works in the public domain (works in which copyright has expired).

Certain federal documents

11.46 Federal statutes, regulations, and court decisions, although under Crown copyright, may be copied without permission.

Exemptions for non-profit institutions

11.47 Non-profit schools, libraries, museums, and archives were exempted from certain provisions of copyright law as of September 1999. The exemptions are specific and very limited. Teachers in non-profit schools, for instance, may copy text onto a blackboard, but without a licence they are still not permitted to copy "handouts" of copyright materials. Non-profit libraries, museums, and archives may, among other things, copy works that must be repaired or replaced because of physical deterioration; and they may make single copies of documents for researchers. For details of the most recent provisions, see the Canadian Heritage or CIPO Web site.

Seeking permission

11.48 Permission or licence to use copyright material may be sought from the copyright owner or from a person or agency to whom the rights have been legitimately transferred: for instance, the publisher, a lawyer, an agent, or an heir.

11.49 A request for permission to reproduce copyright material in another work should be made in writing and should include the information in Figure 11.1.

Figure 11.1 Permission request checklist

About the work to be reproduced:

- title (and title of source, if the work was not published on its own)
- author or creator (of work and source work, if applicable)
- copyright notice
- other facts of publication, if applicable
- number of pages, word count, or other indication of extent or dimensions of the material you wish to reproduce; attach a photocopy if possible
- any proposed alterations (attach to request)

About the forthcoming new work:

- title
- author, editor, or creator
- publisher and publication date
- number of pages, print run, and price (or other indications of your intended use of the work and what benefit, if any, you will derive from that use)

- current or future editions
- language(s) and territories in which the work will be published or distributed

All correspondence and notes of telephone calls, meetings, etc., relating to permission requests should be filed carefully with the publisher.

11.50 Permission to use material prepared by or under the direction of the federal government should be sought from the department responsible, or from Public Works and Government Services Canada (see Sources). Permission to use provincial government materials should be sought from the department responsible or, in Quebec, from Copibec (see Sources). For permission to use the work of Crown corporations, contact the specific corporation.

Finding the unlocatable copyright owner

11.51 Every editor who has handled a permissions file has encountered the frustration of searching for unlocatable copyright owners. For any of dozens of reasons, letters requesting permission go unanswered or are forwarded to an endless chain of addresses.

Copyright for works published in Canada may be registered at the Copyright Office, but since registration is not obligatory, the register is not comprehensive. However, publishers who are unsuccessful in locating copyright owners may apply to the Copyright Board, a related agency. If the board is satisfied that every reasonable effort has been made, it may issue a licence for use of the material in Canada only.

11.52 Publishers frequently include on the acknowledgments page a formula such as: "Every reasonable effort has been made to locate and acknowledge the owners of copyright material reproduced in this volume. The publishers would welcome any information regarding errors or omissions." Such a disclaimer does not absolve the publisher of responsibility for compensating copyright owners, but it demonstrates the publisher's good faith and may help to settle any disputes over ownership more amicably.

11.53 It is important to recall that the death of the author does not end the copyright. Although it sometimes becomes difficult to trace rights after the author's death, those rights remain in force for 50 years in most cases.

Collectives

11.54 CANCOPY, the Canadian Copyright Licensing Agency/Canadian Reprography Collective, grants permission, sets conditions, and collects royalties for photocopying of the published materials in its repertoire (e.g., by schools and universities). Copibec acts as the parallel agency in Quebec. Both organizations have relationships with counterparts in the United States and abroad.

11.55   The Electronic Rights Licensing Agency, TERLA, represents writers, photographers, and illustrators in collective negotiations with commercial publishers who use electronic media. TERLA members can also license the agency to negotiate fees for electronic use of individual copyright works. CANCOPY is also involved in electronic licensing, but with non-commercial users of copyright material.

TRADEMARKS

11.56   Trademarks are words and design elements, such as logos and packages, that a company uses to give distinctive identities to its goods and services. Trademarks may be registered with the federal government, but registration is not required in order for the mark to be protected by law. The company's own name, called a **trade name,** may also be a trademark. **Brand name** is a non-legal term for a trademark.

11.57   Many publishers prefer to substitute generic terms for trademarks when the context allows:

> soft drink or cola *for* Coca-Cola
>
> jeans *for* Levi's
>
> plastic wrap *for* Saran Wrap
>
> photocopy *for* Xerox

The Canadian Press Stylebook lists many generic equivalents as well as a number of former trademarks that are now unprotected and in the public domain. These include **escalator, nylon,** and **raisin bran.** The *CPS* (*Compendium of Pharmaceuticals and Specialties*) lists generic as well as brand names for drugs.

11.58   If a trademark – registered or unregistered – must be specified, use the owner's preferred style:

> Her cold-fighting artillery was on her night table: Extra-Strength Tylenol, a box of Kleenex (the big ones), echinacea, grapefruit juice, and a Harlequin romance.

However, if the owner's style is to use lowercase, all caps, italics, or other graphic flourishes for the mark, a reference in ordinary text may be styled with standard capitalization and type treatment.

> When he was 12, he seemed to live on Pop-Tarts [*not* pop-tarts].
>
> Scrabble [*not* SCRABBLE] games at Lisa's last all night.

11.59   The owner of a mark uses ® if the mark is registered, or ™ if it is unregistered, to indicate its intention to defend the mark. No one else is required to use these symbols.

11.60   A name trademarked in one country might not be trademarked in another. Aspirin, for example, is a trademark in Canada (and uppercased) but not in the United States, where it is now a generic term (and lowercased). To check trademarks for use in Canadian materials, use Canadian references.

   • *Canadian Trade-marks Database:* A searchable online database of registered trade names and marks maintained by the federal government. <strategis.ic.gc.ca/sc_consu/trade-marks/engdoc/cover.html>

   • *Canadian Trade Index:* A searchable database of both registered and unregistered trade names and marks, available online and on CD-ROM. (The print version of the *CTI* no longer lists trade names and marks.) Because participation in the *CTI* is voluntary, it may not be comprehensive. However, it is well established as an authoritative Canadian reference, sponsored for decades by a trade group. <www.ctidirectory.com>

11.61   Using an occasional trademark in most types of writing poses little or no legal risk. But associating one company's trademark with another company's products in a promotional or advertising context – "Try Dandy Diskettes, the Rolls-Royce of storage media" – may well attract the trademark owner's unfavourable attention. As well, derogatory references to a trademark could be construed as defamation.

LIBEL

Statutes and jurisdictions

11.62   Libel law is a provincial matter in Canada; Quebec law differs significantly from that of other provinces and territories. Also, editors should be aware that libel law in the United States is substantially different from Canadian laws, and several principles applicable there have no counterparts in Canada.

11.63   Editors should familiarize themselves with the statute in their province, usually called Libel and Slander Act or Defamation Act. (In *The Journalist's Legal Guide,* Michael Crawford highlights some of the most significant differences among provinces.) Of particular relevance is each statute's definition of the types of publications it governs. As a rule, provincial laws cover broadcast media, newspapers, and some periodicals. All other media, including books, are subject to common law (the accumulation of court decisions on similar matters).

11.64   Editors and publishers sometimes need to be aware of several varieties of libel law as they prepare for publication. A suit can be brought in any jurisdiction to which a plaintiff or a defendant can demonstrate a connection of sufficient significance to satisfy a judge. Potential plaintiffs may live or work in jurisdictions other than the province or country where the work will be published; the author may have a different home base than the publisher; a work may be published in several countries.

Parties to a suit

11.65   In theory, a number of people can be named as defendants in a libel suit – the author, the editor, the publisher, the printer, and the vendor. Often editors are named primarily so that they may be questioned by the plaintiff's lawyers as they gather evidence in examinations for discovery: if the matter proceeds to trial, editors who can offer proof of having exercised care (preferably in the form of written documentation) are unlikely to be held personally liable. (Also, the sensible plaintiff does not sue the impecunious.)

   Normally an editor named in a suit will be treated by the publisher as part of the defence "team" and will not need independent legal advice. However, editors working on sensitive projects would be well advised to check in advance whether the publisher's libel insurance will cover them.

Costs of a libel case

11.66   The costs of defending a libel suit can be considerable, even if the suit fails or is dropped. A publisher may have to withhold, withdraw, or alter a work as a precaution while a legal battle is under way. Legal fees may exceed insurable ceilings. A great deal of time will be diverted from other tasks.

   The costs of settlement may include a substantial payment by the defendant. And a victory for the plaintiff is almost certain to cost the defendant damages as well as compensation to the plaintiff's side for much of their costs.

What constitutes libel?

11.67   In law, a person has a right to her or his good name and a right to defend that name against defamation, which is defined as any statement, written or spoken, or any picture or representation that subjects a person to hatred, ridicule, or contempt. Defamation is an attack on a person's character that attributes to the person some form of disgraceful conduct – dishonesty, cruelty, sexual misbehaviour, irresponsibility, and the like – in either personal or professional concerns.

Defamation and libel are essentially interchangeable terms. (Slander is not likely to be an issue for editors because it refers to a spoken defamation, unpublished by definition.)

11.68 A libel may be unintentional. For example, a pseudonym or the name of a fictional character may turn out to be the name of a real person. If damaging things are said about the character or the person behind the pseudonym and there are other similarities in circumstance, the real person with that name may suffer embarrassment or harm and may have a libel case.

In non-fiction, pseudonyms should be obvious ("Jane Doe") or labelled ("not his real name"). In fiction, when a manuscript editor sees a character with defamatory attributes, it's wise to ask whether the writer has based the character on a real person. Some measures can then be taken to ensure that the identity is adequately disguised: for instance, fictional names can be checked against references such as professional directories, and legal advice can be sought. Unfortunately, disastrous coincidences can still occur, and they can cause just as much damage as statements made deliberately.

11.69 Although one cannot libel a class of persons, a collection of identifiable persons, such as members of a family or of a firm, can be libelled and can sue individually. And although no suit for libel can be brought on behalf of a dead person (except possibly in Quebec), a defamatory statement about a dead person may also damage the reputation of a surviving relative or associate.

Defences against libel

11.70 The principal defences against a charge of libel are three: justification, fair comment, and privilege. If any one defence succeeds, the plaintiff fails.

Justification

11.71 A statement is not libellous if it is true, a defence that the law calls "justification." For purposes of the law, not only must it be true but the defendants (author and publisher) must be able to prove its truth with evidence adequate to satisfy a court (on a balance of probabilities). If the truth of the statement can be established, the plaintiff has no case.

In practice, proving the truth of a statement is often costly and difficult. Witnesses and documents must be available, reliable, and credible, sometimes long after the events in question. With time, memories become clouded and perspectives may change. Editors who expect to rely upon a defence of justification would be wise to examine the writer's evidence thoroughly before publication. "Confidential sources" require the editor's particular attention. When a source will not come forward or a writer will not name a source, the defendants may gain a splendid moral victory for the principle of confidentiality but lose a libel suit.

Fair comment

11.72 The defence of fair comment allows public criticism of creative works, public statements, and the like that are offered to the community for its consideration. With this defence, the comment in question may actually be defamatory, but if it is found to be fair comment (and there is no malice), the case can be dismissed. A number of elements must be present in order to support such a defence.

11.73 First, the statement must be about a matter of public interest or concern. A gratuitous insult or hurtful observation ("She's a mean and spiteful woman whose word cannot be trusted") about a private person who is not offering either his or her character or works for public appraisal cannot be defended as fair comment, because there is no public interest in publishing it.

> "They can say I'm a fat old sod, they can say I'm an untalented bastard, they can call me a poof, but they mustn't lie about me."
>
> – Elton John, upon settling a 1988 libel suit against a British tabloid

11.74 Second, fair comment does not allow people to say anything they want just because they present their thoughts as an "opinion." The comment, although itself an opinion, must be *based on* provable facts. In addition, those facts must be stated in the same context (e.g., in the same book, article, or brochure) as the opinion. A defamatory allegation without a presentation of facts to support the conclusion is not defensible, unless the facts are so widely known as to be "notorious." And if the supposed facts supporting the opinion cannot be proven to be true, the opinion cannot be defended as fair comment.

Note that the fair comment defence cannot be applied to statements of fact. A comment such as "Bloggs is not fit to hold an office of trust" may appear to be stated as a fact, and Bloggs may be able to insist that it be proved to that more stringent standard in court. When such comments are intended to be read as opinion, editors can suggest wording such as "I think" or "It seems" that may help to emphasize the distinction between opinion and fact.

11.75 Further, the comment or opinion damaging to the plaintiff must be honestly believed by the defendant. Even if it seems wrong to others, the comment is fair if the judge can see the possible connection between the opinion and the underlying facts.

11.76　A final restriction pertains to malice. A statement made with malice cannot be defended as fair comment. (If a statement can be successfully defended as true, malice is irrelevant; see 11.71.)

In law, malice involves not only personal ill will or spite but also motives of personal advantage disguised as comment in the public interest. Moreover, it does not mean only the wish to do harm; a reckless disregard of whether harm is done (e.g., the deliberate omission of inconvenient facts) is also construed as malice.

11.77　In Quebec law, the concept of fault – the failure to exercise that degree of care for the interests of others that the law requires – also affects the definition of fair comment.

Privilege

11.78　Under certain circumstances it is considered in the public interest that a person who makes defamatory statements be immune from the charge of libel even though the statements cannot be proved true or defended as fair comment.

11.79　"Absolute" privilege is the protection given to statements made before or during court proceedings. People who make potentially damaging statements in court or in court documents are protected, and so are reporters and publishers recounting these statements as long as their accounts are fair, accurate, without comment, and published contemporaneously. A publisher relying upon this privilege must print, when requested, any response to these statements from people who say they have been damaged by them. The requirement of contemporaneous reporting and of the right of response means that absolute privilege is unlikely to be available to book publishers.

11.80　"Qualified" privilege attaches to the reporting of proceedings of parliamentary or legislative bodies (including municipal councils) and public administrative bodies, and of public meetings of corporations and associations. The same privilege pertains to documents published by these bodies. Reports of these proceedings or publications must be fair and accurate and – a condition not required when absolute privilege applies – without malice (see 11.76).

11.81　Editors should note that a statement protected by absolute privilege upon first publication may not be absolutely privileged upon a later occasion. What appears, for example, in contemporaneous daily newspaper accounts of a trial may be protected by absolute privilege. A later book about that event may be unable to quote those accounts with the same privilege; but qualified privilege remains available if the account is fair, accurate, and without malice (see 11.76).

11.82 The availability of privilege as a defence will often rest less upon the details of what was said than upon interpretations of the circumstances in which it was said. For instance, a shareholders' meeting may be widely considered a "public" meeting if the media are let in; but the corporation can say the meeting was private since it was held by and for shareholders only. The definition of "contemporaneous" may become an issue for a monthly magazine whose stories about a trial cannot be printed as quickly as a daily newspaper's. Editors who expect to call upon privilege as a defence will need a good understanding of the topic and, in all likelihood, legal advice.

Responsibilities of editors and publishers

11.83 Editors are not expected to be legal experts. They can, however, identify in a manuscript any statements that might present a legal risk and draw those statements to the attention of the publisher so that legal opinion can be sought.

11.84 Even before the manuscript is written, it can be valuable for the author and the editor to discuss with a lawyer the general concepts and theses of a sensitive project. At this stage a lawyer can advise the author of potential pitfalls and suggest what supporting material should be accumulated as the research and writing proceeds.

Keeping records

11.85 In the case of a statement broadcast electronically or published in a newspaper, notice of libel must normally be served within six weeks of when the statement comes to the complainant's attention. (Definitions and time limits vary from province to province; the definition of magazines and periodicals is especially unclear.) As noted in 11.63, books and any other publications not covered by statutes are subject to a different legal regime: a suit can be brought as long as six years after the work is published or comes to the complainant's attention. Publishers should maintain files and archives accordingly.

11.86 Publishers and writers should keep all notes, tapes, and other material that can demonstrate the efforts they have made to ensure accuracy. They have no particular obligation to keep archives of materials that were *not* used to produce the eventual publication: out-takes, early drafts, unused research, for instance. Publishers should establish standard procedures for filing or discarding such material and should follow them in every instance. Robert Martin writes in *Media Law,* "What must be avoided is destroying or erasing such material under circumstances where it could be alleged that this was done with the purpose of preventing it becoming evidence in a judicial proceeding."

Drafts that are reviewed by a lawyer should be labelled as such and, like all legal advice, should be kept strictly confidential. If retained in files, these documents are protected by solicitor-client privilege against being divulged to the defence or called into evidence.

PUBLICATION BANS

11.87 Publication of certain material is banned entirely by statutes such as the Official Secrets Act and legislation governing judicial treatment of young offenders. In other criminal matters, bans may be applied to certain phases of a trial or in particular circumstances as ordered by a judge.

11.88 Violation of publication bans amounts to contempt of court: an act or statement that may interfere with the administration of justice.

11.89 Information that might be prejudicial to the outcome of a case is often the subject of publication bans: for example, comment on the character and past criminal record of an accused, other than what has been presented as evidence during a trial. Journalists covering the courts need detailed knowledge of these conventions, and their editors would benefit from familiarity with them, too (see Crawford, *The Journalist's Legal Guide*).

11.90 Timing is often crucial in the decision about what to publish. As in the case of privileged statements, book publishers work in a different legal framework than news media. A publication ban that prohibits the reporting of a defendant's previous convictions during a jury trial will no longer be in effect by the time a book about that trial goes to press, because the trial will probably be over. But a book that reveals prejudicial information about a person before a trial may risk contempt if it is released too close to the trial date.

BREACH OF CONFIDENCE

11.91 A breach of confidence occurs when a person discloses information obtained under an agreement of privacy that derives from the person's position (such as doctor, employer or employee, or public official).

BREACH OF TRADE SECRETS

11.92 A breach of trade secrets occurs when an employee or former employee discloses information that is the property of the employer (such as formulas, processes, client lists).

INVASION OF PRIVACY

11.93   Existing "privacy" legislation mostly outlines the obligation of governments to keep confidential the personal information they have lawfully collected from citizens.

11.94   Laws in four provinces (British Columbia, Manitoba, Newfoundland, and Saskatchewan) dealing with a wider "right to privacy" – a right to keep one's private life out of the media – are relatively new and untested. On the whole, the few cases under these laws as of late 1999 suggest that a strong public interest will justify an invasion of personal privacy. Quebec's privacy laws, also quite recent, seem more restrictive. See Martin, *Media Law,* for a survey of privacy law as of 1997.

SOURCES

Contracting Parties of Treaties Administered by WIPO: Berne Convention [online]. World Intellectual Property Organization (WIPO). [Cited February 17, 2000.] Status as of December 20, 1999. <www.wipo.int/eng/ratific/e-berne.htm>.

Crawford, Michael G. *The Journalist's Legal Guide.* 3rd ed. Scarborough, Ont.: Carswell/Thomson Professional Publishing, 1996.

A Guide to Copyrights. A new edition of this valuable booklet, previously published by Public Works and Government Services Canada in print and electronic formats, is expected in 2000; publication details were not yet confirmed as *Editing Canadian English* went to press. Contact the Canadian Intellectual Property Office (see below).

Harris, Lesley Ellen. *Canadian Copyright Law.* 2nd ed. Toronto: McGraw-Hill Ryerson, 1995. A third edition is expected in 2000.

Law and the Media Series, edited by Stuart H. Robertson. Five short books containing detailed, accessible information on case law, published by the Canadian Bar Association in 1984–86. To order, phone the CBA in Ottawa at 1-800-267-8860.

Martin, Robert. *Media Law.* Concord, Ont.: Irwin Law, 1997. Essentials of Canadian Law Series.

Vaver, David. *Copyright Law.* Toronto: Irwin Law, 2000. Essentials of Canadian Law Series.

————. *Intellectual Property Law.* Concord, Ont.: Irwin Law, 1997. Essentials of Canadian Law Series.

Organizations and agencies

Canadian Copyright Licensing Agency (CANCOPY)
1 Yonge St., Suite 1900
Toronto, ON M5E 1E5
Tel. (416) 868-1620 or 1-800-893-5777; fax (416) 868-1621
<www.cancopy.com>

Canadian Heritage
Copyright Policy Directorate
15 Eddy St., 4th floor
Hull, QC K1A 0M5
Tel. (819) 997-5990; fax (819) 997-5685
<www.pch.gc.ca/culture/cult_ind/copyright.htm>

Canadian Intellectual Property Office (CIPO)
and Copyright Office
Industry Canada
50 Victoria St.
Place du Portage I
Hull, QC K1A 0C9
Tel. (819) 997-1936; fax (819) 953-7620
<cipo.gc.ca> or <strategis.ic.gc.ca/sc_mrksv/cipo/welcome/welcom-e.html>

Copyright Board
56 Sparks St., Suite 800
Ottawa, ON K1A 0C9
Tel. (613) 952-8621; fax (613) 952-8630
<www.cb-cda.gc.ca>

The Electronic Rights Licensing Agency (TERLA)
1 Yonge St., Suite 1900
Toronto, ON M5E 1E5
Tel. (416) 868-0200 or 1-877-557-4616; fax (416) 868-0296
<www.terla.com>

Public Works and Government Services Canada
Crown Copyright Officer
Canadian Government Publishing
350 Albert St., 4th floor
Ottawa, ON K1A 0S5
Tel. (613) 990-2210; fax (613) 998-1450

Société québécoise de gestion collective des droits de reproduction
(Copibec)
1290, rue Saint-Denis, 7ᵉ étage
Montreal, QC H2X 3J7
Tel. (514) 288-1664 or 1-800-717-2022; fax (514) 288-1669
<www.copibec.qc.ca>

United States Copyright Office
Information Section, LM-401
Library of Congress
Washington, DC 20559
Tel. (202) 707-3000; fax (202) 707-6859
<lcweb.loc.gov/copyright>

CHAPTER 12

Et Alia

This chapter presents an alphabetical list of terms that are of special interest in the Canadian context or of general interest in English-language usage.

12.1   **a /an:** In speech, many Canadians suppress the **h** in **historical** and thus say **an** rather than **a** before it. Some treat similarly other words that have an unstressed first syllable beginning with **h** (**hallucination, habitual, hermetic, holistic, hysterical**). Since the habit is highly idiosyncratic, its reproduction in written work creates a major problem of consistency. The editor should normally regard this **an** as a phenomenon of speech and change it to **a** in text.

ABORIGINAL PEOPLES

12.2   A collective name for the original peoples of Canada and their descendants. The Constitution Act, 1982, specifies that the aboriginal peoples in Canada consist of three groups: Indians, Inuit, and Métis. "Indian" is losing favour as a term; however, it remains in the Indian Act, in definitions of Status, Non-Status, Treaty, and Registered Indians, and is used by many in self-reference.

Indians

12.3   Canada makes a legal distinction between **Status Indians** and **Non-Status Indians.** Status Indians are individuals who have legal status as Indian. Who is and who is not a Status Indian and who is eligible and ineligible for status are defined by the Indian Act, a federal statute that governs most administrative aspects of life on reserves in Canada. Status Indians are listed on the official Indian Registry in Ottawa and are issued numbered status cards by the federal government. Status Indians derive social and economic benefits such as subsidized housing and tax exemption on any income derived from employment on the reserve. Many of the benefits that Status Indians receive are the result of treaties or specific federal government policies.

12.4   As a result of changes made to the Indian Act in 1985, a man or woman marrying a Status Indian does not automatically gain Indian status, nor will their children. Before the 1985 changes, only a woman (regardless of her own heritage) who married a man with Indian status would herself have Indian status, as would their children. The 1985 changes also allow a woman with Indian status to keep it if she marries a Non-Status man, and their children also have status. Moreover, women who had earlier lost their status by "marrying out" can reclaim it, although some nevertheless have difficulty in regaining acceptance within the band.

12.5   **Non-Status Indians** are individuals who for various reasons no longer possess Indian status. The absence of status in no way affects their "Indianness," but it does prevent them from owning land on a reserve and receiving benefits that Status Indians receive from the federal government. Non-Status Indians are not normally prohibited from residing on a reserve, but the majority reside off-reserve.

12.6   Those Status Indians who are direct descendants of native peoples who signed a treaty with Canada or with the Crown before Confederation are known as **Treaty Indians.**

12.7   The term **Registered Indians** refers to Status Indians who are either direct descendants of native peoples who did not sign treaties or have not signed a treaty themselves either with Canada or with the Crown before Confederation. Their status as Indians derives from their presence on the official Indian Registry in Ottawa.

12.8   **Band** refers to a specific group of people who reside on a reserve (e.g., the Burns Lake band). Some band members may reside off-reserve and still retain membership in (belong to) the band. There are more than 600 bands in Canada. Many bands are choosing to resurrect their traditional names as replacements for the Eurocentric names and spellings that many explorers, clergy, and fur traders graciously bestowed on their bewildered hosts during the seventeenth and eighteenth centuries. Some examples include Kahnawake for Caughnawaga, Mnjikaning for Rama, and Siksika for Blackfoot. Occasionally, several different contemporary spellings are emerging or have emerged for a band or other grouping to the confusion of many people, including members affected by the changes. A thorough listing of all First Nations bands in Canada can be found at <esd.inac.gc.ca/fnprofiles/FNProfiles_Search.htm> (First Nations Profiles, Department of Indian and Northern Affairs, 1999).

12.9   A **reserve** is land held in trust for a band by the federal government. A band may possess several reserves in addition to the one where band members reside. Normally, only members of a band who have Indian status may own land on the reserve. Ownership of reserve land is either collective (owned by the band) or individual. Owners of reserve land are provided with a Certificate of Possession (commonly referred to as a CP) in lieu of a deed to verify ownership. They can lease their land to anyone, but they are legally prevented from selling land to anyone except other band members. There are 2400 reserves in Canada. The equivalent term for reserve in the United States is **reservation.**

12.10   The **tribe** comprises people who share a language and culture (e.g., the Iroquois tribe or Ojibway tribe). In Canada, **nation** is used in the same sense. Recently, numerous bands throughout Canada have established administrative and political organizations that are referred to as **tribal councils.** They usually consist of several bands that share a geographical proximity in addition to a common language and traditional culture. A list of tribal councils and their member bands can be found at <www.aboriginalcanada.com/firstnation/> (First Nation Information Project, Johnco Group, 1999).

Métis

12.11   The Métis (or Metis) – individuals who are part Indian and part "other" – are one of the three aboriginal peoples recognized by the Canadian Constitution. Historically, Métis emerged from the unions of women from many different Indian tribes and Englishmen, Scotsmen, and Frenchmen. Today, the term is used broadly to describe people with mixed Indian and European ancestry who identify themselves as Métis, distinct from First Nations, Inuit, or non-aboriginal people. Although many Canadians have mixed aboriginal and non-aboriginal ancestry, not all identify themselves as Métis.

12.12   **Half-breed** is a term that is used by some Métis to self-identify. Some Métis regard it and **breed** as pejorative.

Inuit

12.13   The Inuit are the aboriginal people of Arctic Canada. They traditionally lived above the treeline in the area bordered by the Mackenzie Delta in the west, the Labrador coast in the east, the southern shores of Hudson Bay in the south, and the High Arctic Islands in the north. **Inuit** means "the people" in **Inuktitut,** the Inuit language, and it is the term by which the Inuit refer to themselves. An **Inuk** is one Inuit male; an **Inuuk** is one Inuit female. The term "Eskimo," reputedly an Algonkian word for "people who eat raw meat," which early European explorers and Algonkian speakers applied to the Inuit, is no longer commonly used in Canada, although it is common in Alaska.

12.14 There are four principal Inuit settlement areas in Canada: Inuvialuit, Nunavik, Nunavut, and Labrador. Inuvialuit is in the western Arctic and Nunavik in northern Quebec. Nunavut, which became an official territory in 1999, includes three separate settlement areas: Kivalliq, the Keewatin; Kitikmeot, the central Arctic; and Qikiqtaaluk, Baffin Island and the High Arctic Islands. The capital of Nunavut is Iqaluit on Baffin Island.

Note that the Innu of Labrador are not Inuit but rather Cree peoples also known as Naskapi and Montagnais.

collective terms

12.15 The terms **natives** and **native people** have been used widely in reference to the aboriginal people of Canada. While they are still used throughout Canada by aboriginal and non-aboriginal people alike, they are gradually being displaced by the term **aboriginal people** as a collective term, and by **First Nations, Inuit,** and **Métis** to refer to the three aboriginal peoples. Yet there is ongoing debate about which expression refers to whom, and which terms to capitalize (see 8.15–16 and 8.21).

12.16 **First Nations** refers to the people previously referred to as Indians, although the term is not accepted by all Indians throughout Canada. Despite enormous differences in their cultural traditions, political histories, and languages, all First Nations throughout Canada shared several commonalities: they depended on the land for their survival; they were self-governing in that they possessed

> "Whatever term one uses, there will almost certainly be someone who takes exception to it."
>
> – J.R. Miller, "Aboriginals: Introduction," in *Encyclopedia of Canada's Peoples*

separate and independent political, social, and economic institutions; and they engaged in trade and commerce that often extended beyond the present national borders.

12.17 The **Alliance of Manufacturers & Exporters Canada** resulted from a merger of the Canadian Manufacturers' Association and the Canadian Exporters' Association in May 1996.

12.18   Many Canadian **arts awards** are listed in *Sources* and the *Canadian Almanac & Directory*. See also 12.54, "Governor General's Literary Awards."

12.19   **August holiday:** The first Monday in August is celebrated as a holiday in most provinces but comes in many guises: it's Civic Holiday in Manitoba, Saskatchewan, the Northwest Territories, and Ontario (except in Toronto, where it's Simcoe Day); Heritage Day in Alberta; British Columbia Day in British Columbia; New Brunswick Day in New Brunswick; Natal Day in Prince Edward Island and Nova Scotia. Yukon prefers the third Monday for its Discovery Day. St. John's celebrates August 18 as its Civic Holiday, while the rest of Newfoundland does what it wants. Quebec abstains.

12.20   **AWOL (absent without leave):** AWL is no longer the first choice.

12.21   **Bank of Canada:** Canada's central bank is responsible for Canadian monetary policy. It issues bank notes, regulates and supports Canada's principal systems for clearing and settling payments, and acts as a fiscal agent for federal government debt. It does not take deposits, nor does it have branches; <www.bank-banque-Canada.ca>.

12.22   **Beige Paper:** A document prepared by the Quebec Liberal Party during the referendum debate of 1980. Its actual title was *A New Canadian Federation*.

12.23   **Bi and Bi Commission or B and B Commission:** Informal term for the Royal Commission on Bilingualism and Biculturalism (1963–71).

12.24   **Business Development Bank of Canada:** Abbreviated BDC (in both French and English), not BDBC.

12.25   **Canadian Armed Forces:** Made up of Land Force Command, Maritime Command, and Air Command. The bill uniting the forces was passed in May 1967. As of February 1968 the Canadian Army, Royal Canadian Navy, and Royal Canadian Air Force were no longer legally recognized as separate entities. Although **Canadian Armed Forces** remains the complete title and is displayed on most military aircraft, **Canadian Forces** or **CF** is far more commonly used within the organization.

12.26   **Canadian Bill of Rights:** Enacted in 1960 under Prime Minister John Diefenbaker. It applied to federal law only and was not entrenched in the Constitution. When encountered in a post-1982 context, the phrase "Bill of Rights" is often a misnomer for the Canadian Charter of Rights and Freedoms (see 12. 39).

12.27 **Canadian National (CN) and Canadian Pacific (CP):** The Canadian Pacific Railway (CPR) was incorporated in 1880 to build the first transcontinental railway in Canada. Its "last spike" was driven in 1885. The company has since expanded into shipping, real estate, resource development, and hotels and resorts, among other ventures. The parent company is now called Canadian Pacific Limited.

Canadian National Railways was formed by the federal government to consolidate the operations of five railways. It was incorporated in 1919. It too expanded into other industries. CN was privatized in 1995. At the time of writing, CN and Burlington Santa Fe Corp. plan to join into a new company. If the plan receives the necessary approvals, the carrier will be called North American Railways Inc.

12.28 **Canadian Radio-television and Telecommunications Commission (CRTC).**

12.29 **Carleton:** Sir Guy ~; ~ University; ~ Place (Ont.); ~ County (Ottawa area); Mount ~ (N.B.).

12.30 **Carlton:** Ritz-~; ~ (Sask.); ~ St. (Toronto).

12.31 **Cartier, George-Étienne (or George Étienne):** *Not* Georges.

12.32 **Cataloguing in Publication (CIP):** A voluntary program whereby Canadian books are catalogued and the cataloguing information distributed to librarians and booksellers before the books are published. For information, contact: CIP Coordinator, National Library of Canada, 395 Wellington St., Ottawa, ON K1A 0N4; tel. (819) 994-6881; fax (819) 997-7517; <cip@nlc-bcn.ca>.

12.33 **-ceed/-cede/-sede:** accede, antecedent, concede, decedent, exceed, intercede, precede, proceed (*but* procedure), secede, succeed, supersede.

12.34 **chief justice of Canada:** Not "chief justice of the Supreme Court." See also 12.64, "judges and justices."

12.35 **collective nouns:** Terms such as **group, crowd,** and **couple** can take either plural or singular verbs, depending on sense: that is, does the verb apply to the totality or the individuals composing it? Subsequent verbs and pronouns referring to the same noun must then be in the same number.

The mob is growing every minute.

The mob are throwing rotten fruit.

The original Northwest Territories were Rupert's Land and the North-Western Territory.

The Northwest Territories is much smaller since the creation of Nunavut.

The words **government** and **company** are treated as singular in North American usage, but often seen as plural in British material.

Although a quantity expressed in units is plural in form, it takes a singular verb:

Six dollars buys an overdone steak and a limp salad.

Twenty hectares is a sizable estate.

About 125 mL is enough liquid to thin the batter.

12.36 **Confederation:** Capitalized as a term standing for the union of the Canadian provinces in 1867; lowercased if used as a common noun.

Canada began as a confederation of four provinces.

12.37 The **Conference Board of Canada** (a public affairs research group) was called the Conference Board *in* Canada until June 1980. In French: Le Conference Board du Canada.

12.38 **Conservative Party:** Became Progressive Conservative (PC) Party in 1942.

12.39 Canada's **constitution,** since 1982, is officially called the Constitution Act, 1982. The Canadian Charter of Rights and Freedoms constitutes Part I of the Constitution Act, 1982.

12.40 **Criminal Code:** No "Canadian" in the title.

12.41 **Crown corporation and Crown land:** Owned by a government, either federal or provincial.

12.42 **Dene Nation:** Until 1978 known as the Indian Brotherhood of the Northwest Territories. The political organization of the northern Athapaskan-speaking peoples of the western N.W.T., it includes the Chipewyan, Slave, Nahani, Bear Lake, and Dogrib nations.

12.43 **departments and ministries:** Some governments in Canada have departments; some have ministries; some have both. The annual *Canadian*

Almanac & Directory contains reliable listings. See also 12.50, "federal government department names."

12.44 **durum wheat:** *Not* Durham.

12.45 **Eaton's:** With apostrophe at the time of writing. *But* **Eaton** in Quebec.

12.46 **Elliot** Lake; Pierre **Elliott** Trudeau.

12.47 **Erasmus, Georges:** *Not* George.

12.48 **European Monetary Union:** Austria, Belgium, Finland, France, Germany, Ireland, Italy, Luxembourg, the Netherlands, Portugal, Spain. For the euro, see 4.29.

12.49 **European Union:** Austria, Belgium, Denmark, Finland, France, Germany, Greece, Ireland, Italy, Luxembourg, the Netherlands, Portugal, Spain, Sweden, United Kingdom. The European Council, the Council of the European Union, the European Commission, and the European Parliament have different memberships and mandates. For details of their roles and responsibilities within the European Union, consult <europa.eu.int/index-en.htm>.

12.50 **federal government department names:** Under the Federal Identity Program, most government agencies have two name styles. The *legal* title usually includes the word **department:** for instance, Department of Health. The *applied* title usually includes **Canada:** Health Canada. Two departments have applied names that combine the styles: Department of Finance Canada and Department of Justice Canada.

Government agencies must use their applied names except in contexts, such as legislation, where the legal name is required. Editors outside government can choose either style but should apply a consistent pattern. For a list of applied and legal names see <www.tbs-sct.gc.ca/Pubs_pol/ciopubs/TB_FIP/titlesoffedorg1_e.html>.

12.51 **Fleming:** Sir Sandford ~ (railways, founder of time zone system); Donald ~ (federal PC minister); Robert ~ (composer).

12.52 **Flemming:** Hugh John ~ (New Brunswick premier).

12.53   **governor general of Canada:** Addressed as **Right Honourable** for life; incumbent and spouse are styled **Her/His Excellency.** Complete list in *Canadian Oxford* and the *Canadian Almanac & Directory.* See also 12.57, "head of state."

12.54   **Governor General's Literary Awards:** Fourteen annual awards, seven for English and seven for French, in categories of poetry, drama, fiction, non-fiction, children's literature (text), children's literature (illustration), and translation; established 1936.

12.55   **Green Papers** and **White Papers** are types of policy papers prepared by governments. A Green Paper contains discussion of a range of policy alternatives; it is usually sent to a parliamentary committee. A White Paper might follow, narrowing the range of discussion and often indicating the government's preference (but not committing the government to policy or legislation). A term no longer used is Blue Paper, a policy document prepared for a minister.

12.56   **Hansard:** Italicize only when part of an official title; in many Canadian jurisdictions it is not the official title for records of legislative or parliamentary debates.

12.57   Canada's **head of state** is the monarch, not the prime minister, who is the head of government. The prime minister selects the governor general, who is formally appointed by the Queen to act as her representative.

12.58   **honorary:** Correct spelling. "Honourary" is a recent spelling, possibly occurring because some spellchecker programs insisted on "correcting" the u-less spelling. *Canadian Oxford* lists "honourary" as the second choice.

12.59   **Honourables and Right Honourables:** Chief justices of Canada, prime ministers, and governors general are styled **Right Honourable** for life; all other privy councillors (see 12.110), senators, and lieutenant-governors of provinces are styled **Honourable** for life. Judges and justices (see 12.64) are styled **Honourable** during tenure.

12.60   **Hudson** Bay; **Hudson** Strait; **Hudson** Bay Mining and Smelting Co.; **Hudson's** Bay Co.

12.61   **Hydro-Québec.**

Indian: See 12.2–16, "aboriginal peoples."

12.62 **International Standard Book Number (ISBN):** An international system for numbering every book in every edition, designed to provide unique identification for every book published and to improve the exchange of information about books within all segments of the book trade. Includes pamphlets, educational kits, microforms, CD-ROMs, and Braille publications.

The number consists of 10 digits; for example, ISBN 0-7793-4567-5. The first digit is a group identifier representing a national, geographical, or language group. In Canada, English books begin with the digit 0 or 1. ISBN agencies in the U.S.A. and the U.K. also use these prefixes. For French-language identification, the first digit is 2. France and Belgium also use 2 as the prefix.

The ISBN appears on the copyright page and at the bottom of the front or back flap of the jacket, or on the back of a paperback.

For information contact: Canadian ISBN Agency, National Library of Canada, 395 Wellington St., Ottawa, ON K1A 0N4; tel. (819) 994-6872; fax (819) 997-7517; <isbn@nlc-bcn.ca>.

12.63 **International Standard Serial Number (ISSN):** Similar to ISBN, but for newspapers, magazines, journals, and other ongoing publications. Each serial is given a unique eight-digit number (for example, ISSN 0039-9222). The number should appear at the top right-hand corner of the front cover.

For information contact: ISSN Canada, National Library of Canada, 395 Wellington St., Ottawa, ON K1A 0N4; tel. (819) 994-6895; fax (819) 997-6209; <issn@nlc-bcn.ca>.

Inuit: See 12.2–16, "aboriginal peoples."

JUDGES AND JUSTICES

12.64 Practice varies considerably in the style of titles and honorifics for judges in Canada. Editors working for legal publishers, governments, or legal or judicial organizations should consult house style manuals; this section provides guidance for editors of general-interest materials.

The most important principle of title styles, accepted both inside and outside the legal community, is that judges appointed by the federal government have the title **Justice;** judges appointed by provincial and territorial governments have the title **Judge.** (Note the two exceptions, also generally accepted, in the table below.) A justice may be called "a judge" or "the judge" when the term is used without his or her name.

The titles **Right Honourable** and **Honourable** need not be used in general-interest texts, but they should be used in correspondence (for details see the *Canadian Almanac & Directory*). In the legal community the terms are rarely abbreviated. The chief justice of Canada is addressed as **Right Honourable** for life. All other judges are addressed as **Honourable** during tenure. Federally appointed judges may be permitted by the governor general to continue using **Honourable** after retirement, if they so request. The title "His/Her Honour" is no longer used.

For third-person references in general-interest texts, we suggest the following.

FEDERALLY APPOINTED: judges of Supreme Court of Canada, Federal Court of Canada, Court Martial Appeal Court of Canada, and Tax Court of Canada,* and of all provincial and territorial superior courts (see 12.111–23, "provinces and territories")

First reference	Second reference
Chief Justice Dale Wolinsky	Chief Justice Wolinsky
Associate Chief Justice Jan Radu	Justice Radu
Mr. Justice Mohamed Hassan	Justice Hassan
Madam Justice Rita Oliveira	Justice Oliveira

* Exception: Judges of the Tax Court of Canada, although federally appointed, use the same title structure as provincially/territorially appointed judges. However, at the time of writing, legislation was pending that would make their titles the same as those of the other federally appointed judges.

PROVINCIALLY/TERRITORIALLY APPOINTED: judges of provincial* and territorial lower courts (i.e., all courts other than the superior courts)

First reference	Second reference
Chief Judge Kelly Chu	Chief Judge Chu
Associate Chief Judge Pat Morita	Judge Morita
Judge Jean Martin	Judge Martin

* Exception: Judges of the Ontario Court of Justice, although provincially appointed, use the same title structure as federally appointed judges.

12.65 **junior minister:** Informal term for secretaries of state (see 12.135).

12.66 **King's:** ~ Highway; University of ~ College.

12.67 **Laurier, Wilfrid:** *Not* Wilfred; ~ University.

12.68 **Learned Societies:** An umbrella term applied to the numerous scholarly organizations that hold their annual meetings at a specified Canadian university each spring so as to affordably serve a wide range of interests. Frequently referred to as "the Learneds" (and pronounced as two syllables).

12.69 **lieutenant-governor of a province:** Styled **Honourable** for life and **Her/His Honour** while in office.

12.70 **Macdonald:** Sir John A. ~; John Sandfield ~ (Ontario premier); Angus L. ~ (Nova Scotia premier); Sir Hugh John ~ (Manitoba premier); Brian ~ (choreographer); Donald ~ (Royal Commission on Economic Union and Development Prospects for Canada); Jock (J.W.G.) ~ (painter).

12.71 **MacDonald:** Ann-Marie ~ (author); Donald ~ (labour leader); Flora ~ (federal PC minister); J.E.H. ~ (painter); David ~ (PC minister and later NDP candidate).

12.72 **McDonald:** David ~ (Royal Commission of Inquiry into Certain Activities of the Royal Canadian Mounted Police); ~'s restaurants.

12.73 Allan **MacEachen** (Nova Scotia Liberal, federal minister, and later senator); Allan **McEachern** (British Columbia jurist).

12.74 **McIntosh** apple; **Macintosh** computer; **mackintosh** waterproof coat.

12.75 **Mackenzie:** Alexander ~ (explorer, d. 1820); Alexander ~ (prime minister, d. 1892); William Lyon ~ King.

12.76 **McKenzie** Brothers (comedic characters Bob and Doug played by Rick Moranis and Dave Thomas).

12.77 Sarah **McLachlan** (performer); Beverley **McLachlin** (chief justice of Canada); Murray **McLauchlan** (performer); Audrey **McLaughlin** (NDP politician); Robert **McLaughlin** (automotive pioneer).

12.78 *Maclean's* magazine.

12.79 **Macmillan** of Canada (publishing company); **MacMillan** Bloedel (forestry company); Sir Ernest **MacMillan** (musician).

12.80 **Madam Justice/Speaker/Chair:** *Not* Madame.

12.81 **married women's names in Quebec:** Since a reform of family law was implemented in late 1982, Quebec women have retained their birth names upon marriage as their legal names. Women may use their husbands' names for social purposes if they wish.

12.82 **medicare:** In Canada, a generic term for government health insurance plans.

12.83 *The Medium Is the Massage:* "The medium is the message" was Marshall McLuhan's catchphrase and the title of chapter 1 of his landmark *Understanding Media* (1964). An incurable punster, McLuhan named his 1967 book, written with Quentin Fiore and Jerome Agel, *The Medium Is the Massage,* prompting scores of writers, editors, and even reference books to misquote it ever since.

Métis: See 12.2–16, "aboriginal peoples."

12.84 **military titles:** Consult the *Canadian Press Stylebook* or *The Canadian Style.*

12.85 **Miss Edgar's and Miss Cramp's School:** An exclusive girls' school in Montreal.

12.86 **new Canadian:** Outmoded term; see 8.20.

12.87 **New Democratic Party (NDP):** Name changed from Co-operative Commonwealth Federation (CCF) in August 1961.

12.88 The **Newfoundland** House of Assembly unanimously adopted a motion to change the province's name to **Newfoundland and Labrador** on April 29, 1999, in order to recognize common usage in the province. The federal government must pass a constitutional amendment to make the name change official.

NEWSPAPERS

12.89 On mastheads as of January 2000. Source: Canadian Newspaper Association. For when to capitalize **the** in names of newspapers see 3.51.

12.90 **Alberta**
Calgary Herald
The Calgary Sun
Daily Herald-Tribune (Grande Prairie)
The Edmonton Journal

The Edmonton Sun
Fort McMurray Today
Lethbridge Herald
Medicine Hat News
Red Deer Advocate

12.91 **British Columbia**
Alaska Highway News (Fort St. John)
Alberni Valley Times (Port Alberni)
Cranbrook Daily Townsman
The Daily Bulletin (Kimberley)
The Daily Courier (Kelowna)
The Daily News (Prince Rupert)
The Kamloops Daily News
Nanaimo Daily News
Nelson Daily News
Peace River Block News (Dawson Creek)
Penticton Herald
Prince George Citizen
The Province (Vancouver)
Times Colonist (Victoria)
The Trail Times (Trail)
The Vancouver Sun

12.92 **Manitoba**
Brandon Sun
The Daily Graphic (Portage la Prairie)
Flin Flon Reminder
Winnipeg Free Press
Winnipeg Sun

12.93 **New Brunswick**
L'Acadie Nouvelle (Caraquet)
The Daily Gleaner (Fredericton)
Saint John Times Globe
Telegraph Journal (Saint John)
Times & Transcript (Moncton)

12.94 **Newfoundland**
The Telegram (St. John's)
The Western Star (Corner Brook)

12.95 **Nova Scotia**
Amherst Daily News
Cape Breton Post (Sydney)

The Chronicle-Herald/The Mail-Star (Halifax)
The Daily News (Halifax)
The Daily News (Truro)
The Evening News (New Glasgow)

12.96 **Ontario**

The Barrie Examiner
The Beacon Herald (Stratford)
The Brockville Recorder and Times
The Cambridge Reporter
The Chatham Daily News
The Chronicle-Journal (Thunder Bay)
Cobourg Daily Star
Daily Miner and News (Kenora)
The Daily Observer (Pembroke)
The Daily Press (Timmins)
Le Droit (Ottawa)
The Expositor (Brantford)
The Globe and Mail (Toronto)
Guelph Mercury
The Hamilton Spectator
The Intelligencer (Belleville)
The Kingston Whig-Standard
Lindsay Daily Post
The London Free Press
National Post (Toronto)
Niagara Falls Review
The North Bay Nugget
Northern Daily News (Kirkland Lake)
The Observer (Sarnia)
Ottawa Citizen
The Ottawa Sun
The Packet & Times (Orillia)
The Peterborough Examiner
Port Hope Evening Guide
The Record (Kitchener)
St. Thomas Times-Journal
The Sault Star (Sault Ste. Marie)
The Sentinel-Review (Woodstock)
The Simcoe Reformer
The Standard (St. Catharines)
Standard-Freeholder (Cornwall)
The Sudbury Star

The Sun Times (Owen Sound)
The Toronto Star
The Toronto Sun
The Tribune (Welland)
The Windsor Star

12.97 **Prince Edward Island**
The Guardian (Charlottetown)
The Journal-Pioneer (Summerside)

12.98 **Quebec**
Le Devoir (Montreal)
The Gazette (Montreal)
Le Journal de Montréal
Le Journal de Québec (Vanier)
Le Nouvelliste (Trois-Rivières)
La Presse (Montreal)
Le Quotidien (Chicoutimi)
The Record (Sherbrooke)
Le Soleil (Quebec)
La Tribune (Sherbrooke)
La Voix de l'Est (Granby)

12.99 **Saskatchewan**
The LeaderPost (Regina)
Lloydminster Daily Times
Prince Albert Daily Herald
The Times-Herald (Moose Jaw)
The StarPhoenix (Saskatoon)

12.100 **Yukon**
Whitehorse Star

12.101 **normal school:** Old term for teachers' college.

12.102 **northern place names:** The names of several communities in northern Canada have officially been changed to their traditional aboriginal names. Among these are Iqaluit (formerly Frobisher Bay), Kuujjuaq (Fort-Chimo), Kangiqsujuaq (Wakeham Bay or Maricourt), Kugluktuk (Coppermine), Qikiqtarjuaq (Broughton Island), Tulita (Fort Norman), and Wha Ti (Lac la Martre). Other communities, such as Resolute, Pond Inlet, and Clyde River, retain their English names. For a current complete list, place-name searches, and links to related sites, visit the Canadian Permanent Committee on Geographical Names site at <geonames.nrcan.gc.ca>.

12.103 **Ontario courts:** The Ontario Court General Division became the Superior Court of Justice in 1999. The Ontario Court Provincial Division became the Ontario Court of Justice. See also 12.64, "judges and justices."

12.104 **Order of Canada:** Honours Canadian citizens for outstanding achievement. The three levels of membership in descending order of rank are Companion (CC), Officer (OC), and Member (CM).

12.105 **Parti pris:** The name of both a publishing house and a magazine in Quebec during the Quiet Revolution. Its members and associates were called **partipristes.**

12.106 **Petro-Canada, Petrocan.**

12.107 **precedence for Canadian dignitaries:**

1. governor general
2. prime minister
3. chief justice of Canada
4. Speaker of the Senate
5. Speaker of the House of Commons
6. ambassadors, high commissioners, ministers plenipotentiary
7. members of the cabinet (with relative precedence usually governed by the date of their appointment to the Queen's Privy Council)
8. leader of the Opposition

12.108 **prime minister:** Styled **Right Honourable** for life.

12.109 **Prime Minister's Office:** The official names of this office and its opposition counterpart are Office of the Prime Minister and Office of the Leader of the Opposition. In practice, the form Prime Minister's Office (PMO) is widely accepted, even within the office itself. The **Privy Council Office** (PCO) is the office of the Clerk of the Privy Council, who is head of the federal public service and secretary to the cabinet.

12.110 **privy councillors** (members of the Queen's Privy Council of Canada) include the chief justice, the prime minister, provincial premiers, former and present federal cabinet ministers, secretaries of state, and Speakers of the Commons and Senate.

PROVINCES AND TERRITORIES

12.111 **Alberta** (Alta.)
Alberta (*f.*) (Alb.)
capital: Edmonton
created: 1905
historically: North-Western Territory/Rupert's Land
legislature and members: Legislative Assembly, MLAs
superior courts: Court of Appeal, Court of Queen's Bench

12.112 **British Columbia** (B.C.)
Colombie-Britannique (*f.*) (C.-B.)
capital: Victoria
created: 1871
legislature and members: Legislative Assembly, MLAs
superior courts: Court of Appeal, Supreme Court

12.113 **Manitoba** (Man.)
Manitoba (*m.*) (Man.)
capital: Winnipeg
created: 1870
historically: North-Western Territory/Rupert's Land
legislature and members: Legislative Assembly, MLAs
superior courts: Court of Appeal, Court of Queen's Bench

12.114 **New Brunswick** (N.B.)
Nouveau-Brunswick (*m.*) (N.-B.)
capital: Fredericton
in Confederation: 1867
legislature and members: Legislative Assembly, MLAs
superior courts: Court of Appeal, Court of Queen's Bench

12.115 **Newfoundland and Labrador** (Nfld. and Lab.) (see 12.88)
Terre-Neuve (*f.*), Labrador (*m.*) (T.-N., Lab.)
capital: St. John's
in Confederation: 1949
legislature and members: House of Assembly, MHAs
superior courts: Supreme Court (Court of Appeal and Trial Division)

12.116 **Northwest Territories** (N.W.T.)
Territoires du Nord-Ouest (*m.*) (T.N.-O.)
capital: Yellowknife
created: 1870
historically: North-Western Territories/Rupert's Land; the eastern portion
split off to form Nunavut in 1999
legislature and members: Legislative Assembly, MLAs
superior courts: Court of Appeal, Supreme Court

12.117 **Nova Scotia** (N.S.)
Nouvelle-Écosse (*f.*) (N.-É.)
capital: Halifax
in Confederation: 1867
legislature and members: Legislative Assembly, MLAs
superior courts: Court of Appeal, Supreme Court

12.118 **Nunavut**
Nunavut (*m.*)
capital: Iqaluit
created: 1999
historically: North-Western Territory/Rupert's Land; formerly eastern
    portion of Northwest Territories
legislature and members: Legislative Assembly, MLAs
superior courts: Court of Appeal, Court of Justice

12.119 **Ontario** (Ont.)
Ontario (*m.*) (Ont.)
capital: Toronto
created: 1867
historically: Upper Canada 1791–1841; Canada West 1841–67
legislature and members: Legislative Assembly, MPPs
superior courts: Court of Appeal, Superior Court of Justice (see also
    12.103, "Ontario courts")

12.120 **Prince Edward Island** (P.E.I.)
Île du Prince-Édouard *or* Île-du-Prince-Édouard (*f.*) (Î.P.-É. *or* Î.-P.-É.)
capital: Charlottetown
in Confederation: 1873
legislature and members: Legislative Assembly, MLAs
superior courts: Supreme Court (Appeal and Trial Divisions)

12.121 **Quebec** (Que. or P.Q.)
Québec (*m.*) (Qué. *or* Qc)
capital: Quebec City
created: 1867
historically: Quebec to 1791; Lower Canada 1791–1841; Canada East
    1841–67
legislature and members: Assemblée nationale (National Assembly);
    député(e)s (MNAs)
superior courts: Cour d'appel (Court of Appeal); Cour supérieure
    (Superior Court)

12.122 **Saskatchewan** (Sask.)

Saskatchewan (*f.*) (Sask.)
capital: Regina
created: 1905
historically: North-Western Territory/Rupert's Land
legislature and members: Legislative Assembly, MLAs
superior courts: Court of Appeal, Court of Queen's Bench

12.123 **Yukon Territory** (Y.T.)

Territoire du Yukon *or* Yukon (*m.*) (T.Y. *or* Yn)
capital: Whitehorse
created: 1898
historically: North-Western Territories
legislature and members: Legislative Assembly, MLAs
superior courts: Court of Appeal, Supreme Court

12.124 **pure laine ("pure wool")**: Often misspelled in English text, a term some Quebeckers use to define those with "pure" or solely French ancestry.

12.125 A **Quebecker** (preferable to "Quebecer") is a person of or from Quebec province; a **Québécois(e)** is a French Canadian of or from Quebec province. As an adjective in English material, usually capped, as in **Québécois cooking**.

12.126 **Queen's:** ~ Counsel; ~ Park; ~ Plate; ~ University.

12.127 **quoted material:** When should it be edited? The basic rule on editing material from a published source is: Don't. However, there are exceptions.

All authorities agree that the initial letter of a quotation may be changed from capital to lowercase and vice versa, and that the final punctuation mark may be changed to fit the style of the present manuscript.

More problematic are changes to spelling, especially for Canadian editors. American style guides indicate that archaic spellings from older works may be modernized but that the changes should be acknowledged. *Words into Type* adds that modern British spellings may be Americanized in certain contexts – for example, in elementary school texts. No other changes are deemed permissible.

The American rules are premised on the relative rarity of having purely stylistic variations in spelling between an author's text and the material quoted within it. In addition, it will generally be clear when a variation occurs that the quoted material is either British or archaic whereas the main text is American. In Canada, the problem is encountered much more frequently, and its manifestations tend to be less clear-cut. The possible permutations seem infinite: British-style text with American quotations, Canadian-style text with British quotations, text in one Canadian style with quotations in one or more other Canadian styles, and so on.

In other words, quotations with variant spelling often present Canadian editors with a substantial muddifying factor they could do without. The temptation to restyle excerpts and quotations to match the style of the main text is strong, and giving in to it pleases a tidy mind. The practice can also be justified on other grounds: the decisions on spelling style in the quoted material were in all likelihood made by an editor, not the author. These decisions can be compared to certain elements of typography such as display type, which, according to the *Chicago Manual*, "are not an author's doing but the publisher's or the printer's [and] need not, and often should not, be reproduced exactly."

Those who find these arguments dubious are on entirely safe ground in ignoring them and leaving quoted material untouched. In practice, however, many Canadian editors, especially in trade publishing, have accepted them to one degree or another – some wholeheartedly and openly, others covertly. Some editors make other changes of a comparable type on similar grounds: for example, standardizing the spelling out of numbers, and imposing consistency in the use of periods with abbreviations. We note that the right and proper thing to do when changing quoted material is to acknowledge the fact – by a note in the preface such as "Material quoted from published sources has been copy-edited to conform to the style of the text" – although this convention, too, is often ignored.

For quotations of French text, see 6.55–69.

12.128 **Red Book:** Platform document of the Liberal Party of Canada in the 1993 campaign. Its actual title was *Creating Opportunity*. The Liberals produced a sequel for the 1997 campaign, under the title *Securing Our Future Together*; it was commonly referred to as Red Book II.

12.129 **reserve:** *Not* reservation, in Canada (see 12.9, "aboriginal peoples").

12.130 **Royal Canadian Mounted Police (RCMP):** North-West Mounted Police to 1904; Royal North-West or (as the RCMP prefers) Northwest Mounted Police to 1919; merged with Dominion Police, 1919, and renamed Royal Canadian Mounted Police.

12.131 **St. Catharines** (Ont.).

12.132 **Saint John** (N.B.); **St. John's** (Nfld.); **St. John** Ambulance (*not* John's).

12.133 **St. Laurent, Louis:** Some French-language sources give **St-Laurent** as a preferred spelling; however, the first version is widely accepted in English material.

12.134 **school systems:** No assumption of comparability across provinces and territories can be made in the meaning of "public" vs. "separate" or in the division of grades between primary and secondary levels. For an overview, see *The Canadian Encyclopedia.*

12.135 **secretaries of state:** Since November 1993 secretaries of state have been members of the ministry but not of cabinet. They are assigned to assist cabinet ministers in particular areas of responsibility. Having been sworn to the Privy Council, secretaries of state may be addressed as **Honourable.**

Before November 1993 the term **secretary of state** (or **minister of state**) was applied to a wide range of positions, varying from government to government. Some were equivalent to cabinet ministers; others were of lesser rank.

12.136 **Secretary of State for External Affairs** was the title for Canada's minister of foreign affairs until June 1993.

12.137 **senators of Canada:** Styled **Honourable** for life.

12.138 **Simpsons (department store):** No apostrophe. **Simpson** in Quebec.

12.139 **sovereignty-association:** Hyphen, not en dash.

12.140 **split infinitive:** Now generally accepted in preference to awkward phrasing to avoid it.

12.141 **subjunctive:** Three main sorts of subjunctives are encountered, particularly in formal language:

- Formulaic survivals: rather archaic phrases that are fixed in form, such as

    Far be it from me ..., Suffice it to say ..., Long live ..., God save ..., As it were ..., If need be ..., Had I but known ...

- Mandative forms: in formal usage, the subjunctive following such verbs as **demand, require, move, insist, suggest, request,** and **ask.** For example:

    Moved: That the secretary inform the bank of the president's defalcation.

    We insist that she make herself available at any hour of the day or night.

- Contrary-to-fact hypotheticals: sentences in which the content of an **if** or **as though** clause is untrue. For example:

  > If I had a million dollars, I would give it all to you. (*Compare:* If I have the right change, we can park at a meter.)
  >
  > He could enter any hotel as though he were the rightful owner.
  >
  > If she were my child, I'd lock her in her room! (*Compare:* If she is my child, a DNA comparison will prove it.)

This last use of the subjunctive is now considered optional by many authorities, who regard the past indicative as equally acceptable:

> If she was my child, I'd lock her in her room!

Sometimes the subjunctive is used when the **if** clause is not untrue but the tone is tentative:

> If it were to rain, what ever would we do?
>
> If he were to consider raising my salary just a little, I would be so very grateful.

Note that where **if** is equivalent to **whether,** the subjunctive is not used:

> I didn't know if I was going to make it.
>
> We wonder if he knows what he is doing.

12.142 **that/which:** Many writers and editors follow the practice of treating **that** as the relative pronoun used to introduce a restrictive, or defining, clause and **which** to introduce a non-restrictive clause, one that adds information but is not necessary to understanding the main clause. A non-restrictive clause is always set off by commas.

> This is the house that Jack built. (*restrictive*)
>
> Jack's house, which he built himself entirely of organic materials, is much admired for miles around. (*non-restrictive*)

However, language authorities increasingly concede that **which** can introduce either type of clause. See also 5.8–11.

12.143 **this (without antecedent):** Like other pronouns, **this** must have a clear referent in noun form: a noun, a pronoun, a gerund, or a noun phrase. Avoid in particular **this** at the beginning of a sentence when its referent could be any one of a number of preceding thoughts. Consider:

> Many people arrive at suburban hospital emergency departments unattended after accidents that have not been reported to the authorities. This [which?] causes delays.

12.144 **Thompson:** ~ (Man.); David ~ (explorer and fur trader); Judith ~ (playwright); ~ River (major river in British Columbia).

12.145 **Thomson:** Kenneth ~ (financier and newspaper magnate); Tom ~ (painter); Nesbitt ~ (brokerage); Roy ~ Hall (Toronto concert hall).

12.146 There are six **time zones** in Canada reckoning from Greenwich: Newfoundland Standard Time (a half-hour ahead of Atlantic Standard Time); Atlantic Standard Time (Maritime provinces and Labrador); Eastern Standard Time (Quebec and most of Ontario); Central Standard Time (western Ontario to parts of western Saskatchewan); Mountain Standard Time (western Saskatchewan to eastern British Columbia); Pacific Standard Time (British Columbia and the Yukon). Saskatchewan does not switch to daylight saving time.

In some communities "observed" time is not the same as "official" time. See H. David Matthews and Mary Vincent's article "It's about TIME" in the September-October 1998 issue of *Canadian Geographic*. The information in this article is available at <www.cangeo.ca/SO98/geomap.htm>. For more information on official time zones, see <www.nrc.ca/inms/time/tze.html>. (See also 4.25.)

12.147 **Tomson** Highway (author).

12.148 **Toronto Dominion Bank:** The bank's own style is to hyphenate only when **the** precedes the name: **the Toronto-Dominion Bank.**

12.149 **TransCanada:** ~ PipeLines Ltd.; ~ Telephone System; *but* **Trans-Canada** Highway.

12.150 **tuque:** A knitted warm cap, usually coming to a point; a **toque** is a woman's brimless, close-fitted hat or a chef's hat.

12.151 **United Church of Canada:** Church union in 1925 joined primarily the Presbyterians, the Methodists, and the Congregationalists. About one-third of the Presbyterians ("continuing" Presbyterians) rejected union, as did some "continuing" Methodists.

12.152 The **United Kingdom** is a political entity comprising Great Britain and Northern Ireland; Great Britain (or Britain) comprises England, Scotland, and Wales. The British Isles are a geographical entity comprising Britain, Ireland, and adjacent islands.

12.153 **universities:** For a complete list of Canadian degree-granting universities consult the Association of Universities and Colleges of Canada, 600–350 Albert St., Ottawa, ON K1R 1B1; tel. (613) 563-9745; <www.aucc.ca>.

12.154 **Waffle, the:** A splinter group of the NDP created in the 1960s.

12.155 **while:** Should be avoided as an all-purpose conjunction. It refers specifically to time, to simultaneous events:

> The Queen arrived while he was still in the bath.

Be alert for the use of **while** in place of **but, and, whereas,** or **although,** or where a semicolon or a new sentence would be more appropriate. Note particularly the ambiguity possible when undefined **while** begins a sentence: is the meaning in these examples "as long as" or "although"?

> While these serious problems remain, progress is impossible.
> While these serious problems remain, significant progress has nonetheless been made.

12.156 **whisky/whiskey:** Scotch whisky, Canadian rye whisky, and Japanese whisky; Irish and American (bourbon) whiskey.

White Paper: See 12.55, "Green Paper."

12.157 *Who Has Seen the Wind:* No question mark after the title of W.O. Mitchell's novel.

References

The sources below are a selection of those consulted by the committee in writing this book. They are particularly useful or of special interest for work in editing Canadian material. The emphasis is on Canadian resources. Note that not all references cited in this volume appear below; some specialized sources are listed only at the ends of chapters.

Almanacs and encyclopedias

Canadian Almanac & Directory. Toronto: Micromedia, published annually since 1848. Published by Copp Clark 1857–1998, with variations in titles before 1948.

The Canadian Encyclopedia. 2nd ed. Edmonton: Hurtig, 1988. 4 vols.

The Canadian Encyclopedia [CD-ROM]. Toronto: McClelland & Stewart, published annually since 1991. Titles of CD-ROMs vary.

The Canadian Global Almanac. Toronto: Macmillan, published annually since 1987. Title 1987–91 was *Canadian World Almanac & Book of Facts.*

Atlases and gazetteers

Canada Gazetteer Atlas. N.p.: Macmillan of Canada; Energy, Mines and Resources Canada; and the Canadian Government Publishing Centre, Supply and Services Canada, 1980. Accurate but less comprehensive than the *Gazetteer of Canada* series, on which it is based. Published in French under the title *Canada atlas toponymie.*

Canadian Oxford World Atlas. Edited by Quentin Stanford. 4th ed. Don Mills, Ont.: Oxford University Press, 1998.

Gazetteer of Canada/Répertoire géographique du Canada. Prepared by the Canadian Permanent Committee on Geographical Names. Ottawa: Geographical Services Division, Surveys and Mapping Branch, Department of Energy, Mines and Resources, 1952– . Each province (except Quebec: see

Répertoire toponymique du Québec) has a separate volume. This series is the most complete and accurate source of Canadian place names.

GeoNames/Toponymes [online]. Natural Resources Canada/Geomatics Canada, 1999. [Cited January 5, 2000.] Site maintained by the Canadian Permanent Committee on Geographical Names (CPCGN). <geonames. nrcan.gc.ca/>.

National Atlas of Canada [online]. Natural Resources Canada. 6th ed. [Cited December 31, 1999.] <www-nais.ccm.emr.ca/>.

Répertoire toponymique du Québec. Commission de toponymie. [Quebec City]: Éditeur officiel du Québec, 1979. Complements the *Gazetteer of Canada.*

Dictionaries

The Canadian Oxford Dictionary. Edited by Katherine Barber. Toronto: Oxford University Press, 1998.

The Canadian Oxford Spelling Dictionary. Edited by Robert Pontisso and Eric Sinkins. Toronto: Oxford University Press, 1999.

The Concise Oxford Dictionary. 10th ed. Edited by Judy Pearsall. Oxford: Oxford University Press, 1999.

Gage Canadian Dictionary. Edited by Gaelan Dodds deWolf, et al. Revised and expanded. Toronto: Gage Educational Publishing, 1998.

ITP Nelson Canadian Dictionary of the English Language. Toronto: ITP Nelson, 1998. Appendixes include Canadian facts and language concepts.

Merriam-Webster's Collegiate Dictionary. 10th ed. Springfield, Mass.: Merriam-Webster, 1996.

NetLingo [online]. [Cited December 22, 1999.] Online-language dictionary. <www.netlingo.com>.

The Oxford Colour Spelling Dictionary. Edited by Maurice Waite. Oxford: Clarendon Press, 1996.

The Oxford Dictionary of Abbreviations. Oxford and New York: Oxford University Press, 1993.

Grammar

Quirk, Randolph, et al. *A Comprehensive Grammar of the English Language.* London: Longman Group, 1985.

Shaw, Harry. *McGraw-Hill Handbook of English.* Revised by Dave Carley. 4th Canadian ed. Toronto: McGraw-Hill Ryerson, 1986.

Stilman, Anne. *Grammatically Correct: The Writer's Essential Guide to Punctuation, Spelling, Style, Usage and Grammar.* Cincinnati: Writer's Digest Books, 1997.

Multi-reference and research

Newsletter Editors' Resource List [online]. [Cited December 23, 1999.] Reference links for editors and writers; includes links to reference works, libraries, photographers, and cartoonists. <www.tedgoff.com/erlist.html>.

Refdesk.com [online]. 1999. [Cited December 22, 1999.] Lengthy list of links to newspapers, radio, magazines, dictionaries, phone books, and other reference sources. <www.refdesk.com>.

Sources. Toronto: Sources, published since 1977, twice annually.

A Web of On-line Dictionaries [online]. Updated February 17, 2000. [Cited February 17, 2000.] Searchable database for hundreds of dictionaries, thesauruses, and other reference works in dozens of languages. <www.facstaff.bucknell.edu/rbeard/diction.html>.

Style and usage

Barzun, Jacques. *Simple & Direct: A Rhetoric for Writers.* Revised ed. New York: Harper & Row, 1985.

Bernstein, Theodore M. *The Careful Writer: A Modern Guide to English Usage.* New York: Atheneum, 1977.

———. *Dos, Don'ts & Maybes of English Usage.* With the assistance of Marylea Meyersohn and Bertram Lippman. New York: Times Books, 1977.

———. *Miss Thistlebottom's Hobgoblins: The Careful Writer's Guide to the Taboos, Bugbears and Outmoded Rules of English Usage.* New York: Simon and Schuster, 1971.

The Canadian Press Stylebook: A Guide for Writers and Editors. Edited by Patti Tasko. 11th ed. Fully revised and updated. Toronto: Canadian Press, 1999.

The Canadian Style: A Guide to Writing and Editing. Revised and expanded. Toronto: Dundurn Press in cooperation with Public Works and Government Services Canada Translation Bureau, 1997.

The Chicago Manual of Style. 14th ed. Chicago: University of Chicago Press, 1993.

The Chicago Manual of Style: FAQ (and Not So FAQ) [online]. Updated January 2000. [Cited February 17, 2000.] The University of Chicago Press's helpful and entertaining Web site of frequently asked questions. <www.press.uchicago.edu/Misc/Chicago/cmosfaq.html>.

CP Caps and Spelling. Toronto: Canadian Press, 1998.

Follett, Wilson. *Modern American Usage: A Guide*. Edited by Jacques Barzun. New York: Hill and Wang, 1966.

Fowler, H.W. *A Dictionary of Modern English Usage*. Revised by Sir Ernest Gowers. 2nd ed. Oxford: Oxford University Press, 1988.

Garner, Bryan A. *A Dictionary of Modern American Usage*. New York: Oxford University Press, 1998. Includes a chronological list of 350 books on English usage.

The Gazette Style [online]. By Joseph N. Gelmon. Montreal: Gazette. [Cited December 28, 1999.] <www.montrealgazette.com/STYLE/>.

The Globe and Mail Style Book: A Guide to Language and Usage. Edited by J.A. (Sandy) McFarlane and Warren Clements. Toronto: McClelland & Stewart, 1998.

Gowers, Ernest. *The Complete Plain Words*. Revised by Sidney Greenbaum and Janet Whitcut. 3rd ed. London: Penguin, 1987.

Guide to Canadian English Usage. By Margery Fee and Janice McAlpine. Strathy Language Unit, Queen's University. Toronto: Oxford University Press, 1997.

Johnson, Edward D. *The Handbook of Good English*. 2nd ed. New York: Washington Square Press, 1991.

The New Fowler's Modern English Usage. Edited by R.W. Burchfield. 3rd ed. Oxford: Clarendon Press, 1996.

The New York Public Library Writer's Guide to Style and Usage. Edited by Andrea J. Sutcliffe. Alexandria, Va.: HarperCollins, 1994.

The Oxford Dictionary for Writers and Editors. Compiled by the Oxford English Dictionary Department. Oxford: Clarendon Press, 1981. Second edition forthcoming.

Stet! Tricks of the Trade for Writers and Editors. Edited by Bruce O. Boston. Alexandria, Va.: Editorial Experts Inc., 1986. A collection of articles from *The Editorial Eye*, the newsletter on publications standards and practices.

Stet Again! More Tricks of the Trade for Publications People. Alexandria, Va.: EEI Press, 1996. Selections from *The Editorial Eye*.

Strunk, William, and E.B. White. *The Elements of Style*. 3rd ed. New York: Macmillan, 1979.

Williams, Joseph M. *Style: Toward Clarity and Grace*. Chicago: University of Chicago Press, 1995.

Words into Type. Based on studies by Marjorie E. Skillin, Robert M. Gay, and other authorities. 3rd ed. Englewood Cliffs, N.J.: Prentice-Hall, 1974.

Acknowledgments

T he Freelance Editors' Association of Canada sponsored the project that produced the first edition of *Editing Canadian English*, with additional funding coming from the Explorations program of the Canada Council and from the federal Department of Communications. Lydia Burton, who died in 1990, was central in leading the project over the many years of its preparation.

In addition, the following FEAC members and others contributed to the process: Jane Allen, Lee d'Anjou, Eileen Barbeau, Jacques Barzun, Alain Baudot, Chris Bearchell, Naomi Black, Marion Blake, Dennis Bockus, Kathryn Dean, Grace Deutsch, Sue Dickin, David Dunkley, John Eerkes, David Evans, Maureen FitzGerald, Nancy Fleming, Norton Ginsburg, Francess Halpenny, Lesley Harris, Lawrence Haskett, Barbara Hehner, Prue Hemelrijk, Cathleen Hoskins, Jacqueline Hushion, Greg Ioannou, Bernard Kelly, Jean Kerr, Dennis Lane, Susan Lawrence, Willadean Leo, W.C. Lougheed, Ian Montagnes, David Morley, Sharon Nelson, Riça Night, Shaun Oakey, Hélène Papineau, Margaret Parker, Roman Petryshyn, Jean Reavley, Elizabeth Reid, Joe Reid, Lois Reimer, Marilyn Sacks, Eleanor Sinclair, Wendy Spettigue, George Story, Eunice Thorne, Anne Walsh, Avivah Wargon, Kathy Wazana, Bill White, Paul Wilkinson, Michael Williamson, and Jean L. Wilson.

Similarly, the Editors' Association of Canada (the name changed in 1994) has supported this second edition, and once more many editors and others have contributed to its content. Numerous but unnamed here are the many participants in the association's online discussion group who have responded to cries for help from the committee or otherwise provided welcome information on usages, sources, and contentious issues.

For ongoing advice we especially thank Dennis Bockus. Thanks go also to his co-members of the EAC/ACR Advisory Committee who helped out with some of the business aspects of the project: Nancy Flight, Scott Mitchell, Sheila Protti, and Rosemary Tanner. Connie John and Jane

Moore of the EAC National Office provided logistical support, and Krysia Lear helped with publicity and marketing to EAC members. In addition to her liaison duties, Sheila Protti capably orchestrated the contributions of the many and diverse players.

Cynthia Brouse, Peter Jacobsen, Harvey McCue, Jim MacLachlan, Dennis Mills, Shaun Oakey, Robyn Packard, and Karen Staudinger must be singled out for their substantial contributions to the text. For this second edition also, many editors and others volunteered generous amounts of time and effort in the form of research, subject expertise, and critical review of various drafts. A simple alphabetical listing of their names must necessarily obscure the enormous amount of work some individuals took on; nevertheless, we are grateful to the many who did whatever they could: Christopher Adam, Elizabeth d'Anjou, Lee d'Anjou, Rick Archbold, Phyllis Aronoff, Katherine Barber, Jen Birmingham, Susan Bridges, Andy Carroll, Lynda Chiotti, Bruce Couchman, Brian Dillon, John Eerkes, Nancy Flight, Betty Gibbs, Jennifer Glossop, Freya Godard, Mel Graham, Sandy Hamilton, Terry Hemingway, Nancy Holland, Greg Ioannou, Ann James, Bernard Kelly, Bob Kennedy, Fred Kerner, Olive Koyama, Kelly Lamorie, Doug Linzey, Janice McAlpine, Mary McDougall Maude, Perry Millar, Jeff Miller, Aaron Milrad, Peter Moskos, Nicholas d'Ombrain, Jonathan Paterson, Susan Pedwell, Andrea Rush, Lise Saint-André, Edith St-Hilaire, Rosemary Shipton, Anne Stilman, Harry Swain, Rosemary Tanner, Claudette Reed Upton, Robin Van Heck, Karen Virag, Kathy Wazana, Malcolm Williams, and David Zussman.

In preparing the text, we consulted many dictionaries and style guides, and we thank donors of all of these references, notably Oxford University Press, ITP Nelson, Gage, Laurel Amalia at the Canadian Tax Foundation, and Joseph Gelmon at the Montreal *Gazette*.

The clarity and elegance of Robin Brass's text design greatly facilitated the organization of the material. And for copy-editing this new edition as well as the original, we are again grateful for the care and attention of Shaun Oakey, whose broad knowledge, good sense, and tact equip him to be an editors' editor. The thorough and polished index was prepared by Heather Ebbs. Sonia Kuryliw Paine lent a hand with proofreading. Our publisher, Jan Walter of Macfarlane Walter & Ross, has been supportive and encouraging throughout the project, while Laura Siberry has amiably shepherded the text through the publication process.

This book has been in preparation for two and a half years, and during this time the committee members' families patiently shared us with the project. We thank them all: Tony Makepeace; Patrick, Graeme, and Willa Phillips; and Ray, Michel, and Nicholas Protti, whose home was the main meeting venue.

Index